CodeIgniter 2 Cookbook

Over 80 recipes to help you create CodeIgniter-powered applications and solve common coding problems

Rob Foster

PUBLISHING

BIRMINGHAM - MUMBAI

CodeIgniter 2 Cookbook

First published: November 2013

Production Reference: 1191113

Published by Packt Publishing Ltd.
Livery Place
35 Livery Street
Birmingham B3 2PB, UK.

ISBN 978-1-78216-230-8

www.packtpub.com

Cover Image by Feroze Babu (mail@feroze.me)

Credits

Author
Rob Foster

Reviewers
Harpreet Singh Bhatia

Marion Newlevant

Ahmed Samy

John Skoumbourdis

Acquisition Editor
Joanne Fitzpatrick

Lead Technical Editor
Neeshma Ramakrishnan

Technical Editors
Kapil Hemnani

Gauri Dasgupta

Jalasha D'costa

Dipika Gaonkar

Monica John

Edwin Moses

Faisal Siddique

Copy Editors
Brandt D'Mello

Gladson Monteiro

Laxmi Subramanian

Project Coordinator
Navu Dhillon

Proofreaders
Ameesha Green

Linda Morris

Indexer
Monica Ajmera Mehta

Graphics
Rob Parsons

Abhinash Sahu

Production Coordinator
Kyle Albuquerque

Cover Work
Kyle Albuquerque

About the Author

Rob Foster has been working in web development for almost 10 years, focusing on the LAMP stack (although currently rocking a MAC), and has been developing with CodeIgniter for over three years. He has worked in IT for various sectors including public health, charity, new media, and even the gaming industry.

I would like to thank Lucy for all the missed weekends I spent working on the book (at least you got to 62 on Skyrim), Rob Parsons for doing a great job on the images in the book. Thanks to Mum and Dad, Peter and family, Richard (good to have you back again), friends, and family.

About the Reviewers

Harpreet Singh Bhatia is a freelance developer who believes that coding is as much art as it is science, because it not only involve a strong, logical thinking with a care for system resources, but also gives the coder the ability to express himself in order to ensure a smooth flow, making code.

He has a Master's degree in IT and a diploma in Software Engineering from NIIT. He specializes in a wide array of technologies. He is proficient in web application languages, tools, and frameworks including PHP, JavaScript, jQuery, Ajax, CodeIgniter, MySQL, WordPress, CSS3, and HTML5; the Unix environment being his forte.

He has worked in multiple capacities in the IT field. He started off as a teacher/instructor in APTECH. He then switched to development and has served companies such as Screwdriver Infotainment, Kent RO, Design Emporia, Syc Creatives (Malaysia), Multi Design (Norway), and many more. He is also a proud member of "The Group Ry" (Finland).

He has had an enriching experience in software and IT infrastructure development, spanning a wide IT spectrum. This includes web development, application designing, system installation and configuration, and so on.

I would like to thank my father for provoking me to review this book. I would also like to thank the publisher for reaching out to me for this work.

Marion Newlevant started programming at the tail end of the punch card era, and has been doing it ever since. She is a big fan of well-organized code, and started working with CodeIgniter in 2010.

Ahmed Samy is a PHP web developer who is currently working for `Edfa3ly.com`, a superstar e-commerce start-up in Egypt that considers technology as a key player for success.

He has mainly worked with CodeIgniter, Symfony2, Fuel, NoSQL MongoDB, and has recently worked implementing more scalable systems using SOA approaches.

He's also the founder of HypeLabs, a small business that delivers web/mobile app services and is currently in the planning stage of a new start-up idea.

He believes that sharing knowledge with other people is one of the keys to success.

John Skoumbourdis (known as Johnny) is a senior web developer who loves coding. He is always trying to maximize and improve his skills by learning new things in a challenging environment. His mission is to create beautiful and professional websites and help other people to do so by sharing his knowledge. He is currently developing three really famous libraries in CodeIgniter; they are:

- Grocery CRUD (`http://www.grocerycrud.com`)
- Image CRUD (`http://www.grocerycrud.com/image-crud`)
- CodeIgniter Simplicity (`http://www.grocerycrud.com/codeigniter-simplicity`)

If you want to know more about him, you can visit his personal blog at `http://www.web-and-development.com/`.

www.PacktPub.com

Support files, eBooks, discount offers and more

You might want to visit `www.PacktPub.com` for support files and downloads related to your book.

Did you know that Packt offers eBook versions of every book published, with PDF and ePub files available? You can upgrade to the eBook version at `www.PacktPub.com` and as a print book customer, you are entitled to a discount on the eBook copy. Get in touch with us at `service@packtpub.com` for more details.

At `www.PacktPub.com`, you can also read a collection of free technical articles, sign up for a range of free newsletters and receive exclusive discounts and offers on Packt books and eBooks.

`http://PacktLib.PacktPub.com`

Do you need instant solutions to your IT questions? PacktLib is Packt's online digital book library. Here, you can access, read and search across Packt's entire library of books.

Why Subscribe?

- ▶ Fully searchable across every book published by Packt
- ▶ Copy and paste, print and bookmark content
- ▶ On demand and accessible via web browser

Free Access for Packt account holders

If you have an account with Packt at `www.PacktPub.com`, you can use this to access PacktLib today and view nine entirely free books. Simply use your login credentials for immediate access.

Table of Contents

Preface

CodeIgniter 2 Cookbook offers many easy-to-use, easy-to-integrate, and easy-to-adapt recipes using HTTPS, image manipulation, cookie acceptance, form validation, and so on. It is a great resource for 2 AM problems.

What this book covers

Chapter 1, CodeIgniter Basics, takes you through CodeIgniter's download and installation, basic configuration, and so on.

Chapter 2, User Management, focuses on building a basic CRUD interface for managing users.

Chapter 3, Creating E-commerce Features, explores the use of the CodeIgniter Cart class to create a simple storefront, allowing a customer to add items to the cart and checkout.

Chapter 4, Email, HTML Table, and Text Libraries, focuses on sending e-mails using the CodeIgniter Email library, creating interactive tables, and using a few handy HTML functions.

Chapter 5, Managing Data In and Out, deals with form validation, writing files to disk, confirming cookie acceptance from the user, and so on.

Chapter 6, Working with Databases, covers the usage of basic Active Record functions, exporting data from a database query binding, and most of what you might need to work with databases.

Chapter 7, Creating a Secure User Environment, covers escaping user input, switching to and from HTTPS in CodeIgniter, and so on.

Chapter 8, Calendaring, Right Place, and Right Time, deals with creating an interactive calendar that you can add appointments to using fuzzy dates and calculating a person's date of birth (for age verification).

Chapter 9, *Extending the Core*, focuses on using the language class and switching languages on the go, creating hooks, uploading files with FTP, and extending your controllers with MY_Controller.

Chapter 10, *Working with Images*, deals with using the CodeIgniter image manipulation library to crop, rotate, and add watermarks to images and adding CAPTCHA validation to forms.

Chapter 11, *SEO, Caching, and Logging*, deals with caching data from a database, using the CodeIgniter routing methods to alter and amend how URLs are displayed in a browser's address bar, and logging errors and other activities throughout your application.

What you need for this book

You will require the following software:

- An *AMP environment (LAMP, MAMP, WAMP, and so on)
- A copy of the CodeIgniter framework

Who this book is for

CodeIgniter is an easy-to-pick-up framework written in PHP; so, familiarity with PHP and CodeIgniter is advantageous. But, having no experience with CodeIgniter shouldn't be a road block to read the book either. The best thing to do (if you're unsure) is to buy it and just jump in. Having said that, if you are familiar with CodeIgniter, this book can provide immediate sold snippets and recipes you can use for all sorts of day-to-day, CodeIgniter-related tasks.

Conventions

In this book, you will find a number of styles of text that distinguish between different kinds of information. Here are some examples of these styles, and an explanation of their meaning.

Code words in text, database table names, folder names, filenames, file extensions, pathnames, dummy URLs, user input, and Twitter handles are shown as follows: " The `public function index()` function redirects us to the function `public function send_mail()`."

A block of code is set as follows:

```
$this->email->from('from@domain.com', 'Your Name');
$this->email->to('to@domain.com');

$this->email->subject('This is a text email');
$this->email->message('And this is some content for the text
  email.');
```

When we wish to draw your attention to a particular part of a code block, the relevant lines or items are set in bold:

```
function __construct() {
    parent::__construct();
    $this->load->helper('url');
    $this->load->library('email');
}
```

Any command-line input or output is written as follows:

```
C:\path\to\CodeIgniter\file.htaccess" .htaccess
```

New terms and **important words** are shown in bold. Words that you see on the screen, in menus or dialog boxes for example, appear in the text like this: "The user clicks on **View Cart** to view the products they wish to order".

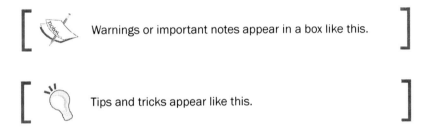

Warnings or important notes appear in a box like this.

Tips and tricks appear like this.

Reader feedback

Feedback from our readers is always welcome. Let us know what you think about this book—what you liked or may have disliked. Reader feedback is important for us to develop titles that you really get the most out of.

To send us general feedback, simply send an e-mail to feedback@packtpub.com, and mention the book title via the subject of your message.

If there is a topic that you have expertise in and you are interested in either writing or contributing to a book, see our author guide on www.packtpub.com/authors.

Customer support

Now that you are the proud owner of a Packt book, we have a number of things to help you to get the most from your purchase.

Downloading the example code

You can download the example code files for all Packt books you have purchased from your account at `http://www.packtpub.com`. If you purchased this book elsewhere, you can visit `http://www.packtpub.com/support` and register to have the files e-mailed directly to you.

Errata

Although we have taken every care to ensure the accuracy of our content, mistakes do happen. If you find a mistake in one of our books—maybe a mistake in the text or the code—we would be grateful if you would report this to us. By doing so, you can save other readers from frustration and help us improve subsequent versions of this book. If you find any errata, please report them by visiting `http://www.packtpub.com/submit-errata`, selecting your book, clicking on the **errata submission form** link, and entering the details of your errata. Once your errata are verified, your submission will be accepted and the errata will be uploaded on our website, or added to any list of existing errata, under the Errata section of that title. Any existing errata can be viewed by selecting your title from `http://www.packtpub.com/support`.

Piracy

Piracy of copyright material on the Internet is an ongoing problem across all media. At Packt, we take the protection of our copyright and licenses very seriously. If you come across any illegal copies of our works, in any form, on the Internet, please provide us with the location address or website name immediately so that we can pursue a remedy.

Please contact us at `copyright@packtpub.com` with a link to the suspected pirated material.

We appreciate your help in protecting our authors, and our ability to bring you valuable content.

Questions

You can contact us at `questions@packtpub.com` if you are having a problem with any aspect of the book, and we will do our best to address it.

1

CodeIgniter Basics

In this chapter, we will cover:

- ▸ Downloading and installing CodeIgniter
- ▸ Basic configuration options
- ▸ Managing CodeIgniter on different environments
- ▸ Managing database settings in different environments
- ▸ Securing system files
- ▸ Removing index.php from the address bar using .htaccess
- ▸ Installing and using Sparks

Introduction

CodeIgniter is an easy to use, easy to set up PHP-based framework which you can use to build pretty much any web-based application you can think of. There is a little bit of configuration needed before we can start to use CodeIgniter; however, this chapter will walk you through downloading, installing, and understanding the basic configuration of CodeIgniter to help you quickly get up and running.

Downloading and installing CodeIgniter

First things first, you will need a copy of CodeIgniter to be getting on with. There are several choices: you can download a nightly build, an older version, or the current stable release. However, it's recommended that you go for the latest stable version.

How to do it...

You can get your hands on the latest stable version of CodeIgniter through the following link:

`http://codeigniter.com/downloads/`

CodeIgniter will be offered as a compressed archive file. Once CodeIgniter has been downloaded, copy the package to your web folder, and unpack it as you would normally unpack an archive on your system. Once you've done this, you'll need to set some configuration options, which we'll look at next.

Basic configuration options

Configuring CodeIgniter is a lot easier than many other web frameworks available and does not require you to resort to using the command line. All you need to quickly get up and running is access to several files in the `application/config/` folder. These are a few of the suggested settings which will get your CodeIgniter installation ready without too much fuss.

How to do it...

Open the file in your localhost of development environment: `/path/to/codeigniter/application/config/config.php` and find the following lines:

    $config["base_url"]:

The value should be the full web address (the address that is written in your browser address bar) to the CodeIgniter installation. So if you are working in your localhost, the value should be: `http://localhost/path/to/codeigniter/`.

 Remember to begin with a `http://` and always put the trailing / slash.

If you've amended your host's file to use a domain name rather than localhost, then be sure to replace localhost with that domain name:

    $config["encryption_key"]

If you wish to use either the `Session` or `Encryption` classes in your application, the encryption key must be set. The encryption key is simply a string of characters used by CodeIgniter to encrypt various types of communication:

    $config["global_xss_filtering"]

The preceding code line specifies whether cross-site script filtering should be applied to the `Get`, `Post`, or `Cookie` variables. For the sake of security, this should be set to `TRUE`, especially in a live environment:

```
$config["csrf_protection"]
```

The preceding code line specifies whether a cookie token is set, which if `TRUE` will be checked every time a form is submitted from the client side. In a live environment, it should be set to `TRUE`:

```
$config["log_threshold"]
```

The preceding code line specifies whether you want to write to logs, and if so, the type of information you wish to write to those logs. For example:

- `0`: No errors are written to logs as logging is deactivated
- `1`: Error messages only (this will include PHP errors also)
- `2`: Debugging messages only
- `3`: Informational messages only
- `4`: All types of messages

The following code line is the path to the folder in which you wish to save log files:

```
$config["log_path"] = "/path/to/log/file"
```

How it works...

CodeIgniter will now respond and function according to the settings provided.

Managing CodeIgniter on different environments

In some cases, it may be useful to adapt your configuration files so that they can function on several servers or environments without having to edit or maintain each time they are moved. For example, the configuration settings you may have on your localhost are very likely to be different than those on a live or production server. Setting the configuration files correctly will save you a lot of time rather than manually switching between the two.

How to do it...

Open the `/path/to/codeigniter/application/config/config.php` file and replace the `$config["base_url"]` line with the following:

```
switch($_SERVER["SERVER_NAME"]) {
    case "localhost":
        $config["base_url"] =
          "http://localhost/path/to/codeigniter/";
        break;
    case "mydomain.com":
        $config["base_url"] = "http://www.mydomain.com/";
        break;
}
```

How it works...

This is simply a case/switch statement with a `SERVER_NAME` check. The `base_url` value is set according to the server that the CodeIgniter application or project is running on.

Managing database settings on different environments

If you plan to use a database for your CodeIgniter application, then you'll need to maintain the correct connection settings. CodeIgniter keeps these settings in the `database.php` config file.

How to do it...

1. Open the `/path/to/codeigniter/application/config/database.php` file. Chances are that the only values that need to change are the standard hostname, username, password of your database server, and the database name.

2. Find the line that defines `$active_group`, which specifies the specific database settings to use for a particular hosting environment. You can switch between settings by a `case/switch` test similar to that used previously, for example, the following code tests for a particular server and loads the appropriate settings:

```
switch($_SERVER["SERVER_NAME"]) {
    case "localhost":
        $active_group = "testing";
        break;
    case "mydomain.com":
```

```
        $active_group = "default"
    break;
}

$db["default"]["hostname"]  = "localhost";
$db["default"]["username"]  = "root";
$db["default"]["password"]  = "";
$db["default"]["database"]  = "database_name";
$db["default"]["dbdriver"]  = "mysql";
$db["default"]["dbprefix"]  = "";
$db["default"]["pconnect"]  = TRUE;
$db["default"]["db_debug"]  = FALSE;
$db["default"]["cache_on"]  = FALSE;
$db["default"]["cachedir"]  = "";
$db["default"]["char_set"]  = "utf8";
$db["default"]["dbcollat"]  = "utf8_general_ci";
$db["default"]["swap_pre"]  = "";
$db["default"]["autoinit"]  = TRUE;
$db["default"]["stricton"]  = FALSE;

$db["testing"]["hostname"]  = "localhost";
$db["testing"]["username"]  = "root";
$db["testing"]["password"]  = "";
$db["testing"]["database"]  = "database_name";
$db["testing"]["dbdriver"]  = "mysql";
$db["testing"]["dbprefix"]  = "";
$db["testing"]["pconnect"]  = TRUE;
$db["testing"]["db_debug"]  = TRUE;
$db["testing"]["cache_on"]  = FALSE;
$db["testing"]["cachedir"]  = "";
$db["testing"]["char_set"]  = "utf8";
$db["testing"]["dbcollat"]  = "utf8_general_ci";
$db["testing"]["swap_pre"]  = "";
$db["testing"]["autoinit"]  = TRUE;
$db["testing"]["stricton"]  = FALSE;

$active_record - Specifies if you require active record
   support.  By default it is set to TRUE.
```

How it works...

All we're doing is defining the environment that the site is running on. In the preceding example, we specify two environments: either default or testing, and apply specific settings for them. So, let's look at some variable definitions.

Common values

The standard database access options are shown in the following table:

Option name	Valid options	Description
$db["default"]["hostname"]	Usually localhost	This is the server that the database sits on
$db["default"]["username"]		The database access username
$db["default"]["password"]		The password for the database
$db["default"]["database"]		The name of the database

Other values

The following table shows the options that normally remain unchanged from the default setting but are here just incase you wish to change them:

Option name	Valid options	Description
$db["default"]["dbdriver"]	mysql	This is the type of DBMS you're using—the recipes in this book use MySQL. The value must be all lowercase.
$db["default"]["dbprefix"]	Default: mysql, but may also be postgre, odbc, and so on	Sometimes you may wish to add a prefix to a database table name, for example, a blogging application might prefix its tables with the word "blog" so the posts table would become blog_posts.
$db["default"]["pconnect"]	TRUE/FALSE	Specifies whether you wish to maintain a persistent connection to the database.
$db["default"]["db_debug"]	TRUE/FALSE	Specifies whether you wish to display database errors on the screen. It is blank by default, but for security purposes should be set to FALSE on a live environment and TRUE while in development.
$db["default"]["cache_on"]	TRUE/FALSE	Specifies whether you want database query caching enabled.

Option name	Valid options	Description
$db["default"]["cachedir"]		Specifies the absolute file path to your database query cache.
$db["default"]["char_set"]	utf8	Specifies the character set that CodeIgniter will use with the database.
$db["default"]["dbcollat"]	utf8_general_ci	Specifies the character collation that CodeIgniter will use with the database.
$db["default"]["port"]	3306	Default MySQL port. This option is not included by default, and if you wish to use a specific port for your database connection, you'll need to manually write in this line and set the value.

We will look at accessing data from a database in more detail in *Chapter 6, Working with Databases*.

Securing the system files

On live environments, it is strongly recommended that you move your system folder out of the web root to prevent malicious access.

How to do it...

1. Move the system folder either by the command line or using your computer's GUI to a folder outside the publicly accessible web folder. The method to do this will be different depending on which system you are using, but I'm sure you know how to move a folder, so we will not discuss that here.

2. After you have moved the system folder, you will need to update the `$system_path` variable in the `path/to/codeigniter/index.php` file. Look for and find the following line:

   ```
   $system_path = "path/to/system/folder";
   ```

   Amend the line to reflect the new location of the system folder. So if, for example, you moved the system folder up one level out of the web root, you should write the following line:

   ```
   $system_path = "../system";
   ```

How it works...

By moving the system folder out of the web root, you are protecting it against access via the Internet (as much as possible). The system folder is much more unlikely to be accessed in a location outside of the web root than inside.

Removing index.php from the address bar using .htaccess

It is possible to remove the `index.php` file from the web browser address bar when CodeIgniter is running.

How to do it...

Create or open a `.htaccess` file. If a `.htaccess` file does not already exist, you can create one as follows:

Linux/Mac

1. Open a terminal window and type: `touch/path/to/CodeIgniter/.htaccess`.

Windows

1. Create a text file in your CodeIgniter root, naming it `file.htaccess`.
2. Press *Windows + R* to open the run dialogue.
3. Enter the following command and click on **OK**:

   ```
   ren "C:\path\to\CodeIgniter\file.htaccess" .htaccess
   ```

4. Once your `.htaccess` file is opened, write the following lines at the top of the file:

   ```
   <IfModule mod_rewrite.c>
   RewriteEngine on
   RewriteCond $1 !^(index\.php|images|robots\.txt)
   RewriteRule ^(.*)$ index.php/$1 [L]
   </IfModule>
   ```

How it works...

This rule in the `.htaccess` file will remove the `index.php` file from the browser's address bar. CodeIgniter's `index.php` file is still called but it is not shown to the user in the address bar of the browser.

Installing and using Sparks

It has been the case for a long time now that to find and use extensions, libraries, and other useful snippets of code for CodeIgniter, you have to search the Internet and download code from various places such as blogs, code repositories, and so on. Useful installations for CodeIgniter were spread across the Internet and as such, may have been hard to locate. Sparks acts as a single point of reference for extensions for CodeIgniter. It's simple to install and use, and contains thousands of useful add-ons for CodeIgniter.

How to do it...

If you are using a MAC or Linux, then the command line interface is open to you.

1. Using the terminal application on your system, navigate to the root of your CodeIgniter application and enter the following line:

   ```
   php -r "$(curl -fsSL http://getsparks.org/go-sparks)"
   ```

   If your installation was successful, you should see something similar to:

   ```
   user@server:/path/to/codeigniter$ php -r "$(curl -fsSL http://
   getsparks.org/go-sparks)"
   Pulling down spark manager from http://getsparks.org/static/
   install/spark-manager-0.0.9.zip ...
   Pulling down Loader class core extension from http://getsparks.
   org/static/install/MY_Loader.php.txt ...
   Extracting zip package ...
   Cleaning up ...
   Spark Manager has been installed successfully!
   Try: `php tools/spark help`
   ```

   If you are using Windows, then you will need to download Sparks and unpack it manually. To do that, perform the following instructions or check out the instructions on the GetSparks website for the latest version:

2. Create a folder named `tools` in the top level (root) of your CodeIgniter directory.
3. Visit the following URL: `http://getsparks.org/install`.
4. Go to the **Normal Installation** section and download the Sparks package.
5. Unpack the download into the `tools` folder you created in step 1.
6. Download the `Loader` class extension from: `http://getsparks.org/static/install/MY_Loader.php.txt`.
7. Rename the `MY_Loader.php.txt` file to `MY_Loader.php` and move it to the `application/core/MY_Loader.php` directory in your CodeIgniter instance.

8. Now that Sparks is installed in your CodeIgniter instance, you can begin to install extensions and packages.

   To install a package from Sparks, type the following in the command line:

   ```
   php tools/spark install [Package Version] Spark Name
   ```

   Here, `Package Version` is the specific version of the Spark you wish to install. You are not required to state the version, and by leaving it out, Sparks will download the latest version by default. `Spark Name` is the name of the Spark you wish to install, so for example, to install the `example-spark` (Version 1.0.0) that comes with the default installation, type in the command line:

   ```
   php tools/spark install -v1.0.0 example-spark
   ```

   If the installation was successful, you should see something similar to:

   ```
   user@server:/path/to/codeigniter$ php tools/spark install -v1.0.0
   example-spark
   [ SPARK ] Retrieving spark detail from getsparks.org
   [ SPARK ] From Downtown! Retrieving spark from Mercurial
   repository at https://url/of/the/spark/repo
   [ SPARK ] Spark installed to ./sparks/example-spark/1.0.0 - You're
   on fire!
   ```

How it works...

You should now be ready to begin making use of your Spark. Be sure to read the `Readme` file or documentation that is included with your Spark for its correct usage.

2
User Management

In this chapter, we will cover:

- ▶ Viewing users
- ▶ Creating users
- ▶ Editing users
- ▶ Deleting users
- ▶ Generating passwords with CodeIgniter
- ▶ Generating passwords with CodeIgniter – the bare bones
- ▶ Forgot password? – resetting passwords with CodeIgniter

Introduction

Chances are that a lot of the sites and apps you'll build with CodeIgniter will need users, and there will be a need to manage them and their details directly, that is create, update, edit, and delete them.

In this chapter, we'll look at basic user management and, build a simple CRUD interface to manage and maintain those users in a database. Later, in *Chapter 7, Creating a Secure User Environment*, we will be looking at securing your user information with login and session functionality, but for now, we will concentrate on building a user management interface.

Before we begin, we'll need to alter some settings in a couple of config files in the `application/config` folder. We'll be editing the following files:

- ▶ `path/to/codeigniter/application/config/config.php`
- ▶ `path/to/codeigniter/application/config/database.php`

Find the following config values in the `path/to/codeigniter/application/config/config.php` file and amend them to reflect the following:

Config item	Change to	Description
`$config['sess_cookie_name']`	ci_session	This should be the name of the cookie written to the users computer.
`$config['sess_expiration']`	7200	This is the number of seconds a session should remain active after a period of no activity before becoming void.
`$config['sess_expire_on_close']`	TRUE	This specifies that if the user closes their browser, the session becomes void.
`$config['sess_encrypt_cookie']`	TRUE	This specifies that if the cookie should be encrypted on the user's computer; for security purposes, this should be set to TRUE.
`$config['sess_use_database']`	TRUE	This specifies whether or not to store sessions in the database. For security purposes, this should be set to TRUE. You will also need to create the session table, which can be found in the *Database schema* section.
`$config['sess_table_name']`	sessions	This specifies the name of the database table used to store session data.
`$config['sess_match_ip']`	TRUE	This specifies CodeIgniter should monitor the IP address of requests and against that of the `session_id`. If the IP of an incoming request doesn't match the previous values, the session is disallowed.
`$config['sess_match_useragent']`	TRUE	This specifies CodeIgniter should monitor the user agent address of requests and against that of the `session_id`. If the user agent of an incoming request doesn't match the previous values, the session is disallowed.

Find the following config values in the `path/to/codeigniter/application/config/database.php` file and amend them to reflect the following:

Config item	Change to value	Description
`$db['default']['hostname']`	localhost	The hostname of your database; this is usually either localhost or an IP address
`$db['default']['username']`	?	The username you wish to use to connect to your database
`$db['default']['password']`	?	The password used to connect to your database
`$db['default']['database']`	?	The name of the database, which you wish to connect to, for example, users

Database schema

Using the method of your choice (command line, phpmyadmin, and so on) enter the following code into your database:

```
CREATE TABLE IF NOT EXISTS `sessions` (
  `session_id` varchar(40) COLLATE utf8_bin NOT NULL DEFAULT '0',
  `ip_address` varchar(16) COLLATE utf8_bin NOT NULL DEFAULT '0',
  `user_agent` varchar(120) COLLATE utf8_bin DEFAULT NULL,
  `last_activity` int(10) unsigned NOT NULL DEFAULT '0',
  `user_data` text COLLATE utf8_bin NOT NULL,
  PRIMARY KEY (`session_id`),
  KEY `last_activity_idx` (`last_activity`)
) ENGINE=InnoDB DEFAULT CHARSET=utf8 COLLATE=utf8_bin;

CREATE TABLE `users` (
  `id` int(11) NOT NULL AUTO_INCREMENT,
  `first_name` varchar(125) NOT NULL,
  `last_name` varchar(125) NOT NULL,
  `email` varchar(255) NOT NULL,
  `created_date` int(11) NOT NULL COMMENT 'unix timestamp',
  `is_active` varchar(3) NOT NULL COMMENT 'yes or no',
  PRIMARY KEY (`id`)
) ENGINE=InnoDB  DEFAULT CHARSET=latin1 AUTO_INCREMENT=1;

INSERT INTO `users` (`id`, `first_name`, `last_name`, `email`,
`created_date`, `is_active`) VALUES
(5, 'First Name', 'Last name', 'first@last.com', 0, '0');
```

What are the columns for and what type of data will we store in them? The following table is a guide to the preceding database schema:

Item name	Attributes	Description
user_id	INTEGER(11)	The table primary key.
user_first_name	VARCHAR(125)	The user's first name.
user_last_name	VARCHAR(125)	The user's last name.
user_email	VARCHAR(255)	The user's e-mail address, for example, name@example.org.
user_created_date	INTEGER(11)	The unix timestamp for the date the user was created within the database.
user_is_active	INTEGER(1)	The Boolean value represented as 0 or 1, if the user is active. This variable specifies whether the user is active within the system. An active user can login, while inactive users cannot.

If you have already created a sessions table, then you can omit that table.

Viewing users

A good place for us to begin is to display a list of our users. We're going to create a model, view, and controller to provide the functionality to do this.

How to do it...

We're going to create the following three files:

- ▶ path/to/codeigniter/application/models/users_model.php: This file gives us CRUD support with the database

- ▶ path/to/codeigniter/application/views/users/view_all_users.php: This file contains a foreach loop, which runs through the results array, writing all users to a table

- ▶ path/to/codeigniter/application/controllers/users.php: This file contains the code necessary to handle the CRUD functionality

1. Copy the following code into the, `path/to/codeigniter/application/controllers/users.php` file:

```php
<?php if (! defined('BASEPATH')) exit('No direct script
  access allowed');

class Users extends CI_Controller {
    function __construct() {
        parent::__construct();
        $this->load->helper('form');
        $this->load->helper('url');
        $this->load->helper('security');
        $this->load->model('Users_model');
        $this->load->database();
    }

    public function index() {
        redirect('users/view_users');
    }

    public function view_users() {
        $data['query'] = $this->Users_model-
          >get_all_users();
        $this->load->view('users/view_all_users', $data);
    }
}
```

2. Copy the following code into the, `path/to/codeigniter/application/models/users_model.php` file:

```php
<?php if ( ! defined('BASEPATH')) exit('No direct script
  access allowed');

class Users_model extends CI_Model {
    function __construct() {
        parent::__construct();
    }

    public function get_all_users() {
        return $this->db->get('users');
    }
}
```

3. Copy the following code into the, `path/to/codeigniter/application/views/users/view_all_users.php` file:

```php
<?php if ($query->num_rows() > 0 ) : ?>
<table border="0">
  <tr>
      <td>ID</td>
      <td>First Name</td>
      <td>Last Name</td>
      <td>Created Date</td>
      <td>Is Active</td>
      <td colspan="2">Actions</td>
  </tr>
  <?php foreach ($query->result() as $row) : ?>
  <tr>
      <td><?php echo $row->id; ?></td>
      <td><?php echo $row->first_name; ?></td>
      <td><?php echo $row->last_name; ?></td>
      <td><?php echo date
         ("d-m-Y", $row->created_date); ?></td>
      <td><?php echo
         ($row->is_active ? 'Yes' : 'No'); ?></td>
      <td><?php echo anchor
          ('users/edit_user/'.$row->id, 'Edit') ; ?></td>
      <td><?php echo anchor
          ('users/delete_user/'.$row->id, 'Delete') ; ?></td>
  </tr>
  <?php endforeach ; ?>
</table>
<?php endif ; ?>
```

How it works...

This is fairly standard stuff and there's nothing complicated going on. We have a controller running the show, which loads some useful helpers to provide support with functions such as `redirect()`, other security functions, and the `Users_model` in its constructor. `public function index()` redirects to `public function view_users()`, which in turn connects to the, `get_all_users()` function in the, `Users_model model`, using the, `$this->Users_model->get_all_users()` syntax to return an Active Record result set. This result set is then passed to the, `users/view_all_users view`, where it is displayed in a `foreach` loop in a table. See...I told you it was simple!

Creating users

You will always need a method to create users yourself from within an application, and will need to; manually enter their data rather than the user entering the data themselves. We're going to build functionality to allow you to create users one by one.

How to do it...

We'll need to create one file:

▸ `path/to/codeigniter/application/views/users/new_user.php`

And amend the following two files:

▸ `path/to/codeigniter/application/controllers/users.php`

▸ `path/to/codeigniter/application/models/users_model.php`

1. Copy the following code into the, `path/to/codeigniter/application/views/users/new_user.php` file:

```php
<?php echo form_open('users/new_user') ; ?>
  <?php if (validation_errors()) : ?>
    <h3>Whoops! There was an error:</h3>
    <p><?php echo validation_errors(); ?></p>
  <?php endif; ?>
  <table border="0">
  <tr>
    <td>User First Name</td>
    <td><?php echo form_input($first_name); ?></td>
  </tr>
  <tr>
    <td>User Last Name</td>
    <td><?php echo form_input($last_name); ?></td>
  </tr>
  <tr>
    <td>User Email</td>
    <td><?php echo form_input($email); ?></td>
  </tr>
  <tr>
    <td>User Is Active?</td>
    <td><?php echo form_checkbox($is_active); ?></td>
  </tr>
</table>
    <?php echo form_submit('submit', 'Create'); ?>
    or <?php echo anchor('users/index', 'cancel'); ?>
<?php echo form_close(); ?>
```

2. Amend the, `path/to/codeigniter/application/controllers/users.php` file, with the following code:

```php
public function new_user() {
    // Load support assets
    $this->load->library('form_validation');
    $this->form_validation->set_error_delimiters
      ('', '<br />');

    // Set validation rules
    $this->form_validation->set_rules
      ('first_name', 'First Name',
        'required|min_length[1]|max_length[125]');
    $this->form_validation->set_rules
      ('last_name', 'Last Name',
        'required|min_length[1]|max_length[125]');
    $this->form_validation->set_rules('email', 'Email',
      'required|min_length[1]|max_length[255]|
        valid_email');
    $this->form_validation->set_rules('is_active',
      'Is Active', 'min_length[1]|max_length[1]|
        integer|is_natural');

    // Begin validation
    if ($this->form_validation->run() == FALSE) {
        // First load, or problem with form
        $data['first_name'] = array('name' =>
          'first_name', 'id' => 'first_name', 'value'
            => set_value('first_name', ''),
              'maxlength'   => '100', 'size' => '35');
        $data['last_name'] = array('name' =>
          'last_name', 'id' => 'last_name', 'value' =>
            set_value('last_name', ''),
              'maxlength'   => '100', 'size' => '35');
        $data['email'] = array('name' => 'email',
          'id' => 'email', 'value' =>
            set_value('email', ''),
              'maxlength'   => '100', 'size' => '35');
        $data['is_active'] = array('name' =>
          'is_active', 'id' => 'is_active',
            'value' => set_value('is_active', ''));

        $this->load->view('users/new_user',$data);
    } else { // Validation passed, now escape the data
        $data = array(
            'first_name' =>
              $this->input->post('first_name'),
            'last_name' =>
              $this->input->post('last_name'),
```

```
                'email' => $this->input->post('email'),
                'is_active' =>
                  $this->input->post('is_active'),
            );

        if ($this->Users_model-
          >process_create_user($data)) {
            redirect('users');
        }
      }
    }
```

3. Amend the, `path/to/codeigniter/application/models/users_model.php` file, with the following code:

```
public function process_create_user($data) {
    if ($this->db->insert('users', $data)) {
      return true;
    } else {
      return false;
    }
}
```

How it works...

There's a little more going on here than with the preceding `view_users` code, but it's still simple and straightforward. `public function new_user()` performs several functions, such as loading the view file, to validating any data inputted after submission, and displaying a view.

If `public function new_user()` is being called for the first time (that is, it is not being called by a form submission), then the validation check (`$this->form_validation->run()`) will equal `FALSE` and the code within the parentheses will be executed. In this case, the code will load the, `cust/new_user` view.

However, if the function is loaded as the result of a form submission, then CodeIgniter will begin checking the user input. The first line of the function loads the necessary library to enable checking the user's input: `$this->library('form_validation')`, and our error delimiters are set with the function, `set_error_deimiters()`. Each item in the form is then checked against the criteria we specify. A full list of validation criteria options are available at: `http://ellislab.com/codeigniter/user-guide/libraries/form_validation.html`

We will also discuss form validation in greater detail in *Chapter 5, Managing Data In and Out.*

If validation isn't passed (the input from the user didn't meet the requirements we set), then `$this->form_validation->run()` will return `FALSE` and the form will be displayed again. The form elements in the view are able to display the user's input (so they don't have to re-enter everything from scratch).

Once validation is passed (`$this->form_validation->run()` returns `TRUE`), then we'll package up the input into an array: `$data`. As we're using Active Record to interact with the database, the keys of the `$data` array must match the column names of our database table. The `$data` array is then sent to the `Users_model` for writing to the database using the syntax: `$this->Users_model->get_all_users()`.

Editing users

You will always need some method to edit users yourself from within an application. In this section, we will look at creating functionality to do just that: to update and edit user details.

How to do it...

We'll need to create one file:

- `path/to/codeigniter/application/views/users/edit_user.php`

And amend the following two files:

- `path/to/codeigniter/application/controllers/users.php`
- `path/to/codeigniter/application/models/users_model.php`

1. Copy the following code to the, `path/to/codeigniter/application/views/users/edit_user.php` file:

```php
<?php echo form_open('users/edit_user') ; ?>
    <?php if (validation_errors()) : ?>
        <h3>Whoops! There was an error:</h3>
        <p><?php echo validation_errors(); ?></p>
    <?php endif; ?>
    <table border="0" >
      <tr>
        <td>User First Name</td>
        <td><?php echo form_input($first_name); ?></td>
      </tr>
      <tr>
        <td>User Last Name</td>
        <td><?php echo form_input($last_name); ?></td>
      </tr>
```

```
<tr>
  <td>User Email</td>
  <td><?php echo form_input($email); ?></td>
</tr>
<tr>
  <td>User Is Active?</td>
  <td><?php echo form_checkbox($is_active); ?></td>
</tr>
<?php echo form_hidden($id); ?>
</table>
<?php echo form_submit('submit', 'Update'); ?>
or <?php echo anchor('users/index', 'cancel'); ?>
<?php echo form_close(); ?>
```

2. Amend the, `path/to/codeigniter/application/controllers/users.php`
   file, with the following code:

```
public function edit_user() {
    // Load support assets
    $this->load->library('form_validation');
    $this->form_validation->set_error_delimiters(
      '', '<br />');

    // Set validation rules
    $this->form_validation->set_rules('first_name',
      'First Name',
        'required|min_length[1]|max_length[125]');
    $this->form_validation->set_rules('last_name',
      'Last Name',
        'required|min_length[1]|max_length[125]');
    $this->form_validation->set_rules('email', 'Email',
      'required|min_length[1]|
        max_length[255]|valid_email');
    $this->form_validation->set_rules('is_active',
      'Is Active', 'min_length[1]|max_length[1]|
        integer|is_natural');

    if ($this->input->post()) {
        $id = $this->input->post('id');
    } else {
        $id = $this->uri->segment(3);
    }

    // Begin validation
    if ($this->form_validation->run() == FALSE) {
      // First load, or problem with form
        $query = $this->Users_model-
          >get_user_details($id);
        foreach ($query->result() as $row) {
            $first_name = $row->first_name;
```

```
                $last_name = $row->last_name;
                $email = $row->email;
                $is_active= $row->is_active;
            }

            $data['first_name'] = array('name' =>
              'first_name', 'id' => 'first_name',
                'value' => set_value('first_name',
                  $first_name), 'maxlength' => '100',
                    'size' => '35');
            $data['last_name'] = array('name' =>
              'last_name', 'id' => 'last_name',
                'value' => set_value('last_name',
                  $last_name), 'maxlength'   => '100',
                    'size' => '35');
            $data['email'] = array('name' => 'email',
              'id' => 'email', 'value' =>
                set_value('email', $email), 'maxlength'
                  => '100', 'size' => '35');
            $data['is_active'] = array('name' =>
              'is_active', 'id' => 'is_active',
                'value' => set_value('is_active',
                  $is_active), 'maxlength'   => '100',
                    'size' => '35');
            $data['id'] = array('id' => set_value(
              'id', $id));

            $this->load->view(
              'users/edit_user', $data);

    } else { // Validation passed, now escape the data
        $data = array(
            'first_name' =>
              $this->input->post('first_name'),
            'last_name' =>
              $this->input->post('last_name'),
            'email' => $this->input->post('email'),
            'is_active' =>
              $this->input->post('is_active'),
        );

        if ($this->Users_model-
          >process_update_user($id, $data)) {
            redirect('users/view_users');
        }
    }
}
```

3. Amend the, `path/to/codeigniter/application/models/users_model.php` file, with the following code:

```
public function process_update_user($id, $data) {
    $this->db->where('id', $id);
    if ($this->db->update('users', $data)) {
      return true;
    } else {
      return false;
    }
}

public function get_user_details($id) {
    $this->db->where('id', $id);
    return $this->db->get('users');
}
```

How it works...

This is similar functionality to creating a new user (mentioned earlier), but instead of writing a row to the users table, we're removing a row based on the user's primary key.

First we'll need to grab the user's ID. At this point, the user's ID is probably coming from an URL, but may also be coming from a post array (for example, if returned `FALSE`). The following code works out how the `$id` variable is coming in (either post or URL), and stores it in the `$id` variable ready for later processing:.

```
if ($this->input->post()) {
    $id = $this->input->post('id');
} else {
    $id = $this->uri->segment(3);
}
```

We then validate the users edited data—if the data passes validation we package up the incoming form data into an associative array (called `$data`). We use the array keys as a mapper to the column names in our database—that is to say that the keys in the array match the database column—stake a look at the following code:

```
$data = array(
    'first_name' => $this->input->post('first_name'),
    'last_name' => $this->input->post('last_name'),
    'email' => $this->input->post('email'),
    'is_active' => $this->input->post('is_active'),
);
```

You can see that the keys of the associative array match the column names in the database table; so the key `first_name` in the array will map to `first_name` column in the table. The key `last_name` in the array will map to the `last_name` column in the table.

Next we write the users edited information to the database. We do this by sending the `$data` array we just created (along with the `$id` variable) to our `Users_model` function `process_update_user()`, which will perform the task of updating.

```php
if ($this->Users_model->process_update_user($id, $data)) {
    redirect('users/view_users');
}
```

Deleting users

It's always a good idea to be able to delete users from an interface rather than removing them from the database directly or not deleting them at all. We're going to create a CRUD interface to allow us to remove users from the database. Here's how to do it.

How to do it...

We'll need to create one file:

▶ path/to/codeigniter/application/views/users/delete_user.php

1. Add the following code into the, `views/users/delete_user.php` file:

```php
<?php echo form_open('users/delete_user'); ?>
    <?php if (validation_errors()) : ?>
        <h3>Whoops! There was an error:</h3>
        <p><?php echo validation_errors(); ?></p>
    <?php endif; ?>
    <?php foreach ($query->result() as $row) : ?>
        <?php echo $row->first_name . ' ' . $row-
          >last_name; ?>
        <?php echo form_submit('submit', 'Delete'); ?>
        or <?php echo anchor('users/index', 'cancel'); ?>
        <?php echo form_hidden('id', $row->id); ?>
    <?php endforeach; ?>
</form>
```

2. Amend the following two files:

   ❑ path/to/codeigniter/application/controllers/users.php
   ❑ path/to/codeigniter/application/models/users_model.php

3. Amend the, `controllers/users.php` file, with the following code:

```php
public function delete_user() {
    // Load support assets
    $this->load->library('form_validation');
    $this->form_validation->set_error_delimiters(
      '', '<br />');

    // Set validation rules
    $this->form_validation->set_rules('id', 'User ID',
      'required|min_length[1]|max_length[11]|
        integer|is_natural');

    if ($this->input->post()) {
        $id = $this->input->post('id');
    } else {
        $id = $this->uri->segment(3);
    }

    if ($this->form_validation->run() == FALSE) {
      // First load, or problem with form

        $data['query'] =
          $this->Users_model->get_user_details($id);

        $this->load->view('users/delete_user', $data);
    } else {
        if ($this->Users_model->delete_user($id)) {
            redirect('users/view_users');
        }
    }
}
```

4. Amend the, `controllers/users_model.php` file, with the following code:

```php
public function delete_user($id) {
    $this->db->where('id', $id);
    if ($this->db->delete('users')) {
        return true;
    } else {
        return false;
    }
}
```

How it works...

This is similar functionality to creating a new user (explained earlier), but instead of writing a row to the users table, we're removing a row based on the user's primary key.

First, we'll need to grab the user's ID. At this point the user's ID is probably coming from an URL, but may also be coming from the post array.

The following code works out how the $id variable is coming in (either from post or by URL) and stores it in the $id variable ready for processing later:

```
if ($this->input->post()) {
  $id = $this->input->post('id');
} else {
  $id = $this->uri->segment(3);
}
```

If `public function delete_user()` is being called for the first time (that is, it is not being called by a form submission), then the user's primary key is passed to `public function delete_user()` from within the URL. It is picked up by `$this->uri->segment(3)` and is sent to the, `users/delete_user.php` view by assigning it in `$this->load->view ('user/delete_user', $data['id])`. Within the view, the $id value is written as a hidden HTML form the element.

It is necessary to assign the user's ID as a hidden element in the form because when the form is submitted, `public function delete_user()` will require the ID of the user. A the form is being submitted rather than a first load, the ID will not be available from `$this->uri->segment(3)`.

`public function delete_user()` performs several functions similar to `public function new_user()`. These are loading the view file, validating any data inputted after submission, and displaying a view.

If `public function delete_user()` is being called as the result of a form submission, CodeIgniter will begin checking and validating the user input; in this case, submitted input consists only of the users ID, which is written as a hidden form element in the view. The first line of the function loads the necessary library to enable checking the user's input: `$this->library('form_validation')`, and our error delimiters are set with the function, `set_error_deimiters()`. The user ID is then checked against the criteria we specify. A full list of validation criteria options are available at:

`http://ellislab.com/codeigniter/user-guide/libraries/form_validation.html`. We will also discuss form validation in greater detail in *Chapter 5, Managing Data In and Out*.

If validation isn't passed (the input from the user didn't meet the requirements we set), then `$this->form_validation->run()` will return `FALSE`, and the form will be displayed again.

Once validation is passed (`$this->form_validation->run()` returns `TRUE`), then we'll package up the input into an array: `$data`. As we're using Active Record to interact with the database, the keys of the `$data` array must match the column names of our database table.

The `$data` array is then sent to the `Users_model` for deletion from the database using the syntax: `$this->Users_model->delete_user($id)`.

Generating passwords with CodeIgniter

There are two ways to explain this. As this is a recipe book, I'm going to give you the structure for a user to register (part of this process is creating a hash from the password the user will provide) and also the signin form (part of this process is to validate a password against a hash). But I'm aware that you won't necessarily need all the following files, the lines which focus on password hashing in the following examples. This way, you can quickly see how the process works and apply it to your situation.

Getting ready

First, let's make the database schema to support the recipe. If you have your own table ready and are just looking for the hashing code, you can probably skip this part. Otherwise, copy the following code into your database:

```
CREATE TABLE IF NOT EXISTS `register` (
  `user_id` int(11) NOT NULL AUTO_INCREMENT,
  `user_first_name` varchar(125) NOT NULL,
  `user_last_name` varchar(125) NOT NULL,
  `user_email` varchar(255) NOT NULL,
  `user_hash` text NOT NULL,
  PRIMARY KEY (`user_id`)
) ENGINE=InnoDB  DEFAULT CHARSET=latin1 AUTO_INCREMENT=1 ;
```

Downloading the example code

You can download the example code files for all Packt books you have purchased from your account at `http://www.packtpub.com`. If you purchased this book elsewhere, you can visit h

The register table description is as follows:

Item name	Attributes	Description
user_id	INTEGER(11)	Table primary key
user_first_name	VARCHAR(125)	The user's first name
user_last_name	VARCHAR(125)	The user's last name
user_email	VARCHAR(255)	The user's e-mail address, for example, name@example.org
user_hash	TEXT	The hash of their password generated by $this->encrypt->sha1($string_ to_hash [, $key])

You'll also have to create a sessions table and ensure that the config file is set up to handle database stored sessions. For instructions on how to do that, see

That's the database done! We're going to use the CodeIgniter **encrypt** library to do the heavy lifting of hashing the password for us, specifically, $this->encrypt->sha1($string_to_ hash [, $key]), where $key is optional. There are a few things we need to set up first. You'll need to decide on the encryption key you want to use: this can either be the encryption key that you've set in $config['encryption_key'] in config.php, or you can pass a new key as a second parameter to CodeIgniter. The presence of this second parameter overrides the value set in $config['encryption_key'].

In the following recipe, we are using the value in $config['encryption_key'] to serve as our encryption key; as such, we won't be passing a second parameter.

When creating a key, try not to use just a single word as this may be cracked using a rainbow table; instead use a fairly long string with random alphanumeric characters.

How to do it...

In this recipe, we're going to create the following seven files:

▸ /path/to/codeigniter/application/controllers/register.php: This file contains a form allowing the user to sign up, and a record is then added to the database table (SQL in the *Getting ready* section)

▸ /path/to/codeigniter/application/models/register_model.php: This file interacts with the database for the controller

▸ /path/to/codeigniter/application/views/register/register.php: This file is for the registration form

- ▶ `/path/to/codeigniter/application/controllers/signin.php`: This file handles the login process, including comparing the password against the hash

- ▶ `/path/to/codeigniter/application/models/signin_model.php`: This file interacts with the database for the controller

- ▶ `/path/to/codeigniter/application/views/signin/signin.php`: This file is for the signin form

- ▶ `/path/to/codeigniter/application/views/signin/loggedin.php`: This file presents a page indicating a successful sign-in

1. Copy the following code into the, `/path/to/codeigniter/application/controllers/register.php` file:

```php
<?php if (!defined('BASEPATH')) exit('No direct script
  access allowed');

class Register extends CI_Controller {
    function __construct() {
        parent::__construct();
        $this->load->helper('form');
        $this->load->helper('url');
        $this->load->helper('security');
        $this->load->model('Register_model');
        $this->load->library('encrypt');
        $this->load->database();
    }

    public function index() {
        redirect('register/register_user');
    }

    public function register_user() {
        // Load support assets
        $this->load->library('form_validation');
        $this->form_validation->set_error_delimiters(
          '', '<br />');

        // Set validation rules
        $this->form_validation->set_rules('first_name',
          'First Name',
            'required|min_length[1]|max_length[125]');
        $this->form_validation->set_rules('last_name',
          'Last Name',
            'required|min_length[1]|max_length[125]');
        $this->form_validation->set_rules('email', 'Email',
          'required|min_length[1]|max_length[255]|
            valid_email');
        $this->form_validation->set_rules('password1',
```

```
                     'Password', 'required|min_length[5]|
                       max_length[15]');
                 $this->form_validation->set_rules('password2',
                   'Confirmation Password', 'required|min_length[5]|
                     max_length[15]|matches[password1]');

                 // Begin validation
                 if ($this->form_validation->run() == FALSE) {
                     // First load, or problem with form
                     $data['page_title'] = "Register";
                     $this->load->view('register/register',$data);
                 } else {
                     // Create hash from user password
                     $hash = $this->encrypt->sha1(
                       $this->input->post('password1'));

                     $data = array(
                         'user_first_name' =>
                           $this->input->post('first_name'),
                         'user_last_name' =>
                           $this->input->post('last_name'),
                         'user_email' =>
                           $this->input->post('email'),
                         'user_hash' => $hash
                     );

                     if ($this->Register_model-
                       >register_user($data)) {
                         redirect('signin');
                     } else {
                         redirect('register');
                     }
                 }
             }
         }
     }
```

2. Copy the following code into the, `/path/to/codeigniter/application/`
    `models/register_model.php` file:

```php
<?php if (! defined('BASEPATH')) exit('No direct script
  access allowed');

class Register_model extends CI_Model {
    function __construct() {
        parent::__construct();
    }

    public function register_user($data) {
        if ($this->db->insert('register', $data)) {
            return true;
```

```
        } else {
            return false;
        }
    }

    public function update_user($data, $email) {
        $this->db->where('user_email', $email);
        $this->db->update('register', $data);
    }
}
```

3. Copy the following code into the, `/path/to/codeigniter/application/views/register/register.php` file:

```php
<?php echo form_open('register/register_user') ; ?>
    <?php if (validation_errors()) : ?>
        <h3>Whoops! There was an error:</h3>
        <p><?php echo validation_errors(); ?></p>
    <?php endif; ?>
    <table border="0" >
        <tr>
            <td>First Name</td>
            <td><?php echo form_input(array('name' =>
                'first_name', 'id' => 'first_name',
                    'value' => set_value('first_name', ''),
                        'maxlength' => '100', 'size' => '50',
                            'style' => 'width:100%')); ?></td>
        </tr>
        <tr>
            <td>Last Name</td>
            <td><?php echo form_input(array('name' =>
                'last_name', 'id' => 'last_name',
                    'value' => set_value('last_name', ''),
                        'maxlength' => '100', 'size' => '50',
                            'style' => 'width:100%')); ?></td>
        </tr>
        <tr>
            <td>User Email</td>
            <td><?php echo form_input(array('name' =>
                'email', 'id' => 'email',
                    'value' => set_value('email', ''),
                        'maxlength' => '100', 'size' => '50',
                            'style' => 'width:100%')); ?></td>
        </tr>
        <tr>
            <td>Password</td>
            <td><?php echo form_password(array('name' =>
                'password1', 'id' => 'password1',
                    'value' => set_value('password1', ''),
                        'maxlength' => '100', 'size' => '50',
```

```
                            'style' => 'width:100%')); ?></td>
        </tr>
        <tr>
            <td>Confirm Password</td>
            <td><?php echo form_password(array('name' =>
                'password2', 'id' => 'password2',
                 'value' => set_value('password2', ''),
                    'maxlength' => '100', 'size' => '50',
                        'style' => 'width:100%')); ?></td>
        </tr>
    </table>
    <?php echo form_submit('submit', 'Submit'); ?>
    or <?php echo anchor('form', 'cancel'); ?>
<?php echo form_close(); ?>
```

4. Copy the following code in to the, `/path/to/codeigniter/application/ controllers/signin.php` file:

```php
<?php if (!defined('BASEPATH')) exit('No direct script
  access allowed');

class Signin extends CI_Controller {

  function __construct() {
    parent::__construct();
    $this->load->helper('form');
    $this->load->helper('url');
    $this->load->helper('security');
  }

  public function index() {
    redirect('signin/login');
  }

    public function login() {
    if ($this->session->userdata('logged_in') == TRUE) {
      redirect('signin/loggedin');
    } else {
      $this->load->library('form_validation');

      // Set validation rules for view filters
      $this->form_validation->set_rules('email', 'Email',
        'required|valid_email|min_length[5]|
          max_length[125]');
      $this->form_validation->set_rules('password',
        'Password ', 'required|min_length[5]|
          max_length[30]');

      if ($this->form_validation->run() == FALSE) {
        $this->load->view('signin/signin');
```

```php
    } else {
      $email = $this->input->post('email');
      $password = $this->input->post('password');

      $this->load->model('Signin_model');
      $query =
        $this->Signin_model->does_user_exist($email);

      if ($query->num_rows() == 1) {
        // One matching row found
        foreach ($query->result() as $row) {
          // Call Encrypt library
          $this->load->library('encrypt');

          // Generate hash from a their password
          $hash = $this->encrypt->sha1($password);

          // Compare the generated hash with that in the
          // database
          if ($hash != $row->user_hash) {
            // Didn't match so send back to login
            $data['login_fail'] = true;
            $this->load->view('signin/signin', $data);
          } else {
            $data = array(
              'user_id' => $row->user_id,
              'user_email' => $row->user_email,
              'logged_in' => TRUE
            );

            // Save data to session
            $this->session->set_userdata($data);
            redirect('signin/loggedin');
          }
        }
      }
    }
  }

  function loggedin() {
    if ($this->session->userdata('logged_in') == TRUE) {
      $this->load->view('signin/loggedin');
    } else {
      redirect('signin');
    }
  }
}
```

5. Copy the following code in to the, `/path/to/codeigniter/application/models/signin_model.php` file:

```php
<?php if ( ! defined('BASEPATH')) exit('No direct script
  access allowed');

class Signin_model extends CI_Model {
    function __construct() {
        parent::__construct();
    }

    public function does_user_exist($email) {
        $this->db->where('user_email', $email);
        $query = $this->db->get('register');
        return $query;
    }
}
```

6. Then copy the following code in to the, `/path/to/codeigniter/application/views/signin/signin.php` file:

```php
<?php echo form_open('signin/login') ; ?>
    <?php if (validation_errors()) : ?>
        <h3>Whoops! There was an error:</h3>
        <p><?php echo validation_errors(); ?></p>
    <?php endif; ?>

    <?php if (isset($login_fail)) : ?>
        <h3>Login Error:</h3>
        <p>Username or Password is incorrect,
          please try again.</p>
    <?php endif; ?>

    <table border="0" >
        <tr>
            <td>User Email</td>
            <td><?php echo form_input(array('name' =>
              'email', 'id' => 'email',
                'value' => set_value('email', ''),
                  'maxlength' => '100', 'size' => '50',
                    'style' => 'width:100%')); ?></td>
        </tr>
        <tr>
            <td>Password</td>
            <td><?php echo form_password(array('name' =>
              'password', 'id' => 'password',
                'value' => set_value('password', ''),
                  'maxlength' => '100', 'size' => '50',
```

```
                       'style' => 'width:100%')); ?></td>
            </tr>
        </table>
        <?php echo form_submit('submit', 'Submit'); ?>
        or <?php echo anchor('signin', 'cancel'); ?>
    <?php echo form_close(); ?>
```

7. Then copy the following code in to the, `/path/to/codeigniter/application/views/signin/loggedin.php` file:

```
Success!  Logged in as <?php echo
    $this->session->userdata('user_email'); ?>
```

How it works...

Okay, there's a lot going on in this example but it's actually fairly simple. Take a look at the preceding code again—specifically the lines which are highlighted as these are the lines that are password specific. The files created in the preceding section show the creation of a user and the logging in of that user. Of course, your code will be different; but let's concentrate on those highlighted lines.

They show the code that performs the hashing and comparison of passwords (a concise version can be found in the following recipe).

Firstly, let's look at the register user process. The register controller accepts user-submitted information from the `/path/to/codeigniter/application/views/register/register.php` view. Upon successfully passing the following validation line:

```
$hash = $this->encrypt->sha1($password);
```

will generate a hashed value using the password the user supplied, this hashed value is stored in the, `$hash` variable (obvious huh?).

`$hash` is then added to the `$data` array for insertion into the database as follows:

```
// Create hash from user password
$hash = $this->encrypt->sha1($this->input->post('password1'));

$data = array(
    'user_first_name' => $this->input->post('first_name'),
    'user_last_name' => $this->input->post('last_name'),
    'user_email' => $this->input->post('email'),
    'user_hash' => $hash
);
```

Now let's take a look at the sign-in process. `public function login()` accepts the e-mail address and password from the user (from the, `/path/to/codeigniter/application/ views/signin/signin.php` view), and upon successfully passing validation, we look up the user-supplied e-mail address in the register table as follows:

```
$this->load->model('Signin_model');
$query = $this->Signin_model->does_user_exist($email);

if ($query->num_rows() == 1) {
  // One matching row found
  foreach ($query->result() as $row) {
  ..
}
```

If the e-mail exists, we generate a hash from the user-supplied password. This process is the same as the functionality found in the registration process as follows:

```
// Call Encrypt library
$this->load->library('encrypt');

// Generate hash from a their password
$hash = $this->encrypt->sha1($password);

// Compare the generated hash with that in the
// database
if ($hash != $row->user_hash) {
  // Didn't match so send back to login
  $data['login_fail'] = true;
  $this->load->view('signin/signin', $data);
} else {
  $data = array(
      'user_id' => $row->user_id,
      'user_email' => $row->user_email,
      'logged_in' => TRUE
  );

  // Save data to session
  $this->session->set_userdata($data);
  redirect('signin/loggedin');
}
```

Now, take a look at the highlighted line in the preceding code. We're comparing the hash we generated from the user-supplied password against `user_hash` in the record we pulled from the register table. If the two hashes do not match, then the user must not have supplied the correct password, so we send them back to the signin form and wait for another attempt. However, if the two hashes do match, then the user must have supplied the correct password, so we'll start a session for them and redirect them to `public function loggedin()`. In this case, it is a brief message, indicating that they are successfully logged in. However, in your application, this would be some sort of password protected member area, perhaps a dashboard.

Generating passwords with CodeIgniter – the bare bones

Okay, this is just the bare bones process. If you want a full example, then the preceding recipe is for you. This recipe is for people who already have a create-user process, but wish to integrate some password protection into an existing process.

How to do it...

If you don't need the preceding recipe and only require the bare bones of hashing/comparing; please refer to the following steps:

Generating a hash

To generate a hash, perform the following steps:

1. Generate a hash with a key in `$config['encryption_key']` as follows:

```
// Call Encrypt library
$this->load->library('encrypt');

$hash = $this->encrypt->sha1($text_to_be_hashed);
```

2. Generate a hash with a key other than that in `$config['encryption_key']` as follows:

```
// Call Encrypt library
$this->load->library('encrypt');

$key = "This-is-the-key";
$hash = $this->encrypt->sha1($text_to_be_hashed, $key);
```

 In a production environment, replace the `$key` value (`This-is-the-key`) with a realistic value. Make it a long string of alphanumeric characters; the more random the better!

Comparing hashed values

The hash values are compared as follows:

```
// Call Encrypt library
$this->load->library('encrypt');

// Generate hash from a their password
$hash = $this->encrypt->sha1($password);

// Compare the generated hash with that in the database
if ($hash != $row->user_hash) {
    // Didn't match so send back to login
    redirect('signin/login');
} else {
    // Did match so log them in if you wish
}
```

How it works...

Generating a hash with the $config['encryption_key'] value: First, we load the encrypt library with `$this->load->library('encrypt')`, then we call the `sha1` function in the encrypt library and pass to it the, `$text_to_be_hashed` variable. The key used to encrypt the `$text_to_be_hashed` string, comes from the value set in the config array item, `$config['encryption_key']`, in the `config.php` file. `$this->encrypt->sha1 ($text_to_be_hashed)` will return a string that we'll store in the, `$hash` variable.

Generating a hash without the $config['encryption_key'] value (that is adding a second parameter): First, we load the encrypt library with `$this->load->library('encrypt')`, then we call the `sha1` function in the encrypt library and pass to it the, `$text_to_be_hashed`, and also an encryption key as a second parameter:

```
$this->encrypt->sha1($text_to_be_hashed, $key)
```

Adding this key as a second parameter (`$key`) will cause CodeIgniter to use that key rather than any value set in `$config['encryption_key']`. `$this->encrypt->sha1($text_to_be_hashed, $key)` will return a string that we'll store in the variable, `$hash`.

After loading the encryption support library with `$this->load->library('encrypt')`, a string of text (in this case, in the, `$password` variable) is passed to the `sha1` function in the encrypt library, storing its product in the, `$hash` variable. We can now use this variable to compare a stored value, such as from a database select result. In this example, we compare `$hash` with the value in `$row->user_hash`. If they do not match, we send `redirect()` to the login screen, but you could easily code any action, such as logging the event or displaying a message rather than a redirect. If the `$hash` and `$row->user_hash` values do match, then you could perform an action based on this confirmation; an example would be logging the user in.

Forgot password? – resetting passwords with CodeIgniter

Everyone forgets their password from time to time and it's likely that a user may wish to be reminded of their password. However, we cannot send them their password as we don't have it; we are only storing a hash of it—the password isn't actually stored in the database. The user will have to reset their password; generating a new hash as they do so.

Getting ready

We want to be sure that a user has genuinely requested a new password, therefore, we're going to add a column in the register table to support this. The new column called `forgot_password` will contain a code which we will generate when a new password is requested; and we will check that code when the user is redirected back to the site from a url in an e-mail, which we will also send to them. Copy the following code into your database:

```
ALTER TABLE register ADD forgot_password INT(11) AFTER user_hash;
```

How to do it...

We're going to create the following two files:

- `/path/to/codeigniter/application/views/signin/forgot_password.php`
- `/path/to/codeigniter/application/views/signin/new_password.php`

And amend the following three files:

- `/path/to/codeigniter/application/controllers/signin.php`
- `/path/to/codeigniter/application/models/signin_model.php`
- `/path/to/codeigniter/application/views/signin/signin.php`

1. Copy the following code into `/path/to/codeigniter/application/views/signin/forgot_password.php`:

```php
<?php echo form_open('signin/forgot_password') ; ?>
    <?php if (validation_errors()) : ?>
        <h3>Whoops! There was an error:</h3>
        <p><?php echo validation_errors(); ?></p>
    <?php endif; ?>
    <?php if (isset($submit_success)) : ?>
        <h3>Email Sent:</h3>
        <p>An email has been sent to the address
          provided.</p>
```

```php
<?php endif; ?>
<table border="0" >
    <tr>
        <td>User Email</td>
        <td><?php echo form_input(array('name' =>
            'email', 'id' => 'email',
                'value' => set_value('email', ''),
                    'maxlength' => '100', 'size' => '50',
                        'style' => 'width:100%')); ?></td>
    </tr>
</table>
<?php echo form_submit('submit', 'Submit'); ?>
or <?php echo anchor('form', 'cancel'); ?>
<?php echo form_close(); ?>
```

2. Copy the following code into /path/to/codeigniter/application/views/
   signin/new_password.php:

```php
<?php echo form_open('signin/new_password') ; ?>
    <?php if (validation_errors()) : ?>
        <h3>Whoops! There was an error:</h3>
        <p><?php echo validation_errors(); ?></p>
    <?php endif; ?>
    <h2>Reset your password</h2>

    <table border="0">
        <tr>
            <td>User Email</td>
            <td><?php echo form_input(array('name' =>
                'email', 'id' => 'email', 'value' =>
                    set_value('email', ''), 'maxlength' =>
                        '100', 'size' => '50',
                            'style' => 'width:100%')); ?></td>
        </tr>
        <tr>
            <td>Password</td>
            <td><?php echo form_password(array('name' =>
                'password1', 'id' => 'password1',
                    'value' => set_value('password1', ''),
                        'maxlength' => '100', 'size' => '50',
                            'style' => 'width:100%')); ?></td>
        </tr>
        <tr>
            <td>Confirm Password</td>
            <td><?php echo form_password(array('name' =>
                'password2', 'id' => 'password2',
                    'value' => set_value('password2', ''),
                        'maxlength' => '100', 'size' => '50',
```

```
                    'style' => 'width:100%')); ?></td>
        </tr>

            <?php echo form_hidden('code', $code) ; ?>
    </table>
    <?php echo form_submit('submit', 'Submit'); ?>
    or <?php echo anchor('form', 'cancel'); ?>
<?php echo form_close(); ?>
```

3. Amend /path/to/codeigniter/application/controllers/signin.php, adding the following code:

```
public function forgot_password() {
    $this->load->library('form_validation');
    $this->form_validation->set_rules('email', 'Email',
      'required|valid_email|min_length[5]|
        max_length[125]');

    if ($this->form_validation->run() == FALSE) {
      $this->load->view('signin/forgot_password');
    } else {
      $email = $this->input->post('email');

      $this->db->where('user_email', $email);
      $this->db->from('register');
      $num_res = $this->db->count_all_results();

      if ($num_res == 1) {
        // Make a small string (code) to assign to the user
        // to indicate they've requested a change of
        // password
        $code = mt_rand('5000', '200000');
        $data = array(
          'forgot_password' => $code,
        );

        $this->db->where('user_email', $email);
        if ($this->db->update('register', $data)) {
          // Update okay, send email
          $url = "http://
            www.domain.com/signin/new_password/".$code;
          $body = "\nPlease click the following link to
            reset your password:\n\n".$url."\n\n";
          if (mail($email, 'Password reset', $body,
            'From: no-reply@domain.com')) {
            $data['submit_success'] = true;
            $this->load->view('signin/signin', $data);
          }
```

```
      } else {
        // Some sort of error happened, redirect user
        // back to form
        redirect('singin/forgot_password');
      }
    } else {
      // Some sort of error happened, redirect user back
      // to form
      redirect('singin/forgot_password');
    }
  }
}

public function new_password() {
  $this->load->library('form_validation');
  $this->form_validation->set_rules('code', 'Code',
    'required|min_length[4]|max_length[7]');
  $this->form_validation->set_rules('email', 'Email',
    'required|valid_email|min_length[5]|
      max_length[125]');
  $this->form_validation->set_rules('password1',
    'Password', 'required|min_length[5]|max_length[15]');
  $this->form_validation->set_rules('password2',
    'Confirmation Password', 'required|min_length[5]|
      max_length[15]|matches[password1]');

  // Get Code from URL or POST and clean up
  if ($this->input->post()) {
    $data['code'] = xss_clean($this->input-
      >post('code'));
  } else {
    $data['code'] = xss_clean($this->uri->segment(3));
  }

  if ($this->form_validation->run() == FALSE) {
    $this->load->view('signin/new_password', $data);
  } else {
    // Does code from input match the code against the
    // email
    $this->load->model('Signin_model');
    $email = xss_clean($this->input->post('email'));
    if (!$this->Signin_model-
      >does_code_match($data['code'], $email)) {
      // Code doesn't match
      redirect ('signin/forgot_password');
    } else {// Code does match
      $this->load->model('Register_model');
```

```
$hash = $this->encrypt->sha1($this->input-
  >post('password1'));

$data = array(
  'user_hash' => $hash
);

if ($this->Register_model->update_user(
  $data, $email)) {
  redirect ('signin');
  }
 }
}
}
```

4. Then, amend `/path/to/codeigniter/application/models/signin_model.php`, adding the following code:

```
public function update_user($data, $email) {
    $this->db->where('user_email', $email);
    $this->db->update('register', $data);
}

public function does_email_exist($email) {
  $this->db->where('user_email', $email);
  $this->db->from('register');
  $num_res = $this->db->count_all_results();
    if ($num_res == 1) {
      return TRUE;
  } else {
      return FALSE;
  }
}

public function does_code_match($code, $email) {
  $this->db->where('user_email', $email);
  $this->db->where('forgot_password', $code);
  $this->db->from('register');
    $num_res = $this->db->count_all_results();

    if ($num_res == 1) {
      return TRUE;
  } else {
      return FALSE;
  }
}
```

5. Then, amend /path/to/codeigniter/application/views/signin.php, adding the following code:

```php
<?php echo form_open('signin/login') ; ?>
    <?php if (validation_errors()) : ?>
        <h3>Whoops! There was an error:</h3>
        <p><?php echo validation_errors(); ?></p>
    <?php endif; ?>

    <?php if (isset($login_fail)) : ?>
        <h3>Login Error:</h3>
        <p>Username or Password is incorrect, please try
            again.</p>
    <?php endif; ?>

    <table border="0" >
        <tr>
            <td>User Email</td>
            <td><?php echo form_input(array('name' =>
                'email', 'id' => 'email',
                    'value' => set_value('email', ''),
                        'maxlength' => '100', 'size' => '50',
                            'style' => 'width:100%')); ?></td>
        </tr>
        <tr>
            <td>Password</td>
            <td><?php echo form_password(array('name' =>
                'password', 'id' => 'password',
                    'value' => set_value('password', ''),
                        'maxlength' => '100', 'size' => '50',
                            'style' => 'width:100%')); ?></td>
        </tr>
    </table>
    <?php echo form_submit('submit', 'Submit'); ?>
    or <?php echo anchor('signin', 'cancel'); ?>
    <?php echo anchor('signin/forgot_password',
        'Forgot Password'); ?>
<?php echo form_close(); ?>
```

We're only changing one line from this file: the highlighted line is an anchor() statement, which displays a link to the forgot password form.

How it works...

Firstly, take a look at the following flowchart:

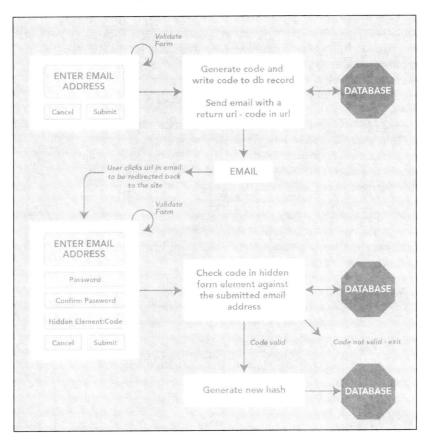

Now, let's imagine that a user has forgotten their password and wishes to be reminded of it. The user will click on the forgot password link in the amended signin form (`/path/to/codeigniter/application/views/signin/signin.php`), which redirects them to `public function forgot_password()` in the signin controller. The `forgot_password()` function immediately displays the, `/path/to/codeigniter/application/views/signin/forgot_password.php` view. The user enters an e-mail address and submits the form using the **Submit** button.

Next the `forgot_password()` function will validate the input supplied by the user and if that input passes the validation rules the `forgot_password()` function will look in the database to see if a row exists in the register table whose e-mail matches the supplied e-mail in the form submission. If a match is found a tracking code (this is used for the hidden form element in the form view file) is generated and assigned to the `$data` array. This code is then written to the row in the database we just looked for, and an e-mail is sent to the e-mail address associated with the account (or row). In this case we're using the PHPs `mail()` function rather than CodeIgniter's mail functionality; you can of course use CodeIgniter to send the e-mail rather than PHP `mail()`—we discuss sending e-mails in CodeIgniter in *Chapter 4, Email, HTML Table, and Text Libraries*, anyway—back to the story.

Next, it's over to our user. They should look in their e-mail inbox for the e-mail we've just sent them, if they do they'll see a link in that e-mail directing them back to our system and to `public function new_password()`. Clicking on that link will open the, `/path/to/codeigniter/application/views/signin/new_password.php view`, which will display the reset password form.

Remember that the `$code` we parameter generated? `$code` was the third URL parameter and is now set as a hidden form element. The user enters their e-mail and password (twice to confirm) and clicks on **Submit**. The form then posts to `public function new_password()`, which validates for form.

Upon passing validation, the e-mail address and code are looked up in the register table. If found (and they match), a new `$hash` array is made and saved to their record in the database. Finally, they're redirected to the signin form, where they can log()in using their new password.

3
Creating E-commerce Features

In this chapter, we will cover:

- ▸ Amending configuration settings to run sessions in a database
- ▸ Creating a basic cart
- ▸ Adding and searching by product categories
- ▸ Saving the cart to the database

Introduction

The `Cart` class in CodeIgniter provides basic shopping cart functionality, such as adding items, amending the cart, displaying cart details, and removing items within the cart. In this chapter, we'll look at creating a simple shop using the CodeIgniter `Cart` class.

Amending configuration settings to run sessions in a database

"Why do I need to do this; I'm not using sessions at the moment and besides, I have already covered sessions in another recipe?" I know; I hear you; but the CodeIgniter `Cart` class makes use of sessions in order to build a cart for the customer or user. We'll go over sessions here with the `Cart` class in mind. If you've already implemented sessions, you can probably skip this recipe.

Getting ready

Before we launch into the cart example, we need to do a little housekeeping. First, we'll alter some config settings, which will allow CodeIgniter to save Cart information to the database, and then we'll create a simple database schema to handle products, and so on.

How to do it...

There are some configuration changes we need to apply before we start, they are as follows:

1. Open the, `application/config/config.php` file, in a text editor and make the following amendments:

Config variable	Value	Explanation
`$config['encryption_ key'] = ''`	Alphanumeric	Specifies the encryption key CodeIgniter should use when encrypting sessions. The value can be alphanumeric and you must decide on a string for its value.
`$config['sess_encrypt_ cookie']`	TRUE/FALSE	Specifies whether or not to encrypt the sessions in the database; for this example, it should be set to TRUE.
`$config['sess_use_ database]`	TRUE/FALSE	Specifies whether or not to store sessions in the database; for this example, it should be set to TRUE.
`$config['sess_table_ name']`	Alphanumeric	The name of the table in the database that is used to store sessions. For this example, it should be set to sess_cart.

2. There are some tables required to support this recipe, and also some dummy data. Copy the following SQL code into your database:

```
CREATE TABLE IF NOT EXISTS `sessions` (
  `session_id` varchar(40) COLLATE utf8_bin NOT NULL
    DEFAULT '0',
  `ip_address` varchar(16) COLLATE utf8_bin NOT NULL
    DEFAULT '0',
  `user_agent` varchar(120) COLLATE utf8_bin DEFAULT NULL,
  `last_activity` int(10) unsigned NOT NULL DEFAULT '0',
  `user_data` text COLLATE utf8_bin NOT NULL,
  PRIMARY KEY (`session_id`),
  KEY `last_activity_idx` (`last_activity`)
```

```
) ENGINE=InnoDB DEFAULT CHARSET=utf8 COLLATE=utf8_bin;

CREATE TABLE IF NOT EXISTS `products` (
  `product_id` int(11) NOT NULL AUTO_INCREMENT,
  `product_name` varchar(255) NOT NULL,
  `product_code` int(11) NOT NULL,
  `product_description` varchar(255) NOT NULL,
  `category_id` int(11) NOT NULL,
  `product_price` int(11) NOT NULL,
  PRIMARY KEY (`product_id`)
) ENGINE=InnoDB  DEFAULT CHARSET=latin1 AUTO_INCREMENT=3;

INSERT INTO `products` (`product_id`, `product_name`,
  `product_code`, `product_description`, `category_id`,
    `product_price`) VALUES
(1, 'Running Shoes', 423423, 'These are some shoes', 2,
  50),
(2, 'Hawaiian Shirt', 34234, 'This is a shirt', 1, 25);

CREATE TABLE IF NOT EXISTS `categories` (
  `cat_id` int(11) NOT NULL AUTO_INCREMENT,
  `cat_name` varchar(50) NOT NULL,
  PRIMARY KEY (`cat_id`)
) ENGINE=InnoDB  DEFAULT CHARSET=latin1 AUTO_INCREMENT=3;

INSERT INTO `categories` (`cat_id`, `cat_name`) VALUES
(1, 'Shirts'),
(2, 'Footware');
```

How it works...

Okay so what have we just made? The following is a description of both tables:

Categories table

The categories table stores information about the category groups that each product (in the products table) is associated with. They are as follows:

Item name	Attributes	Description
cat_id	INTEGER(11)	Table primary key.
cat_name	VARCHAR(50)	Name of the category.

Products table

The products table stores information about each product for sale in the cart. It is linked to the categories table by the foreign key (`category_id`). The following is the product table:

Item name	Attributes	Description
`product_id`	`INTEGER(11)`	Table primary key
`product_name`	`VARCHAR(125)`	Name of the product
`product_code`	`INTEGER(11)`	A code for the product, which could be used as an internal stock code
`product_description`	`VARCHAR(255)`	Detailed description of the product
`category_id`	`INTEGER(11)`	The products category ID() as a foreign key from the category table
`product_price`	`INTEGER(11)`	The value of the product.

Creating a basic cart

In this section, we will be creating the basic files necessary to run a cart. Later in the chapter, we will be adding greater functionality to it, but first let's prepare. We will be creating the following four files:

- `path/to/codeigniter/application/controllers/shop.php`: This controller will handle any customer interaction between the views and the model, such as handling any forms and controlling the customer's journey through the cart.

- `path/to/codeigniter/application/models/shop_model.php`: This model will handle any database interaction between the controller and the database. It will contain functions to fetch products and, product categories, and later in the chapter, to save the cart to the database.

- `path/to/codeigniter/application/views/shop/display_cart.php`: This view will display a summary of a customer's cart at any one time, and allow that customer to amend the quantities of items in their cart.

- `path/to/codeigniter/application/views/shop/view_products.php`: This view will display products from the `cart.products` table in the database, and provide options to allow the customer to add items to their cart.

How to do it...

We're going to create the following four files:

- /path/to/codeigniter/application/controllers/shop.php
- /path/to/codeigniter/application/models/shop_model.php
- /path/to/codeigniter/application/views/shop/display_cart.php
- /path/to/codeigniter/application/views/shop/display_products.php

1. Copy the following code into the, /path/to/codeigniter/application/
   controllers/shop.php file:

```php
<?php if (!defined('BASEPATH')) exit('No direct script
  access allowed');

class Shop extends CI_Controller {
    function __construct() {
        parent::__construct();
        $this->load->library('cart');
        $this->load->helper('form');
        $this->load->helper('url');
        $this->load->helper('security');
        $this->load->model('Shop_model');
    }

    public function index() {
        $data['query'] =
          $this->Shop_model->get_all_products();
        $this->load->view('shop/display_products', $data);
    }

    public function add() {
        $product_id = $this->uri->segment(3);
        $query = $this->Shop_model-
          >get_product_details($product_id);
        foreach($query->result() as $row) {
            $data = array(
                'id'   => $row->product_id,
                'qty' => 1,
                'price'  => $row->product_price,
                'name' => $row->product_name,
            );
        }

        $this->cart->insert($data);
```

```
        $this->load->view('shop/display_cart', $data);
    }

    public function update_cart() {
        $data = array();
        $i = 0;

        foreach($this->input->post() as $item) {
                $data[$i]['rowid']  = $item['rowid'];
                $data[$i]['qty']    = $item['qty'];
                $i++;
        }

        $this->cart->update($data);
        redirect('shop/display_cart');
    }

    public function display_cart() {
        $this->load->view('shop/display_cart');
    }

    public function clear_cart() {
        $this->cart->destroy();
        redirect('index');
    }
}
```

2. Then copy the following code to the, `/path/to/codeigniter/application/` `models/shop_model.php` file:

```php
<?php if ( ! defined('BASEPATH')) exit('No direct script
  access allowed');

class Shop_model extends CI_Model {

    function __construct() {
        parent::__construct();
        $this->load->helper('url');
    }

    public function get_product_details($product_id) {
        $this->db->where('product_id', $product_id);
        $query = $this->db->get('products');
        return $query;
    }

    public function get_all_products() {
        $query = $this->db->get('products');
        return $query;
    }
}
```

3. Then copy the following code to the, `path/to/codeigniter/application/`
    `views/shop/display_cart.php` file:

```php
<?php echo form_open('shop/update_cart'); ?>

<table cellpadding="6" cellspacing="1"
  style="width:50%" border="1">

  <tr>
    <th>Quantity</th>
    <th>Description</th>
    <th>Item Price</th>
    <th>Sub-Total</th>
  </tr>

  <?php $i = 1; ?>

  <?php foreach ($this->cart->contents() as $items): ?>

    <?php echo form_hidden(
      $i . '[rowid]', $items['rowid']); ?>

    <tr>
      <td><?php echo form_input(array('name' =>
        $i . '[qty]', 'value' => $items['qty'],
          'maxlength' => '3', 'size' => '5')); ?></td>
      <td>
        <?php echo $items['name']; ?>

        <?php if ($this->cart->has_options(
          $items['rowid']) == TRUE): ?>

          <p>
            <?php foreach ($this->cart->product_options(
              $items['rowid']) as $option_name =>
                $option_value): ?>

              <strong><?php echo $option_name; ?>:</strong>
                <?php echo $option_value; ?><br/>

            <?php endforeach; ?>
          </p>

        <?php endif; ?>

      </td>
      <td><?php echo $this->cart->format_number(
        $items['price']); ?></td>
      <td>$<?php echo $this->cart->format_number(
        $items['subtotal']); ?></td>
```

```
    </tr>

    <?php $i++; ?>

  <?php endforeach; ?>

  <tr>
    <td colspan="2"> </td>
    <td><strong>Total</strong></td>
    <td>$<?php echo $this->cart->format_number(
       $this->cart->total()); ?></td>
  </tr>

</table>

<p><?php echo form_submit('', 'Update Cart'); ?></p>
<?php echo form_close() ; ?>
```

4. Finally, copy the following code to the, `path/to/codeigniter/application/ views/shop/display_products.php` file:

```
<body>
    <table>
    <?php foreach ($query->result() as $row) : ?>
        <tr>
        <td><?php echo $row->product_id ; ?></td>
        <td><?php echo $row->product_name ; ?></td>
        <td><?php echo $row->product_description ; ?></td>
        <td><?php echo anchor('shop/add/'.$row->product_id,
           'Add to cart') ; ?></td>
        </tr>
    <?php endforeach ; ?>
    </table>
</body>
```

How it works...

Okay, there's a lot going on here; so rather than discussing what's going on in each file, we'll break it down into user actions. There are several actions users can perform when interacting with the cart. The most common are as follows:

▸ User browses the catalogue

▸ User adds an item to the cart

▸ User updates or removes items in the cart

User browses the catalogue

`public function index()` in `controllers/shop.php` loads all the products from the database by calling the `$this->Cart_model->get_all_products()` function from `Shop_model`, and passes it to the, `views/shop/display_products.php` view, via `$this->load->view('shop/display_products', $data)`.

User adds an item to the cart

User clicks on the **Add to cart** link in the, `views/shop/display_products.php` file, next to the item they wish to purchase, which calls `public function add()` in `controllers/shop.php`. `public function add()` fetches the product ID passed to it in the URL by `$this->uri->segment(3)`. Using this, `$product_id` looks up the product details from the database by `$this->Shop_model->get_product_details($product_id)`. This data is then written to the cart by `$this->cart->insert($data)`. Finally, the user is redirected to the cart with `$this->load->view('shop/display_cart', $data)` so they can view their item in the cart and make any amendments if they wish to.

User updates or removes items in the cart

This covers two actions: adding more items to the cart or completely removing an item or all items from the cart. They are described as follows:

- **Adding to or subtracting items from the cart**: When the user views their cart, he they see a table with the quantities of each item in their cart to the left. The user can change the quantity of items by changing the values in this textbox. If the user increases or decreases the current quantity of a particular item and presses the, **Update Cart** button, then we run the shop controller function, `update_cart()`. `update_cart()` loops through the post array looking at each item and its new or desired quantity. It will track each item with the rowed value in the `$data` array, ensuring that the correct item is updated with the correct new quantity.

- **Removing items from the cart**: This functions the same way as adding or removing items as previously described. However, the difference is that if the quantity chosen by the user is `0 (zero)`, then CodeIgniter will remove the item completely from the cart.

Adding and searching by product categories

From a customer perspective, it is useful to be able to narrow down your catalogue by viewing products by category, such as shoes, shirts, coats, and so on. If you wish to add this functionality, you'll need to amend the database. If you require this feature, copy the code in the following *Getting ready* section.

Getting ready

In order to support searching and filtering by categories, we'll need to add a categories table. If you haven't already done this during the *Getting ready* section earlier in the chapter, create the following table in your database:

```
CREATE TABLE IF NOT EXISTS `categories` (
  `cat_id` int(11) NOT NULL AUTO_INCREMENT,
  `cat_name` varchar(50) NOT NULL,
  PRIMARY KEY (`cat_id`)
) ENGINE=InnoDB  DEFAULT CHARSET=latin1 AUTO_INCREMENT=3;


INSERT INTO `categories` (`cat_id`, `cat_name`) VALUES
(1, 'Shirts'),
(2, 'Footware');
```

How to do it...

We'll now need to make amendments to the following files:

- `/path/to/codeigniter/views/shop/display_products.php`: This added a small menu allowing the user to click on different categories; the results will be filtered accordingly.

- `/path/to/codeigniter/views/shop/display_cart.php`: This added a small menu allowing the user to click on different categories; the results will be filtered accordingly.

- `/path/to/codeigniter/application/controllers/shop.php`: This added code that will display categories and also look for a user's category choice in a form submission.

- `/path/to/codeigniter/application/models/shop_model.php`: This added the code that, pulls categories from the database according to a category ID.

1. Copy the following code at the top of the, `path/to/codeigniter/application/views/shop/display_cart.php` file:

```php
<?php echo form_open('shop/index') ; ?>
  <select name="cat">
    <?php foreach ($cat_query->result() as $cat_row) : ?>
      <option value="<?php echo $cat_row->cat_id;?>">
        <?php echo $cat_row->cat_name;?></option>
    <?php endforeach ; ?>
  </select>
<?php echo form_submit('', 'Search') ; ?>
    <?php echo form_close() ; ?>
```

2. Copy the following code at the top of the, `path/to/codeigniter/application/`
   `views/shop/display_products.php` file:

```php
<?php echo form_open('shop/index') ; ?>
    <select name="cat">
        <?php foreach ($cat_query->result() as
          $cat_row) : ?>
            <option value="<?php echo $cat_row-
              >cat_id;?>"><?php echo $cat_row-
                >cat_name;?></option>
        <?php endforeach ; ?>
    </select>
<?php echo form_submit('', 'Search') ; ?>
<?php echo form_close() ; ?>
```

3. Replace `public function index()` in the shop controller with the following:

```php
public function index() {
    $this->load->library('form_validation');
    $this->form_validation->set_error_delimiters(
      '', '<br />');

    if ($this->input->post()) {
        $category_id = $this->input->post('cat');
    } else {
        $category_id = null;
    }

    $this->form_validation->set_rules('cat',
      'Category', 'required|min_length[1]|
        max_length[125]|integer');

    if ($this->form_validation->run() == FALSE) {
        $data['query'] = $this->Shop_model-
          >get_all_products($category_id);
        $data['cat_query'] =
          $this->Shop_model->get_all_categories();
        $this->load->view(
          'shop/display_products', $data);
    } else {
        $data['query'] = $this->Shop_model-
          >get_all_products($category_id);
        $data['cat_query'] =
          $this->Shop_model->get_all_categories();
        $this->load->view(
          'shop/display_products', $data);
    }
}
```

4. Replace the shop controller function, `add()`, with the following code (the changes are highlighted):

```
public function add() {
        $product_id = $this->uri->segment(3);
        $query = $this->Shop_model-
          >get_product_details($product_id);
        foreach($query->result() as $row) {
            $data = array(
                'id' => $row->product_id,
                'qty' => 1,
                'price' => $row->product_price,
                'name' => $row->product_name,
            );
        }

        $this->cart->insert($data);
        $data['cat_query'] =
          $this->Shop_model->get_all_categories();

        $this->load->view('shop/display_cart', $data);
    }
```

5. Replace the controller function, `displat_cart()`, with the following code (the changes are highlighted):

```
public function display_cart() {
        $data['cat_query'] =
          $this->Shop_model->get_all_categories();
        $this->load->view('shop/display_cart', $data);
    }
```

6. Replace `public function get_all_products()` in the `shop_model` with the following code:

```
public function get_all_products($category_id = null) {
        if ($category_id) {
            $this->db->where('category_id', $category_id);
        }
        $query = $this->db->get('products');
        return $query;
    }
```

7. Add the following function, `get_all_categories()`, to the `shop_model` as follows:

```
public function get_all_categories() {
        $query = $this->db->get('categories');
        return $query;
    }
```

We've amended `public function index()` so that we can filter the user's browsing results by `$category_id` (which is the primary key of each category in the database). If the page is being loaded for the first time (not as a submission), then the code:

```
if ($this->input->post()) {
        $category_id = $this->input->post('cat');
    } else {
        $category_id = null;
    }
```

will automatically set `$category_id` to null so `$this->Shop_model->get_all_products($category_id)` will return all products regardless of `category_id`. However, if `$category_id` is passed with a form submission, then `$this->Shop_model->get_all_products($category_id)` will return only the products that are assigned to that category.

Saving the cart to the database

Before your customers are ready to proceed to payment, you need to take their details for payment, delivery, and your own records, and then move their cart that is in the session table to a specific table that will store orders.

Once the order has been saved and the customer details are supplied, a unique order code is generated and stored in `orders.order_fulfilment_code`. This can be used by a payment provider (for example, PayPal, GoCardless, Stripe, and so on) to keep track of the payment processing through their system and back into yours.

1. First, create the following tables in your database:

```
CREATE TABLE IF NOT EXISTS `customer` (
  `cust_id` int(11) NOT NULL AUTO_INCREMENT,
  `cust_first_name` varchar(125) NOT NULL,
  `cust_last_name` varchar(125) NOT NULL,
  `cust_email` varchar(255) NOT NULL,
  `cust_created_at` int(11) NOT NULL,
  `cust_address` text NOT NULL COMMENT 'card holder
    address',
  PRIMARY KEY (`cust_id`)
) ENGINE=InnoDB DEFAULT CHARSET=latin1 AUTO_INCREMENT=1 ;

CREATE TABLE `orders` (
```

```
`order_id` int(11) NOT NULL AUTO_INCREMENT,
`cust_id` int(11) NOT NULL,
`order_details` text NOT NULL,
`order_created_at` int(11) NOT NULL,
`order_closed` int(1) NOT NULL COMMENT '0 = open, 1 = closed',
`order_fulfilment_code` varchar(255) NOT NULL COMMENT
  'the unique code sent to a payment provider',
`order_delivery_address` text NOT NULL,
PRIMARY KEY (`order_id`)
) ENGINE=InnoDB  DEFAULT CHARSET-latin1 AUTO_INCREMENT=1;
```

2. Now that we have created the database tables to store your customers and orders, let's create the files to support this new functionality. We're going to create the following two files:

   ❑ `/path/to/codeigniter/application/controllers/cust.php`
   ❑ `/path/to/codeigniter/application/models/cart_model.php`

3. Create the, `/path/to/codeigniter/application/controllers/cust.php` controller and add the following code to it:

```php
<?php if (!defined('BASEPATH')) exit(
  'No direct script access allowed');

class Cust extends CI_Controller {
    function __construct() {
        parent::__construct();
        $this->load->library('cart');
        $this->load->helper('form');
        $this->load->helper('url');
        $this->load->helper('security');
        $this->load->model('Shop_model');
    }

    public function index() {
        redirect('cust/user_details');
    }

    public function user_details() {
        $this->load->library('form_validation');
        $this->form_validation->set_error_delimiters();

        // Set validation rules
        $this->form_validation->set_rules('first_name',
          'First Name', 'required|min_length[1]|
            max_length[125]');
        $this->form_validation->set_rules('last_name',
          'Last Name', 'required|min_length[1]|
            max_length[125]');
        $this->form_validation->set_rules('email',
```

```
        'Email Address', 'required|min_length[1]|
          max_length[255]|valid_email');
      $this->form_validation->set_rules('email_confirm',
        'Comfirmation Email Address',
          'required|min_length[1]|max_length[255]|
            valid_email|matches[email]');
      $this->form_validation->set_rules(
        'payment_address', 'Payment Address',
          'required|min_length[1]|max_length[1000]');
      $this->form_validation->set_rules(
        'delivery_address', 'Delivery Address',
          'min_length[1]|max_length[1000]');

      // Begin validation
      if ($this->form_validation->run() == FALSE) {
          $this->load->view('shop/user_details');
      } else {
          $cust_data = array(
          'cust_first_name' =>
            $this->input->post('cust_first_name'),
          'cust_last_name' =>
            $this->input->post('cust_last_name'),
          'cust_email'=>
            $this->input->post('cust_email'),
          'cust_address'   =>
            $this->input->post('payment_address'),
          'cust_created_at' => time());

          $payment_code = mt_rand();

          $order_data = array(
          'order_details' => serialize(
            $this->cart->contents()),
          'order_delivery_address' =>
            $this->input->post('delivery_address'),
          'order_created_at' => time(),
          'order_closed' => '0',
          'order_fulfilment_code' => $payment_code,
          'order_delivery_address' =>
            $this->input->post('payment_address'));

          if ($this->Shop_model->save_cart_to_database(
            $cust_data, $order_data)) {
              echo 'Order and Customer saved to DB';
          } else {
              echo 'Could not save to DB';
          }
      }
    }
}
```

4. Add `public function save_cart_to_db()` to the `models/shop_model.php` model as follows:

```php
public function save_cart_to_database(
  $cust_data, $order_data) {
    $this->db->insert('customer', $cust_data);
    $order_data['cust_id'] = $this->db->insert_id();
    if ($this->db->insert('orders', $order_data)) {
        return true;
    } else {
        return false;
    }
}
```

5. Amend the, `views/shop/display_cart.php` file. At the top of the page, add the following line:

```php
<?php echo anchor('cust/user_details',
  'Proceed to checkout') ; ?>
```

6. Create the `filepath/to/codeigniter/application/views/shop/user_details.php` file and add the following code into it:

```php
<body>
    <?php echo validation_errors(); ?>
    <?php echo form_open('/cust/user_details') ; ?>
        <?php echo form_input(array('name' => 'first_name',
          'value' => 'First Name', 'maxlength' => '125',
            'size' => '50')); ?><br />
        <?php echo form_input(array('name' => 'last_name',
          'value' => 'Last Name', 'maxlength' => '125',
            'size' => '50')); ?><br />
        <?php echo form_input(array('name' => 'email',
          'value' => 'Email Address', 'maxlength' => '255',
            'size' => '50')); ?><br />
        <?php echo form_input(array('name' =>
          'email_confirm', 'value' => 'Confirm Email',
            'maxlength' => '255', 'size' => '50')); ?>
              <br />
        <?php echo form_textarea(array('name' =>
          'payment_address', 'value' => 'Payment Address',
            'rows' => '6', 'cols' => '40',
              'size' => '50')); ?><br />
        <?php echo form_submit('', 'Enter') ; ?><br />
        <?php echo form_close() ; ?>
    </form>
</body>
```

How it works...

To explain what's happening here, let's look at this from the customer's perspective. The customer has taken a look around the store and has selected a few items and placed them into the cart. The next step is to convert that cart into an order. So, the user clicks on **View Cart** to view the products they wish to order (we've already covered this, so we won't go into it again.) When the user clicks on **Proceed to checkout**, the public function, `user_details()`, is called, which displays `views/shop/user_details.php` to the customer. This asks them to enter some information; in this case, their name, e-mail address, payment, delivery address, and so on. On successfully submitting the form (that is, no validation errors), their order is moved from the cart to the database and matched with their submitted user details.

A tracking code is also created with the line, `$payment_code = mt_rand()`, which can be used to track the payment through a payment providers system.

4

Email, HTML Table, and Text Libraries

In this chapter, you will learn:

- ▶ Sending plain e-mails with CodeIgniter Email
- ▶ Sending HTML e-mails with CodeIgniter Email
- ▶ Sending attachments with CodeIgniter Email
- ▶ Sending bulk e-mails with CodeIgniter Email
- ▶ Using an HTML table with DataTable
- ▶ Using an HTML table with DataTable and a database
- ▶ Using `word_limiter()` for table output
- ▶ Using `word_censor()` for cleaning input

Introduction

CodeIgniter comes with some useful libraries and functions for handling many aspects of application development. In this chapter we will look at Email and HTML tables. The CodeIgniter Email library is capable of sending plain text and HTML e-mails, with and without attachments that can be used (with a little configuration) instead of the standard PHP `mail()` function. CodeIgniter's HTML Table library is excellent at generating the HTML necessary for pretty much most of what you will need a table for—and, together with DataTable, can provide excellent interactive tables for your users.

Sending plain e-mails with CodeIgniter Email

It's always useful to be able to send e-mails and CodeIgniter comes with an excellent library for sending e-mails. There are a few recipes in this chapter, which deal with sending e-mails. However, this is the basic Hello World type example that is very simple.

How to do it...

A simple way to send plain e-mails using CodeIgniter Email is as follows:

1. Create a file `email.php` at `path/to/codeigniter/application/controllers/`.

2. Add the following code to the controller file `email.php`:

```php
<?php if ( ! defined('BASEPATH')) exit('No direct script access allowed');

class Email extends CI_Controller {
    function __construct() {
        parent::__construct();
        $this->load->helper('url');
        $this->load->library('email');
    }

    public function index() {
        redirect('email/send_email');
    }

    public function send_email() {
        $config['protocol'] = 'sendmail';
        $config['mailpath'] = '/usr/sbin/sendmail';
        $config['charset'] = 'iso-8859-1';
        $config['wordwrap'] = TRUE;
        $config['mailtype'] = 'text';

        $this->email->initialize($config);
        $this->email->from('from@domain.com', 'Your Name');
        $this->email->to('to@domain.com');
        $this->email->subject('This is a text email');
        $this->email->message('And this is some content for
          the text email.');

        $this->email->send();

        echo $this->email->print_debugger();
    }
}
```

How it works...

In the constructor controller we load the Email library (highlighted in the following code), which provides support to send e-mails:

```
function __construct() {
    parent::__construct();
    $this->load->helper('url');
    $this->load->library('email');
}
```

Next, `public function index()` redirects us to the function `public function send_mail()`, which sets some initial configuration variables for CodeIgniter Email library to work with, such as the system used to send the e-mail (in this case, `sendmail`), the path to send e-mail on your system, the `mailtype` variable (text or HTML), and so on. Take a look at the following line of code:

```
$config['mailtype'] = 'text';
```

Here, we're telling CodeIgniter to send the e-mail as just plain text rather than HTML.

These configuration settings are initialized (that is, passed to the Email library), and we begin to build the e-mail by setting the `to`, `from`, `subject`, and `message` attributes:

```
$this->email->from('from@domain.com', 'Your Name');
$this->email->to('to@domain.com');

$this->email->subject('This is a text email');
$this->email->message('And this is some content for the text
  email.');
```

Then, send the e-mail:

```
$this->email->send();
```

If all works out as planned, you should see an output similar to the following one:

```
User-Agent: CodeIgniter
Date: Fri, 4 Oct 2013 08:51:03 +0200
From: "Your Name" <from@domain.com>
Return-Path: <from@domain.com>
To: to@domain.com
Subject: =?iso-8859-1?Q?This_is_a_text_email?=
Reply-To: "from@domain.com" <from@domain.com>
X-Sender: from@domain.com
X-Mailer: CodeIgniter
X-Priority: 3 (Normal)
Message-ID: <524e6557968c5@domain.com>
```

```
Mime-Version: 1.0


Content-Type: text/plain; charset=iso-8859-1
Content-Transfer-Encoding: 8bit

And this is some content for the text email.
```

Sending HTML e-mails with CodeIgniter Email

There might be times when you wish to display formatted e-mails rather than just plain text, so you may wish to include images, text formatting, and URLs in the body of your e-mail. HTML e-mails will allow you to do this and CodeIgniter Email library can easily be set to do just that.

How to do it...

HTML e-mails can be sent by executing the following steps:

1. Create a file `email.php` at `/path/to/codeigniter/application/controllers/`.

2. Add the following code to the controller file `email.php`:

```php
<?php if ( ! defined('BASEPATH')) exit('No direct script access allowed');

class Email extends CI_Controller {
    function __construct() {
        parent::__construct();
        $this->load->helper('url');
        $this->load->library('email');
    }

    public function index() {
        redirect('email/send_email');
    }

    public function send_email() {
        $config['protocol'] = 'sendmail';
        $config['mailpath'] = '/usr/sbin/sendmail';
        $config['charset'] = 'iso-8859-1';
        $config['wordwrap'] = TRUE;
```

```
            $config['mailtype'] = 'html';

            $this->email->initialize($config);

            $this->email->from('from@domain.com', 'Your Name');
            $this->email->to('to@domain.com');

            $this->email->subject('This is a html email');
            $html = 'This is an <b>HTML</b> email';
            $this->email->message($html);

            $this->email->send();

            echo $this->email->print_debugger();
        }
    }
```

How it works...

In the constructor controller we load the Email library (highlighted in the following code), which provides support for us to send e-mails:

```
function __construct() {
    parent::__construct();
    $this->load->helper('url');
    $this->load->library('email');
}
```

Next, `public function index()` redirects us to the function `public function send_mail()`, which sets some initial configuration variables for CodeIgniter Email library to work with, such as the system used to send the e-mail (in this case, `sendmail`), the path to send e-mail on your system, the `mailtype` variable (text or HTML), and so on. Take a look at the following line of code:

```
$config['mailtype'] = 'html';
```

Here, we're telling CodeIgniter to send the e-mail as HTML rather than as text.

These configuration settings are initialized (that is, passed to the Email library) and we begin to build the e-mail by setting the `to`, `from`, `subject`, and `message` attributes:

```
$this->email->from('from@domain.com', 'Your Name');
$this->email->to('to@domain.com');
$this->email->subject('This is a text email');
$this->email->message('And this is some content for the text
  email.');
```

Then, send the e-mail using the following code:

```
        $this->email->send();
```

If all works out as planned, you should see an output similar to the following code:

```
Your message has been successfully sent using the following protocol:
sendmail
User-Agent: CodeIgniter
Date: Fri, 4 Oct 2013 08:56:59 +0200
From: "Your Name" <from@domain.com>
Return-Path: <from@domain.com>
To: to@domain.com
Subject: =?iso-8859-1?Q?This_is_a_html_email?=
Reply-To: "from@domain.com" <from@domain.com>
X-Sender: from@domain.com
X-Mailer: CodeIgniter
X-Priority: 3 (Normal)
Message-ID: <524e66bbf282f@domain.com>
Mime-Version: 1.0


Content-Type: multipart/alternative; boundary="B_ALT_524e66bbf2868"

This is a multi-part message in MIME format.
Your email application may not support this format.

--B_ALT_524e66bbf2868
Content-Type: text/plain; charset=iso-8859-1
Content-Transfer-Encoding: 8bit

This is an HTML email


--B_ALT_524e66bbf2868
Content-Type: text/html; charset=iso-8859-1
Content-Transfer-Encoding: quoted-printable

This is an <b>HTML</b> email

--B_ALT_524e66bbf2868--
```

Sending attachments with CodeIgniter Email

There might be times when you wish to send an attachment along with the e-mail, such as an invoice to a customer for a recent purchase or perhaps an image. The CodeIgniter Email library can easily be set to do just that.

How to do it...

You can send attachments with CodeIgniter Email by executing the following steps:

1. Create a file `email.php` at `/path/to/codeigniter/application/controllers/`.

2. Add the following code to the controller file, `email.php`:

```php
<?php if ( ! defined('BASEPATH')) exit('No direct script access
    allowed');
class Email extends CI_Controller {
    function __construct() {
        parent::__construct();
        $this->load->helper('url');
        $this->load->library('email');
}

    public function index() {
        redirect('email/send_email');
    }
    public function send_email() {
        $config['protocol'] = 'sendmail';
        $config['mailpath'] = '/usr/sbin/sendmail';
        $config['charset'] = 'iso-8859-1';
        $config['wordwrap'] = TRUE;
        $config['mailtype'] = 'html';
        $this->email->initialize($config);
        $this->email->from('from@domain.com', 'Your Name');
        $this->email->to('to@domain.com');
        $this->email->subject('This is a html email');
        $html = 'This is an <b>HTML</b> email with an attachment,
            <i>lovely!</i>';
        $this->email->message($html);
        $this->email->attach('/path/to/attachment');
        $this->email->send();
        echo $this->email->print_debugger();
    }
}
```

How it works...

In the constructor controller we load the Email library (highlighted in the following code), which provides support to send e-mails:

```
function __construct() {
    parent::__construct();
    $this->load->helper('url');
    $this->load->library('email');
}
```

Next, `public function index()` redirects us to the function, `public function send_mail()`, which sets some initial configuration variables for the CodeIgniter Email library to work with, such as the system used to send the e-mail (in this case, `sendmail`), the path to send mail on your system, the `mailtype` variable (text or HTML), and so on. These configuration settings are initialized (that is, passed to the Email library) and we begin to build the e-mail; setting the `to`, `from`, `subject`, and `message` attributes, as well as the path to the attachment we're sending in the e-mail (highlighted in the following code):

```
$this->email->from('from@domain.com', 'Your Name');
$this->email->to('to@domain.com');
$this->email->subject('This is a html email');
$html = 'This is an <b>HTML</b> email with an attachment,
    <i>lovely!</i>';
$this->email->message($html);
$this->email->attach('/path/to/attachment');
```

Then, send the e-mail using the following code:

```
$this->email->send();
```

Sending bulk e-mails with CodeIgniter Email

There may be times when you wish to send out bulk e-mails; perhaps to all the people who have paid to go on a tour. You may wish to send them each a personalized e-mail, and also add an attachment. You may also want to pull their e-mail preference (plain text or HTML) from the account on your database and send them the correct format of e-mail. That's what we're going to do here.

Getting ready

We need to know each person's preferences such as whether they want HTML e-mails or text, and also their individual reference number (or booking ID) for their trip. As per this requirement, we are going to have a database to hold all the information; so copy the following code into your database:

```
CREATE TABLE `bookers` (
    `id` int(11) NOT NULL AUTO_INCREMENT,
    `firstname` varchar(50) NOT NULL,
    `lastname` varchar(50) NOT NULL,
    `email` varchar(255) NOT NULL,
    `email_pref` varchar(4) NOT NULL,
    `booking_ref` varchar(10) NOT NULL,
    PRIMARY KEY (`id`)
) ENGINE=InnoDB  DEFAULT CHARSET=latin1 AUTO_INCREMENT=3 ;
INSERT INTO `bookers` (`id`, `firstname`, `lastname`, `email`,
  `email_pref`, `booking_ref`) VALUES
(1, 'Robert', 'Foster', 'example1@domain1.com', 'html', 'ABC123'),
(2, 'Lucy', 'Welsh', 'example2@domain2.com', 'html', 'DEF456');
```

How to do it...

1. Create a file email.php at /path/to/codeigniter/application/ controllers/.

2. Add the following code to the controller file, email.php:

```php
<?php if ( ! defined('BASEPATH')) exit('No direct script
  access allowed');
class Email extends CI_Controller {
    function __construct() {
        parent::__construct();
        $this->load->helper('url');
        $this->load->library('email');
    }
    public function index() {
        redirect('email/send_email');
    }
    public function send_email() {
        $config['protocol'] = 'sendmail';
        $config['mailpath'] = '/usr/sbin/sendmail';
        $config['charset'] = 'iso-8859-1';
        $config['wordwrap'] = TRUE;
        $query = "SELECT * FROM bookers ";
        $result = $this->db->query($query);
```

```
foreach ($result->result() as $row) {
    $this->email->clear();
    if ($row->email_pref == 'text') {
        $config['mailtype'] = 'text';
        $body = 'Hi ' . $row->firstname . ',
            Thanks you for booking with us, please
            find attached the itinerary for your
            trip. This is your booking reference
            number: ' . $row->booking_ref . '
            Thanks for booking with us, have a
            lovely trip.';
    } else {
        $config['mailtype'] = 'html';
        $body = 'Hi ' . $row->firstname . ',
            <br /><br />Thanks you for booking with
            us, please find attached the itinerary
            for your trip. </p>This is your booking
            reference number: <b>' .
            $row->booking_ref . '</b><br />
            <br />Thanks for booking with us,
            have a lovely trip.';
    }

    $this->email->initialize($config);
    $this->email->to($row->email);
    $this->email->from('
        bookings@thecodeigniterholidaycompany.com');
    $this->email->subject('
        Holiday booking details');

    $this->email->message($body);
    $this->email->send();
    }

    echo $this->email->print_debugger();
    }
}
```

How it works...

In the constructor controller we load the Email library (highlighted in the following code), which provides support for us to send e-mails:

```
function __construct() {
    parent::__construct();
    $this->load->helper('url');
    $this->load->library('email');
}
```

Next, `public function index()` redirects us to the function, `public function send_mail()`, which sets some initial configuration variables for CodeIgniter Email library to work with, such as the system used to send the e-mail (in this case, `sendmail`), the path to send mail from your system.

We then query the database for each of the customer's booking details:

```
$query = "SELECT * FROM bookers ";
$result = $this->db->query($query);

foreach ($result->result() as $row) {

}
```

The query will loop through each result and send a specific e-mail based on the values retrieved from the database in each loop.

Firstly, we give ourselves a clean slate by clearing all the settings and variables from a previous loop iteration by using the CodeIgniter `email` function:

```
$this->email->clear();
```

We then look at their e-mail preference and set the e-mail sending (`mailtype`) variable accordingly, along with the text for the body of the e-mails. So, if someone prefers HTML, we look for that preference and define the body of the HTML e-mail, otherwise for a text e-mail, we look for the text e-mail preference and define the body for the text e-mail:

```
if ($row->email_pref == 'text') {
    $config['mailtype'] = 'text';
    $body = 'Hi ' . $row->firstname . ',
      Thank you for booking with us, please find attached the
      itinerary for your trip.
      This is your booking reference number: ' .
      $row->booking_ref . '
      Thanks for booking with us, have a lovely trip.';
} else {
    $config['mailtype'] = 'html';
    $body = 'Hi ' . $row->firstname . ',<br /><br />
      Thank you for booking with us, please find attached the
      itinerary for your trip. </p>
      This is your booking reference number: <b>' .
      $row->booking_ref . '</b><br /><br />
      Thanks for booking with us, have a lovely trip.';
}
```

After this, we initialize the configuration variables. Those of you who have looked at the previous few recipes will notice that the initialization takes place later in the code of this recipe than in others. This is because we cannot initialize the `config` variables earlier as some of the variables rely on the preferences of individual customers, which are fetched from the database. So, we have to wait until each user's details are fetched from a database to initialize each iteration of the configuration settings. And finally, we send the e-mail:

```
$this->email->send();
```

If all goes well, you should see an output similar to the following:

```
Your message has been successfully sent using the following protocol:
sendmail
User-Agent: CodeIgniter
Date: Fri, 4 Oct 2013 20:06:13 +0200
To: to@domain.com
From: <bookings@thecodeigniterholidaycompany.com>
Return-Path: <bookings@thecodeigniterholidaycompany.com>
Subject: =?iso-8859-1?Q?Holiday_booking_details?=
Reply-To: "bookings@thecodeigniterholidaycompany.com" <bookings@
thecodeigniterholidaycompany.com>
X-Sender: bookings@thecodeigniterholidaycompany.com
X-Mailer: CodeIgniter
X-Priority: 3 (Normal)
Message-ID: <524f0395942a2@thecodeigniterholidaycompany.com>
Mime-Version: 1.0


Content-Type: multipart/alternative; boundary="B_ALT_524f0395942bb"

This is a multi-part message in MIME format.
Your email application may not support this format.

--B_ALT_524f0395942bb
Content-Type: text/plain; charset=iso-8859-1
Content-Transfer-Encoding: 8bit

Hi RobertThanks you booking with us,
 please find attached the itinerary for your trip.
 This is your booking reference number:
 ABC123
 Thanks for booking with us, have a lovely trip.


--B_ALT_524f0395942bb
```

```
Content-Type: text/html; charset=iso-8859-1
Content-Transfer-Encoding: quoted-printable

Hi Robert<br /><br />Thanks you booking with us,=20
            please find attached the itinerary for your trip.
            </p>This is your booking reference number:=20
            <b>ABC123</b><br /><br />
            Thanks for booking with us, have a lovely trip.

--B_ALT_524f0395942bb--
```

Using an HTML table with DataTable

DataTable is a free to use library that turns your normal looking html table into an interactive marvel with sortable and searchable columns and a whole lot more; we're going to use it with CodeIgniter, merging DataTable and CodeIgniter table functionality. It's simple to use and is able to handle most of the things you will need it for. Here, in this recipe, we're going to use it with DataTable to create an interactive HTML table that is sortable and searchable. It has pagination too! If you want database results, move on to the next recipe, *Using an HTML table with DataTable and a database*, where we'll look at populating a table from a database query.

Getting ready

For this recipe, you will need to follow the given procedure:

1. Ensure that you've downloaded DataTable from the following link:

    `https://datatables.net/download/`

2. Unzip the downloaded `.zip` file, and move the files to a location on your web server or localhost, which will be accessible by CodeIgniter. For this recipe, I have put the folder at `application/views`; but you can make your own choice if you wish.

How to do it...

1. Create four files as given:

    ❑   `/path/to/codeigniter/application/controllers/table.php`

    ❑   `/path/to/codeigniter/application/views/table_header.php`

    ❑   `/path/to/codeigniter/application/views/table_body.php`

    ❑   `/path/to/codeigniter/application/views/table_footer.php`

2. Create the controller file, `table.php`, and add the following code to it:

```php
<?php if ( ! defined('BASEPATH')) exit('No direct script
  access allowed');

class Table extends CI_Controller {

    function __construct() {
        parent::__construct();
        $this->load->library('table');
}

    public function index() {
        $tmpl = array (
            'table_open'            => '<table border="0"
              cellpadding="4" cellspacing="0"
              id="example">',

            'heading_row_start'     => '<tr>',
            'heading_row_end'       => '</tr>',
            'heading_cell_start'    => '<th>',
            'heading_cell_end'      => '</th>',

            'row_start'             => '<tr>',
            'row_end'               => '</tr>',
            'cell_start'            => '<td>',
            'cell_end'              => '</td>',

            'row_alt_start'         => '<tr>',
            'row_alt_end'           => '</tr>',
            'cell_alt_start'        => '<td>',
            'cell_alt_end'          => '</td>',

            'table_close'           => '</table>'
        );

        $this->table->set_template($tmpl);

        $this->table->set_heading(array('ID',
          'First Name', 'Last Name'));

        $this->table->add_row(array('1', 'Rob', 'Foster'));
        $this->table->add_row(array('2', 'Lucy', 'Welsh'));
        $this->table->add_row(array('3', 'George',
          'Foster'));
        $this->table->add_row(array('4', 'Jackie',
          'Foster'));
        $this->table->add_row(array('5', 'Antony',
          'Welsh'));
```

```
$this->table->add_row(array('6', 'Rowena',
  'Welsh'));
$this->table->add_row(array('7', 'Peter',
  'Foster'));
$this->table->add_row(array('8', 'Jenny',
  'Foster'));
$this->table->add_row(array('9', 'Oliver',
  'Welsh'));
$this->table->add_row(array('10', 'Felicity',
  'Foster'));
$this->table->add_row(array('11', 'Harrison',
  'Foster'));
$this->table->add_row(array('12', 'Mia',
  'The Cat'));

$data['table'] = $this->table->generate();

$this->load->view('tables/table_header');
$this->load->view('tables/table_body',$data);
$this->load->view('tables/table_footer');
    }

  }
```

3. Create the view file, `table_header.php`, and add the following code to it:

```html
<html>
    <head>
        <style type="text/css" title="currentStyle">
            @import "<?php echo $this->
              config->item('base_url') ;
              ?>application/views/
              DataTables-1.9.4/media/css/
              demo_page.css";
            @import "<?php echo $this->
              config->item('base_url') ;
              ?>application/views/DataTables-1.9.4/media/
              css/jquery.dataTables.css";
        </style>
        <script type="text/javascript"
          language="javascript"
          src="<?php echo $this->config->item('base_url') ;
          ?>application/views/DataTables-1.9.4/media/
          js/jquery.js"></script>
        <script type="text/javascript" language="javascript"
          src="<?php echo $this->config->item('base_url') ;
          ?>application/views/DataTables-1.9.4/media/
          js/jquery.dataTables.js"></script>
        <script type="text/javascript" charset="utf-8">
```

```
          $(document).ready(function() {
              $('#example').dataTable();
          } );
      </script>
  </head>
  <body>
```

Take a look at the `<script>` tag:

```
<script type="text/javascript" charset="utf-8">
    $(document).ready(function() {
        $('#example').dataTable();
    } );
</script>
```

The `#example` parameter is the ID of the table (detailed in the following *How it works...* section). Ensure that the value `example` in `<script>` and table markup is the same.

4. Create the view file, `table_body.php`, and add the following code to it:

```
<?php echo $table ; ?>
```

5. Create the controller file, `table_footer.php`, and add the following code to it:

```
    </body>
</html>
```

How it works...

The constructor in the table controller loads the CodeIgniter's Table library:

```
function __construct() {
    parent::__construct();
    $this->load->library('table');
}
```

The `public function index()` function is called. We then define how we want our HTML table markup to appear. This is where you can place any markup for the specific CSS, using which you can style the elements of the table:

```
$tmpl = array (
    'table_open'            => '<table border="0" cellpadding="4"
      cellspacing="0" id="example">',

    'heading_row_start'     => '<tr>',
    'heading_row_end'       => '</tr>',
    'heading_cell_start'    => '<th>',
```

```
    'heading_cell_end'      => '</th>',

    'row_start'             => '<tr>',
    'row_end'               => '</tr>',
    'cell_start'            => '<td>',
    'cell_end'              => '</td>',

    'row_alt_start'         => '<tr>',
    'row_alt_end'           => '</tr>',
    'cell_alt_start'        => '<td>',
    'cell_alt_end'          => '</td>',

    'table_close'           => '</table>'
);
```

Take a closer look at the `table_open` element of the `$tmpl` array. Look for the item highlighted in the preceding code. The `id="example"` item is used by DataTable (in the `<script>` tag of the file `table_header.php`) to apply its CSS and functionality. You can, of course, name it anything you like, but be sure to reflect that change in the JavaScript.

We then call `$this->table->set_template()` to apply the HTML table markup:

```
$this->table->set_template($tmpl);
```

We then set the table headers and apply the data for our rows. Ensure that the number of items in the table headers is the same as the number of items in the table data:

```
$this->table->set_heading(array('ID', 'First Name',
  'Last Name'));

$this->table->add_row(array('1', 'Rob', 'Foster'));
$this->table->add_row(array('2', 'Lucy', 'Welsh'));
$this->table->add_row(array('3', 'George', 'Foster'));
$this->table->add_row(array('4', 'Jackie', 'Foster'));
$this->table->add_row(array('5', 'Antony', 'Welsh'));
$this->table->add_row(array('6', 'Rowena', 'Welsh'));
$this->table->add_row(array('7', 'Peter', 'Foster'));
$this->table->add_row(array('8', 'Jenny', 'Foster'));
$this->table->add_row(array('9', 'Oliver', 'Welsh'));
$this->table->add_row(array('10', 'Felicity', 'Foster'));
$this->table->add_row(array('11', 'Harrison', 'Foster'));
$this->table->add_row(array('12', 'Mia', 'The Cat'));
```

We then generate the table. The `$this->table->generate()` function will return a string of HTML, which we save in `$data['table']`.

```
$data['table'] = $this->table->generate();
```

The `$data` array is then passed to our view files for rendering to the browser:

```
$this->load->view('tables/table_header');
$this->load->view('tables/table_body',$data);
$this->load->view('tables/table_footer');
```

Using an HTML table with DataTable and a database

CodeIgniter comes with a useful library to handle HTML tables. It's simple to use and is able to handle most of the things you would need it for. Here, in this recipe, we're going to use it with DataTable to create an interactive HTML table that is sortable and searchable. It even has pagination! This recipe populates the table using a database query. If you're not looking for that and just want a simple table, try the preceding recipe—*Using an HTML table with DataTable*.

Getting ready

For this recipe, you will have to:

1. Ensure that you've downloaded DataTable from `https://datatables.net/download/`.

2. Unzip the downloaded `.zip` file, and move the files to a location on your web server or localhost, which will be accessible by CodeIgniter. For this recipe, I have put the folder in the `application/views` folder; but you can make your own choice if you wish.

3. As we're using CodeIgniter's HTML Table library to create a table for us with data from a table, we will first need to create that table; so, copy the following code into your database:

```
CREATE TABLE IF NOT EXISTS `person` (
    `id` int(11) NOT NULL AUTO_INCREMENT,
    `first_name` varchar(50) NOT NULL,
    `last_name` varchar(50) NOT NULL,
    `email` varchar(255) NOT NULL,
    PRIMARY KEY (`id`)
) ENGINE=InnoDB  DEFAULT CHARSET=latin1 AUTO_INCREMENT=5 ;
INSERT INTO `person` (`id`, `first_name`, `last_name`,
    `email`) VALUES
(1, 'Rob', 'Foster', 'rfoster@dudlydog.com'),
(2, 'Lucy', 'Welsh', 'lwelsh@cocopopet.com'),
```

```
(3, 'Chloe', 'Graves', 'cgraves@mia-cat.com'),
(4, 'Claire', 'Strickland',
  'cstrickland@an-other-domain.com');
```

How to do it...

1. Create four files as given:

   ❏ /path/to/codeigniter/application/controllers/table.php

   ❏ /path/to/codeigniter/application/views/table_header.php

   ❏ /path/to/codeigniter/application/views/table_body.php

   ❏ /path/to/codeigniter/application/views/table_footer.php

2. Create the controller file, table.php, and add the following code to it:

```php
<?php if ( ! defined('BASEPATH')) exit('No direct script
  access allowed');

class Table extends CI_Controller {

    function __construct() {
        parent::__construct();
        $this->load->library('table');
        $this->load->database();
    }

    public function index() {
        $tmpl = array (
            'table_open'          => '<table border="0"
              cellpadding="4" cellspacing="0"
              id="example">',

            'heading_row_start'   => '<tr>',
            'heading_row_end'     => '</tr>',
            'heading_cell_start'  => '<th>',
            'heading_cell_end'    => '</th>',

            'row_start'           => '<tr>',
            'row_end'             => '</tr>',
            'cell_start'          => '<td>',
            'cell_end'            => '</td>',

            'row_alt_start'       => '<tr>',
            'row_alt_end'         => '</tr>',
            'cell_alt_start'      => '<td>',
            'cell_alt_end'        => '</td>',

            'table_close'         => '</table>'
```

```
        );

        $this->table->set_template($tmpl);

        $this->table->set_heading(array('ID', 'First Name',
          'Last Name', 'Email'));
        $query = $this->db->query("SELECT * FROM person");
        $data['table'] = $this->table->generate($query);

        $this->load->view('tables/table_header');
        $this->load->view('tables/table_body',$data);
        $this->load->view('tables/table_footer');
    }
}
```

3. Create the view file, `table_header.php`, and add the following code to it:

```html
<html>
    <head>
        <style type="text/css" title="currentStyle">
            @import "<?php echo
              $this->config->item('base_url') ;
              ?>application/views/
              DataTables-1.9.4/media/css/demo_page.css";
            @import "<?php echo
              $this->config->item('base_url') ;
              ?>application/views/
              DataTables-1.9.4/media/css/
              jquery.dataTables.css";
        </style>
        <script type="text/javascript"
          language="javascript" src="<?php echo
          $this->config->item('base_url') ;
          ?>application/views/
          DataTables-1.9.4/media/js/jquery.js"></script>
        <script type="text/javascript"
          language="javascript" src="
          <?php echo $this->config->item('base_url') ;
          ?>application/views/
          DataTables-1.9.4/media/js/jquery.dataTables.js">
          </script>
        <script type="text/javascript" charset="utf-8">
        $(document).ready(function() {
            $('#example').dataTable();
            } );
        </script>
    </head>
    <body>
```

The #example parameter is the ID of the table (detailed in the following *How it works* section). Ensure that the value example in <script> and the table markup is the same.

4. Create the view file table_body.php and add the following code to it:

```php
<?php echo $table ; ?>
```

5. Create the controller file table_footer.php and add the following code to it:

```html
    </body>
</html>
```

How it works...

The constructor in the table controller loads CodeIgniter's Table library:

```php
function __construct() {
    parent::__construct();
    $this->load->library('table');
}
```

The public function index() function is called. We then define how we want our HTML table markup to look. This is where you can place any markup for the specific CSS, using which you can style the elements of the table:

```php
$tmpl = array (
    'table_open'          => '<table border="0" cellpadding="4"
      cellspacing="0" id="example">',

    'heading_row_start'   => '<tr>',
    'heading_row_end'     => '</tr>',
    'heading_cell_start'  => '<th>',
    'heading_cell_end'    => '</th>',

    'row_start'           => '<tr>',
    'row_end'             => '</tr>',
    'cell_start'          => '<td>',
    'cell_end'            => '</td>',

    'row_alt_start'       => '<tr>',
    'row_alt_end'         => '</tr>',
    'cell_alt_start'      => '<td>',
    'cell_alt_end'        => '</td>',

    'table_close'         => '</table>'
);
```

Take a closer look at the `table_open` element of the `$tmpl` array. Look for the item I've highlighted in the preceding code. The `id="example"` item is used by DataTable (in the `<script>` tag of the file, `table_header.php`) to apply its CSS and functionality. You can, of course, name it anything you like but be sure to reflect that change in the JavaScript code.

We then call `$this->table->set_template()` to apply the HTML table markup:

```
$this->table->set_template($tmpl);
```

We then set the table headers and apply the data for our rows from a database query. Ensure that the number of items in the table headers is the same as the number of items in the table data:

```
$this->table->set_heading(array('ID', 'First Name',
    'Last Name', 'Email'));
$query = $this->db->query("SELECT * FROM person");
$data['table'] = $this->table->generate($query);
```

We then generate the table. The `$this->table->generate()` function will return a string of HTML, which we save in `$data['table']`.

```
$data['table'] = $this->table->generate();
```

The `$data` array is then passed to our view files for rendering to the browser:

```
$this->load->view('tables/table_header');
$this->load->view('tables/table_body', $data);
$this->load->view('tables/table_footer');
```

Using word_limiter() for table output

Suppose that you're making a CMS or some sort of admin interface and you're currently making a view which lists—oh I don't know—articles. Suppose that there are some articles in your database and you have to list them. It might be considered useful to the user of the CMS to provide them with a brief preview of the article so that they can be sure that they're deleting, editing, or just looking at the correct one. A preview—similar to the one found in an e-mail client—displays the first few lines, so that a user can be sure of what they're looking at. CodeIgniter comes with a handy function for limiting the number of words displayed from a string of text; this function is perfect for such a purpose. Here, we're going to build a very small example for our recipe of a view, listing some articles and previewing the first few lines of each article.

Getting ready

As the articles will be stored in the database we will need to build a table to store them in; this will be just a simple table containing the articles. In any application, you'll likely build the database tables for the articles and article management (or whatever content you're hosting) yourself and have many more tables of a different design and schema than is in the example recipe here. However, this is merely a brief example—feel free to adapt and amend the recipe as you require:

Create the following table in your database:

```
CREATE TABLE `articles` (
    `id` int(11) NOT NULL AUTO_INCREMENT,
    `title` varchar(255) NOT NULL,
    `body` text NOT NULL,
    `created_at` int(11) NOT NULL,
    PRIMARY KEY (`id`)
) ENGINE=InnoDB  DEFAULT CHARSET=latin1 AUTO_INCREMENT=3 ;
```

Insert the following entries into the table:

```
INSERT INTO `articles` (`id`, `title`, `body`, `created_at`)
  VALUES
(1, 'Article One', '
<p>It suddenly struck me that that tiny pea, pretty and blue,
  was the Earth. I put up my thumb and shut one eye,
  and my thumb blotted out the planet Earth.
  I didn't feel like a giant. I felt very, very small.</p>\r\n
  <p>Houston, Tranquillity Base here. The Eagle has landed.</p>
  \r\n<p>That's one small step for [a] man, one giant leap for
  mankind.</p>', 1381009509),
(2, 'Article Two', '<p>Space, the final frontier. These are the
  voyages of the Starship Enterprise. Its five-year mission: to
  explore strange new worlds, to seek out new life and new
  civilizations, to boldly go where no man has gone before.</p>
  \r\n<p>We choose to go to the moon in this decade and
  do the other things, not because they are easy, but because
  they are hard, because that goal will serve to organize and
  measure the best of our energies and skills, because that
  challenge is one that we are willing to accept, one we are
  unwilling to postpone, and one which we intend to
  win.</p>\r\n<p>The sky is the limit only for those who aren't
  afraid to fly!</p>', 1381003509);
```

We're displaying articles here (which in general are fairly long). So, to save on space in the book and limit the amount of typing you need to do, I've only included 2 short articles. I got the text for the articles from the Space Ipsum website (http://spaceipsum.com/). If you don't want to type all that text from the preceding code (and why would you), you can go to Space Ipsum and get your own article content for this recipe. Either way it's good.

How to do it...

We will be creating the following three files:

- ▸ `limit.php` at `/path/to/codeigniter/application/controllers/`: This will be running the show for us, calling the model and passing data to the view file `view_all.php` under `limit/`

- ▸ `/path/to/codeigniter/application/views/limit/view_all.php`: This will display a table summary of each article with the content for the body field limited by `word_limiter()`

- ▸ `/path/to/codeigniter/application/models/limit_model.php`: This will retrieve the articles from the database with Active Record

1. We will be creating the following three files: Create the controller file, `limit.php`, and add the following code to it:

```php
<?php if ( ! defined('BASEPATH')) exit('No direct script
  access allowed');

class Limit extends CI_Controller {
    function __construct() {
        parent::__construct();
        $this->load->helper('url');
        $this->load->helper('text');
        $this->load->model('Limit_model');
    }

    public function index() {
        redirect('limit/view_all');
    }

    public function view_all() {
        $data['query'] = $this->Limit_model->get_all();
        $this->load->view('limit/view_all', $data);
    }
}
```

2. Create the view file, `views/limit/view_all.php`, and add the following code to it:

```php
<table>
    <tr>
        <td><b>Title</b></td>
        <td><b>Preview</b></td>
        <td><b>Created At</b></td>
    </tr>
    <?php foreach ($query->result() as $row) : ?>
        <tr>
            <td><?php echo $row->title ; ?></td>
```

```
            <td><?php echo word_limiter($row->body, 15) ;
              ?></td>
            <td><?php echo $row->created_at ; ?></td>
          </tr>
        <?php endforeach ; ?>

    </table>
```

3. Create the model file, `limit_model.php`, and add the following code to it:

```
<?php if ( ! defined('BASEPATH')) exit('No direct script
  access allowed');

class Limit_model extends CI_Model {
    function __construct() {
        parent::__construct();
    }

    function get_all() {
        $query = $this->db->get('articles');
        return $query;
    }
}
```

How it works...

We start by loading the support assets in the constructor:

```
function __construct() {
    parent::__construct();
    $this->load->helper('url');
    $this->load->helper('text');
    $this->load->model('Limit_model');
}
```

The `url` and `text` variable will provide support for the `redirect()` and `word_limit()` functions respectively, and the `Limit_model` class will support access with the database for us.

The `public function index()` function redirects us to the public function `view_all`, which calls the `get_all()` function of `Limit_model`:

```
$data['query'] = $this->Limit_model->get_all();
$this->load->view('limit/view_all', $data);
```

The `get_all()` function will query the database with Active Record and pull out the contents, passing this back to our controller and saving it in the `$data` array (highlighted in the following code) where it is passed to the `limit/view_all` view file:

```
$data['query'] = $this->Limit_model->get_all();
$this->load->view('limit/view_all', $data);
```

If all works out as planned, you should see something similar to the following screenshot:

Title	Preview	Created At
Article One	It suddenly struck me that that tiny pea, pretty and blue, was the Earth. I...	1381009509
Article Two	Space, the final frontier. These are the voyages of the Starship Enterprise. Its five-year mission:...	1381003509

You can see that the word count of the **Preview** column is limited to 15 words, where it is capped and appended with three periods (**...**).

Using word_censor() for cleaning input

There may be times when you're building your application that you'll need to not only validate against unwanted data, but also check the content of that data for any unwanted words or phrases. For example, imagine that you're building a simple blogging engine and you don't want people replying to your blog posts with rude words and phrases—fair enough. So, what you need to do is to be able to look through the user input and filter out any unwanted content that might be present. CodeIgniter provides just this facility with the function `word_censor()`. Let's look at how to use it.

Getting ready

We're going to store our censored words in a database; so, we'll look for words that we'll use in place of actual rude words, such as `rude_word_number_1`, and so on.

Run the following MySQL code in your database:

```
CREATE TABLE `censored_words` (
    `id` int(11) NOT NULL AUTO_INCREMENT,
    `word` varchar(255) NOT NULL,
    PRIMARY KEY (`id`)
) ENGINE=InnoDB  DEFAULT CHARSET=latin1 AUTO_INCREMENT=5 ;

INSERT INTO `censored_words` (`id`, `word`) VALUES
(1, 'rude_word_number_1'),
(2, 'rude_word_number_2'),
(3, 'rude_word_number_3'),
(4, 'rude_word_number_4');
```

We will store the censored text in another table. For want of a better title, I've called that table `censor`. The following code is the schema for that table, which you can run in your database:

```
CREATE TABLE `censor` (
    `id` int(11) NOT NULL AUTO_INCREMENT,
    `name` varchar(255) NOT NULL,
    `body` text NOT NULL,
    PRIMARY KEY (`id`)
) ENGINE=InnoDB DEFAULT CHARSET=latin1 AUTO_INCREMENT=1 ;
```

How to do it...

1. Create three files as shown:

    ❑   /path/to/codeigniter/application/controllers/censor.php

    ❑   /path/to/codeigniter/application/views/censor/create.php

    ❑   /path/to/codeigniter/application/models/censor_model.php

2. Create the controller file, `censor.php`, and add the following code to it:

```php
<?php if ( ! defined('BASEPATH')) exit('No direct script
  access allowed');

class Censor extends CI_Controller {
    function __construct() {
        parent::__construct();
        $this->load->helper('url');
        $this->load->helper('text');
        $this->load->model('Censor_model');
    }

    public function index() {
        redirect('censor/create');
    }

    public function create() {
        $this->load->library('form_validation');
        $this->form_validation->set_error_delimiters('',
          '<br />');
        $this->form_validation->set_rules('name', 'Name',
          'required|min_length[1]|max_length[225]|trim');
        $this->form_validation->set_rules('body', 'Body',
          'required|min_length[1]|max_length[2000]|trim');

        if ($this->form_validation->run() == FALSE) {
            $this->load->view('censor/create');
        } else {
```

```
        $query =
          $this->Censor_model->get_censored_words();
        $censored_words = array();

        foreach ($query->result() as $row) {
            $censored_words[] = $row->word;
        }

        $data = array(
            'name' => $this->input->post('name'),
            'body' => word_censor(
              $this->input->post('body'),
              $censored_words, 'BOOM')
        );

        if ($this->Censor_model->create($data)) {
            echo 'Entered into DB:<br /><pre>';
            var_dump($data);
            echo '</pre>';
        }
    }
  }
}
```

3. Create the view file `create.php` at `/path/to/codeigniter/application/views/censor/` and add the following code to it:

```
<?php echo validation_errors() ; ?>
<?php echo form_open('censor/create');?>
    <input type="text" name="name" size="20"
      value="<?php echo set_value('body') ; ?>" />
    <br />
    <textarea name="body"><?php echo set_value('body') ;
      ?></textarea>
    <br />
<?php echo form_submit('submit','Submit!') ; ?>
<?php echo form_close() ; ?>
```

4. Create the model file `censor_model.php` at `/path/to/codeigniter/application/models/` and add the following code to it:

```
<?php if ( ! defined('BASEPATH')) exit('No direct script
    access allowed');

class Censor_model extends CI_Model {
    function __construct() {
        parent::__construct();
    }

    function get_censored_words() {
```

```
        $query = $this->db->get('censored_words');
        return $query;
    }

    function create($data) {
        if ($this->db->insert('censor', $data)) {
            return true;
        } else {
            return false;
        }
    }
}
```

How it works...

The constructor in our `Censor` class loads our support files: the helpers `url` and `text`, and our model `Censor_model`:

```
function __construct() {
    parent::__construct();
    $this->load->helper('url');
    $this->load->helper('text');
    $this->load->model('Censor_model');
}
```

The `public function index()` function redirects us to `public function create()` where we begin form validation. We load the form validation library and set the error delimiters, after which we set the rules for the form elements in the view file `create.php` at `/path/to/codeigniter/application//views/censor/`.

If there is an error, or the controller is being accessed for the first time, `$this->form_validation->run()` will equal `FALSE` and we shall just display the view file for the user to fill in.

However, once the form has been submitted (and assuming that there were no errors picked up by CodeIgniter's validation functionality), we now want to check the input for any unwanted words. To do that, we must first get a list of the unwanted words. As we're storing those words in the database table `censored_words`, we also should fetch them. So, we grab them from the database with the `censor_model` function `get_censored_words()`, and add them to an array called `$censored_words`:

```
$query = $this->Censor_model->get_censored_words();
$censored_words = array();

foreach ($query->result() as $row) {
    $censored_words[] = $row->word;
}
```

We then build the $data array ready to be passed to the Censor_model function, create(). Take a look at the body element of the array, which I've highlighted in the following code:

```
$data = array(
    'name' => $this->input->post('name'),
    'body' => word_censor($this->input->post('body'),
      $censored_words, 'BOOM')
    );
```

Here, we call the text helper function, word_censor(), passing the string that we wish to check. In this case, the body forms items from the submitted form, along with the array of censored words as a second parameter; the third parameter is optional. Leaving the third parameter blank will cause CodeIgniter to replace a censored word with the default string ####. However, for this recipe we're replacing each censored word with the string BOOM.

The $data array is then written to the database table, censor (I really must think of a better name for that table).

Let's take it for a spin. Run the censor controller in your browser and you should see an output similar to the following screenshot:

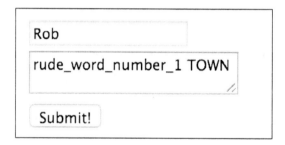

Here, we have entered the values Rob and rude_word_number_1 TOWN. When you click on the **Submit** button you should see the array var_dump of $data showing:

```
Entered into DB:
array(2) {
  ["name"]=>
  string(3) "Rob"
  ["body"]=>
  string(9) "BOOM TOWN"
}
```

If you see **BOOM TOWN**, you know it has worked!

5
Managing Data In and Out

In this chapter, we will cover:

- Sending different data to multiple views
- Validating user input
- Preparing user input
- Sticky form elements in CodeIgniter
- Displaying errors next to form items
- Reading files from the filesystem
- Writing files to the filesystem
- Creating and downloading ZIP files
- Uploading files with CodeIgniter
- Creating and using validation callbacks
- Using the language class
- Using the language class – switching a language on the fly
- Confirming cookie acceptance from the user

Introduction

Managing data is an important subject covering not only the format of output data, database structure, and access methods but also security; any discussion of data and managing that data will obviously feature discussions of security and the protection of your system and its data. As such, there will be some cross-over with the security chapter and I recommend that you also read that chapter alongside this.

Sending different data to multiple views

Someone recently asked me if they could send different data to different views in the same browser page and have the data displayed in its own section. Luckily, this can be done easily; you can pass more than one array of data to more than one view at the same time.

This can be really useful if your web page is split into sections with each section displaying its own data. For example, you may want a section displaying most read articles with another displaying most shared articles.

Getting ready

As we're going to be pulling data from a database we will need to ensure that a few `config` variables are set to allow us to do this. Open up the `/path/to/codeigniter/application/config/database.php` file and find the following settings. Then, amend them to match your requirements:

Option Name	Valid Options	Description
`$db['default']['hostname']`	Usually localhost	This is the server on which the database sits
`$db['default']['username']`	?	The database access username
`$db['default']['password']`	?	The password for the database
`$db['default']['database']`	?	The name of the database

Now that we've configured CodeIgniter to connect to a database, copy the following code into your database:

```
CREATE TABLE IF NOT EXISTS `articles` (
  `article_id` int(11) NOT NULL AUTO_INCREMENT,
  `article_title` varchar(255) NOT NULL,
  `article_body` text NOT NULL,
  `is_main` varchar(3) NOT NULL,
  PRIMARY KEY (`article_id`)

);

INSERT INTO `articles` (`article_id`, `article_title`,
  `article_body`, `is_main`) VALUES
(1, 'Article One', 'Article One Body', 'yes'),
(2, 'Article Two', 'Article Two Body', 'no'),
(3, 'Article Three', 'Article Three Body', 'no'),
(4, 'Article Four', 'Article Four Body', 'no'),
(5, 'Article Five', 'Article Five Body', 'no'),
(6, 'Article Six', 'Article Six Body', 'no');
```

How to do it...

We're going to create four files:

- ► `/path/to/codeigniter/application/controllers/articles.php`

- ► `/path/to/codeigniter/application/models/content_model.php`

- ► `/path/to/codeigniter/application/views/articles/left.php`

- ► `/path/to/codeigniter/application/views/articles/right.php`

1. Create the `/path/to/codeigniter/application/controllers/articles.php` file and copy the following code into it:

```
<?php if (!defined('BASEPATH')) exit('No direct script
  access allowed');
class Articles extends CI_Controller {
  function __construct() {
    parent::__construct();
    $this->load->helper('url');
  }

  public function index() {
    // Load content model
    $this->load->model('content_model');

    // Fetch stuff from database and store in specific
      arrays
```

```
$left_data['main_article'] = $this->content_model-
   >get_main_article();
$right_data['article_list'] = $this->content_model-
   >get_article_list();

// Load views and pass data to them
$this->load->view('articles/left', $left_data);
$this->load->view('articles/right', $right_data);
    }
}
```

2. Create the `/path/to/codeigniter/application/models/content_model.php` file and copy the following code into it:

```
class Content_model extends CI_Model {
  function get_main_article() {
    $this->db->where('is_main', 'yes');
    return $this->db->get('articles');
  }

  function get_article_list() {
    return $this->db->get('articles');
  }
}
```

3. Create the `/path/to/codeigniter/application/views/articles/left.php` file and copy the following code into it:

```
<?php foreach ($main_article->result() as $main_row) : ?>
    <h2><?php echo $main_row->article_title ; ?></h2>
    <p><?php echo $main_row->article_body ; ?></p>
<?php endforeach ; ?>
```

4. Create the `/path/to/codeigniter/application/views/articles/right.php` file and copy the following code into it:

```
<?php foreach ($article_list->result() as $list_row) : ?>
    <?php echo anchor('#', $list_row->article_title) ;
       ?><br />
<?php endforeach ; ?>
```

How it works...

`public function index()` loads the `content_model` by `$this->load->model('content_model');` and calls the two model functions `get_main_article()` and `get_article_list()`. The `get_main_article()` function fetches the row for the left-hand view and stores it in the `$left_data` array and `get_article_list()` fetches results for the right-hand view and stores it in the `$right_data` array:

```
// Fetch stuff from database and store in $data
```

```
$left_data['main_article'] = $this->content_model-
  >get_main_article();
$right_data['article_list'] = $this->content_model-
  >get_article_list();
```

Both left and right views are called and both the arrays ($left_data and $right_data) passed to them:

```
// Load views and pass $data variable to them
$this->load->view('articles/left', $left_data);
$this->load->view('articles/right', $right_data);
```

Each view will then loop through the specific array outputting the fields we want.

Validating user input

Validating user input allows you to set rules against which input coming in from the user can be judged. For example, you may wish to enforce certain conditions on an e-mail field, most obviously checking for a valid e-mail syntax, but also the minimum and maximum length, and whether it is required. CodeIgniter can even look into a database and check for duplicate values. In this recipe, we're going to build a controller and view, which together will allow the user to input data and have it validated against rules that will be set; errors, if any, will be reported back to the user.

Getting ready

You'll need to be aware of a few things before getting started. The following is a table of all available CodeIgniter validation rules:

Rule	Parameter	Description
required	No	It specifies if the specific form element must have data when submitted by the user. It will return FALSE if empty.
matches	Yes	It compares the data between two form elements to see if they match. It will return FALSE if they don't match and TRUE if they do. Example use:
		`$this->form_validation->set_rules('item1', 'Item1', '');` `$this->form_validation->set_rules('item2', 'Item2', 'matches[Item1]');`

Rule	Parameter	Description
is_unique	Yes	It queries a database to see if the value of a table record item matches the value of the form element being submitted. It will return FALSE if the form element is not unique. Example use: ```$this->form_validation->set_rules('item1', 'Item1', 'matches [users.username]');```
min_length	Yes	It checks the length of the value in the form element to see if it is less than the parameter specified. It will return FALSE if the form element is smaller than the value specified. Example use: ```$this->form_validation->set_rules('item1', 'Item1', 'min_length[12]');```
max_length	Yes	It is the reverse of min_length; it checks if the length of the value in the form element is greater than the parameter specified. It will return FALSE if the form element is greater than the value specified. Example use: ```$this->form_validation->set_rules('item1', 'Item1', 'max_length[12]');```
exact_length	Yes	It checks if the length of the value in the form element is the exact value as compared to the specified parameter. It will return FALSE if the form element is anything other than what is specified. Example use: ```$this->form_validation->set_rules('item1', 'Item1', 'exact_length [12]');```
greater_than	Yes	It checks if the value in the form element is greater than a supplied parameter. It will return FALSE if the form element is less than the parameter value or that value is not numeric. Example use: ```$this->form_validation->set_rules('item1', 'Item1', 'greater_than[12]');```

Rule	Parameter	Description
less_than	Yes	It is the reverse of greater_than. It checks if the value in the form element is less than a supplied parameter. It will return `FALSE` if the form element is greater than the parameter value or that value is not numeric. Example use: ```$this->form_validation->set_rules('item1', 'Item1', 'less_than[12]');```
alpha	No	It checks if the value in the form element contains alphabetical characters only. It will return `FALSE` if the form element value is anything other than that.
alpha_numeric	No	It checks if the value in the form element contains alphabetical and integer values only. It will return `FALSE` if the form element value is anything other than that.
alpha_dash	No	It checks if the value of the form element contains anything other than alpha-numeric characters, underscores or dashes. It will return `FALSE` if it contains any other value.
numeric	No	It checks if the value of the form element contains anything other than numeric characters. It will return `FALSE` if the form element contains anything other than that.
integer	No	It checks if the value of the form element contains anything other than integer values. It will return `FALSE` if the form element contains anything other than that.
decimal	Yes	It checks if the value of the form element contains a decimal value, that is a number separated with a decimal point (`.`), otherwise it will return `FALSE`.
is_natural	No	It checks if the value of the form element contains anything other than natural numbers—that is to say anything other than 1, 2, 3, 4, 5, and so on. It will return `FALSE` if the form element contains anything other than that.
is_natural_no_zero	No	It checks if the value of the form element contains anything other than natural numbers, which are greater than zero. It will return `FALSE` if the value is anything other than natural numbers or zero.
valid_email	No	It checks if the value of the form element contains a valid e-mail as calculated by Regular Expression within CodeIgniter. It will return `FALSE` if the form element does not contain a valid e-mail address.

Rule	Parameter	Description
valid_emails	No	It checks if the value of the form element contains valid e-mail addresses as calculated by Regular Expression within CodeIgniter. It will return FALSE if the form element does not contain a valid e-mail address.
valid_ip	No	It checks if the supplied IP address is valid.
valid_base64	No	It returns FALSE if the supplied string contains anything other than valid Base64 characters.

There are also some basic config changes we'll need to make before we start working through our recipes. We're going to amend the `path/to/codeigniter/application/config/config.php` file.

Config Item	Change to Value	Description
`$config['global_xrsf_filtering']`	TRUE	It specifies whether CodeIgniter always filters for Cross-Site Scripting. For security purposes it is recommended that this is set to TRUE.
`$config['csrf_protection']`	TRUE	It specifies whether to use Cross-Site Request Forgery protection. For security purposes it is recommended that this is set to TRUE.
`$config['csrf_token_name']`	Your own string	It specifies that if the user closes his/her browser the session becomes void.
`$config['csrf_cookie_name']`	Another string of your choice	It specifies whether the cookie should be encrypted on the user's computer. For security purposes this should be set to TRUE.
`$config['csrf_expire']`	7200	It specifies the length of time in seconds.

How to do it...

Create the following files in your CodeIgniter install:

- `/path/to/codeigniter/application/controllers/form.php`
- `/path/to/codeigniter/application/views/new_record.php`

1. Add the following code into the `path/to/codeigniter/application/controllers/form.php` file:

```php
<?php if (!defined('BASEPATH')) exit('No direct script
  access allowed');

class Form extends CI_Controller {
  function __construct() {
    parent::__construct();
    $this->load->helper('form');
    $this->load->helper('url');
    $this->load->helper('security');
    $this->load->library('form_validation');
  }

  public function index() {
    redirect('form/submit_form');
  }

  public function submit_form() {
    $this->form_validation->set_error_delimiters('', '<br
      />');

    $this->form_validation->set_rules('first_name', 'First
      Name', 'required|min_length[1]|max_length[125]');
    $this->form_validation->set_rules('last_name', 'Last
      Name', 'required|min_length[1]|max_length[125]');
    $this->form_validation->set_rules('email', 'Email',
      'required|min_length[1]|max_length[255]
        |valid_email');
    $this->form_validation->set_rules('contact', 'Contact',
      'required|min_length[1]|max_length[1]|
        integer|is_natural');
    $this->form_validation->set_rules('answer', 'Question',
      'required|min_length[1]|max_length[2]|
        integer|is_natural');

    // Begin validation
    if ($this->form_validation->run() == FALSE) { //
      First load, or problem with form
      $this->load->view('new_record');
    }
    else {
      // Validation passed, now escape the data
      $data = array(
        'first_name'    => $this->input-
          >post('first_name'),
        'last_name'     => $this->input->post('last_name'),
        'email'         => $this->input->post('email'),
        'contact'       => $this->input->post('contact'),
```

```
                'answer'          => $this->input->post('answer')
            );

        echo '<pre>';
        var_dump($data);
        echo '</pre>';
        }
    }
}
```

2. Add the following code into the path /to/codeigniter/application/views/
   new_record.php file:

```
<?php echo form_open('form/submit_form') ; ?>
    <?php if (validation_errors()) : ?>
        <h3>Whoops! There was an error:</h3>
        <p><?php echo validation_errors(); ?></p>
    <?php endif; ?>
    <table border="0" >
        <tr>
            <td>First Name</td>
            <td><?php echo form_input(array('name' => 'first_
name', 'id' => 'first_name', 'value' => '', 'maxlength' => '100',
'size' => '50', 'style' => 'width:100%')); ?></td>
        </tr>
        <tr>
            <td>Last Name</td>
            <td><?php echo form_input(array('name' => 'last_name',
'id' => 'last_name', 'value' => '', 'maxlength' => '100', 'size'
=> '50', 'style' => 'width:100%')); ?></td>
        </tr>
        <tr>
            <td>User Email</td>
            <td><?php echo form_input(array('name' => 'email',
'id' => 'email', 'value' => '', 'maxlength' => '100', 'size' =>
'50', 'style' => 'width:100%')); ?></td>
        </tr>
        <tr>
            <td>Do you want to be contacted in the future?</td>
            <td><?php echo 'Yes'.form_checkbox('contact', '1',
TRUE).'No'.form_checkbox('contact', '0', FALSE); ?></td>
        </tr>
        <tr>
            <td>What is 10 + 5?</td>
            <td><?php echo form_input(array('name' => 'answer',
```

```
'id' => 'answer', 'value' => '', 'maxlength' => '100', 'size' =>
'50', 'style' => 'width:100%')); ?></td>
        </tr>
      </table>
      <?php echo form_submit('submit', 'Submit'); ?>
      or <?php echo anchor('form', 'cancel'); ?>
  <?php echo form_close(); ?>
```

How it works...

CodeIgniter will first run `public function index()`, which will immediately redirect to `public function submit_form()`. The `submit_form()` function will set our error delimiters with the line `$this->form_validation->set_error_delimiters('', '<br />');` and then list the validation rules for each form element:

```
$this->form_validation->set_rules('first_name', 'First Name',
   'required|min_length[1]|max_length[125]');
$this->form_validation->set_rules('last_name', 'Last Name',
   'required|min_length[1]|max_length[125]');
$this->form_validation->set_rules('email', 'Email',
   'required|min_length[1]|max_length[255]|valid_email');
$this->form_validation->set_rules('contact', 'Contact',
   'required|min_length[1]|max_length[1]|integer|is_natural');
$this->form_validation->set_rules('answer', 'Question',
   'required|min_length[1]|max_length[2]|integer|is_natural');
```

As the form is being run for the first time `$this->form_validation->run()` will return `FALSE` and so load the view file `$this->load->view('new_record');`, which will render the form to the user. The user can then enter his/her details into the form. Once the user clicks on the **Submit** button, CodeIgniter again loads public function `submit_form()`, but this time, as the form is being submitted the validation rules are applied to the data being submitted. CodeIgniter will compare the data submitted against the rules and return `FALSE` if that data fails to match the rules in validation. If those rules are not met, the user will see error messages in the view. The following code checks if there are any validation errors, if so it will display them one by one:

```
<?php if (validation_errors()) : ?>
    <h3>Whoops! There was an error:</h3>
    <p><?php echo validation_errors(); ?></p>
<?php endif; ?>
```

Preparing user input

The validation rules can also be used to prepare input for you. For example, you can `trim()` whitespace from the input or apply `htmlspecialchars()`. Any PHP function can be used, as long as that function accepts one parameter as an argument by default.

How to do it...

Let's assume that we want to `trim()` whitespaces from the beginning and end of the input and generate an md5 hash of the input:

```
$this->form_validation->set_rules('input_name', 'Input Name',
    'trim|md5');
```

Sticky form elements in CodeIgniter

It is good for user experience to offer feedback; we do this in the preceding sections with `validation_errors()`, but it is also useful to keep user data in form elements to save them having to re-type everything, should there be an error. To do this, we need to use CodeIgniter's `set_value()` function.

Getting ready

Make sure that you load `$this->load->helper('form');` from within the `__constructor()` of the controller; however, you can always autoload the helper from `/path.to/codeigniter/application/config/autoload.php`.

How to do it...

We're going to edit the `/path/to/codeigniter/application/views/new_record.php` file.

1. Amend the file to show the following (changes in bold):

```
<?php echo form_open('form/submit_form') ; ?>
    <?php if (validation_errors()) : ?>
        <h3>Whoops! There was an error:</h3>
        <p><?php echo validation_errors(); ?></p>
    <?php endif; ?>
    <table border="0" >
        <tr>
            <td>First Name</td>
            <td><?php echo form_input(array('name' => 'first_
```

```
name', 'id' => 'first_name', 'value' => set_value('first_
name', ''), 'maxlength' => '100', 'size' => '50', 'style' =>
'width:100%')); ?></td>
            </tr>
            <tr>
                <td>Last Name</td>
                <td><?php echo form_input(array('name' => 'last_name',
'id' => 'last_name', 'value' => set_value('last_name', ''),
'maxlength' => '100', 'size' => '50', 'style' => 'width:100%'));
?></td>
            </tr>
            <tr>
                <td>User Email</td>
                <td><?php echo form_input(array('name' => 'email',
'id' => 'email', 'value' => set_value('email', ''), 'maxlength' =>
'100', 'size' => '50', 'style' => 'width:100%')); ?></td>
            </tr>
            <tr>
                <td>Do you want to be contacted in the future?</td>
                <td><?php echo 'Yes'.form_checkbox('contact', '1',
TRUE).'No'.form_checkbox('contact', '0', FALSE); ?></td>
            </tr>
            <tr>
                <td>What is 10 + 5?</td>
                <td><?php echo form_input(array('name' => 'answer',
'id' => 'answer', 'value' => set_value('answer', ''), 'maxlength'
=> '100', 'size' => '50', 'style' => 'width:100%')); ?></td>
            </tr>
        </table>
        <?php echo form_submit('submit', 'Submit'); ?>
        or <?php echo anchor('form', 'cancel'); ?>
<?php echo form_close(); ?>
```

How it works...

Essentially, it is exactly the same functionality as the *Validating User Input* recipe, except that now the CodeIgniter function, set_value(), populates the form element value with the data submitted previously by the user.

Displaying errors next to form items

In the preceding example, we displayed errors one by one at the top of the HTML page; however, you may wish to display each individual error closer to the form element to which it refers.

How to do it...

We're going to amend the `/path/to/codeigniter/application/views/new_record.php` file.

1. Amend the code to reflect the following (changes in bold):

```php
<?php echo form_open('form/submit_form') ; ?>
    <?php if (validation_errors()) : ?>
        <h3>Whoops! There was an error:</h3>
    <?php endif; ?>
    <table border="0" >
        <tr>
            <td>First Name</td>
        <?php if (form_error('first_name')) : ?>
            <?php echo form_error('first_name') ; ?>
        <?php endif ; ?>
            <td><?php echo form_input(array('name' => 'first_
name', 'id' => 'first_name', 'value' => set_value('first_
name', ''), 'maxlength' => '100', 'size' => '50', 'style' =>
'width:100%')); ?></td>
        </tr>
        <tr>
            <td>Last Name</td>
        <?php if (form_error('last_name')) : ?>
            <?php echo form_error('last_name') ; ?>
        <?php endif ; ?>
            <td><?php echo form_input(array('name' => 'last_name',
'id' => 'last_name', 'value' => set_value('last_name', ''),
'maxlength' => '100', 'size' => '50', 'style' => 'width:100%'));
?></td>
        </tr>
        <tr>
            <td>User Email</td>
        <?php if (form_error('email')) : ?>
            <?php echo form_error('email') ; ?>
        <?php endif ; ?>
            <td><?php echo form_input(array('name' => 'email',
'id' => 'email', 'value' => set_value('email', ''), 'maxlength' =>
'100', 'size' => '50', 'style' => 'width:100%')); ?></td>
        </tr>
        <tr>
```

```
<?php if (form_error('contact')) : ?>
  <?php echo form_error('contact') ; ?>
<?php endif ; ?>
        <td>Do you want to be contacted in the future?</td>
        <td><?php echo 'Yes'.form_checkbox('contact', '1',
TRUE).'No'.form_checkbox('contact', '0', FALSE); ?></td>
      </tr>
      <tr>
        <td>What is 10 + 5?</td>
        <td><?php echo form_input(array('name' => 'answer',
'id' => 'answer', 'value' => set_value('answer', ''), 'maxlength'
=> '100', 'size' => '50', 'style' => 'width:100%')); ?></td>
      </tr>
    </table>
    <?php echo form_submit('submit', 'Submit'); ?>
    or <?php echo anchor('form', 'cancel'); ?>
<?php echo form_close(); ?>
```

How it works...

Essentially, it's exactly the same validation functionality as the preceding recipe; the only change is how we're displaying the errors. We have removed the line `<p><?php echo validation_errors(); ?></p>`, as we're not listing the errors one by one. We have added the CodeIgniter's `form_error()` statement, passing it the name of the HTML form element so that if CodeIgniter's validation class discovers that the posted form data does not meet the parameters assigned to it as validation rules, an error will be displayed above the form element.

Reading files from the filesystem

Although you're probably going to be writing and reading data in a database you will certainly come in contact with the requirement to write something to the disk, and read from files stored on it. CodeIgniter can support several methods for interacting with files.

Getting ready

There are no configuration options to change here, but ensure that you load the file helper in your controller constructor (and also the `url` helper):

```
function __construct() {
    parent::__construct();
    $this->load->helper('url');
    $this->load->helper('file');
}
```

We're going to read files from the disk and display details about them to a view.
Firstly, we're going to create two files:

- `/path/to/codeigniter/application/controllers/file.php`
- `/path/to/codeigniter/application/views/file/view_file.php`

1. Add the following code into `/path/to/codeigniter/application/controllers/file.php`:

```php
<?php if (!defined('BASEPATH')) exit('No direct script access
allowed');

class File extends CI_Controller {
    function __construct() {
        parent::__construct();
        $this->load->helper('url');
        $this->load->helper('file');
    }

    public function index() {
        redirect('file/view_all_files');
    }

    public function view_all_files() {
        $data['dir'] = '/full/path/to/read';
        $data['files'] = get_dir_file_info($data['dir']);
        $this->load->view('files/view_file', $data);
    }
}
```

2. Add the following code into `/path/to/codeigniter/application/views/files/view_file.php`:

```html
<html>
    <head>
        <title>Viewing Files</title>
    </head>
    <body>
        <?php echo anchor('file/create_file', 'Create File'); ?>
        <?php echo anchor('file/read_file', 'Read File'); ?>
        <?php echo anchor('file/view_all_files', 'View Files'); ?>
        <table border="1">
            <tr>
                <td><b>Filename</b></td>
                <td><b>Size</b></td>
                <td><b>Created</b></td>
                <td colspan="3">Actions</td>
```

```
                </tr>
                <?php foreach ($files as $file) : ?>
                    <tr>
                        <td>
                            <?php if (is_dir($file['server_path'])) :
    ?>
                                <b><?php echo $file['name']; ?></b>
                            <?php else : ?>
                                <?php echo $file['name']; ?>
                            <?php endif; ?>
                        </td>
                        <td>
                            <?php echo $file['size']; ?>
                        </td>
                        <td>
                            <?php echo date("d/m/Y H:i:s",
    $file['date']); ?>
                        </td>
                        <td>
                            <?php echo anchor('file/edit_file/' .
    $file['name'], 'Edit'); ?> 
                            <?php echo anchor('file/delete_file/' .
    $file['name'], 'Delete'); ?> 
                            <?php echo anchor('file/view_file/' .
    $file['name'], 'View'); ?>
                        </td>
                    </tr>
                <?php endforeach; ?>
            </table>
    </body>
    </html>
```

How it works...

The business end of this is the controller, `function view_all_files()`. We're doing three things. First, is setting the target directory with which we wish to read the line `$data['dir']` `= '/full/path/to/read';` obviously replacing `'/full/path/to/read'` with the actual path.

We then pass `$data['dir']` to the CodeIgniter function, which does the heavy lifting for us, `get_dir_file_info()` returns an array for every item in the target directory. We store this in `$data['files']`.

`$this->load->view('files/view_file', $data);` calls the HTML template, passing to it the files array, which in turn loops through the `$files` array, outputting to an HTML table.

We also use the PHP function `is_dir()` to test whether an item is a directory or not; if it is, we make it bold in the HTML code—for no other reason than it's good to know what you're looking at.

It would be a great idea to move much of this functionality to a library or helper so that it can be more easily shared by other parts of your application if necessary.

Writing files to the filesystem

If you're reading from a disk (as we have seen previously), you'll probably want to write to a disk. Now, we'll look at creating several types of files and writing them to a location on the disk.

How to do it...

We're going to amend the file:

▸ `/path/to/codeigniter/application/controllers/write_file.php`

Amend `/path/to/codeigniter/application/controllers/file/file.php` to reflect the following:

```
public function write() {
  // Set data
  $data_to_write = 'This is text which will be written to
    the file';
  // Define path for file
  $path = "/path/to/write/to/with/filename.extension";

  if (!write_file($path, $data_to_write)) { // Error
    echo 'Error writing to file: ' . $path;
  } else { // Everything worked
  echo 'Data written to '. $path;
  }
}
```

How it works...

The `public function write()` function sets the `$data_to_write` variable to a string; however, this could be amended to accept user input, database results, and so on. The `$path` array is also defined, this should be the full path with the file extension. The destination directory should have enough permissions to allow CodeIgniter to write to it. Then, we test for the return result of the CodeIgniter function, `write_file()`. If there was an error, we display a short message; however, you can amend this, perhaps report to the error log. If successful it displays a success message; again this can also be amended to other behavior.

Creating and downloading ZIP files

You may wish to generate ZIP folders from your application and force a download for your users; for example, if you have a group of files, such as a press pack, which you wish to be kept together, or a set of CSV files. Saving them into a ZIP file and allowing a download is a great way to do this.

How to do it...

We're going to create a new file:

▸ /path/to/codeigniter/application/controllers/zip.php

And copy the following code into it:

```php
<?php if (!defined('BASEPATH')) exit('No direct script access
allowed');
class Zip extends CI_Controller {
  function __construct() {
    parent::__construct();
    $this->load->helper('form');
    $this->load->helper('url');
    $this->load->library('zip');
  }

  public function index() {
    redirect('zip/zipme');
  }

  public function zipme() {

  $file_name = '/path/to/zip/tozip.txt';

  // Create some data for the file
  $data = 'This is a string of text which we will use to write to
    the file in the variable $file_name';

  // Set the time (to be used as ZIP filename)
  $date = date("d-m-Y", time());

  // Save some data to the ZIP archive
  $this->zip->add_data($file_name, $data);

  // Create the ZIP archive on your server - make sure this path
    is
  // outside of your web root
```

```
$this->zip->archive('/path/in/zip/'.$date.'.zip');

// Download the ZIP archive
$this->zip->download($date.'.zip');

// Clear the cached ZIP archive
$this->zip->clear_data();
    }
}
```

How it works...

This is actually quite simple, we start by declaring a `$file_name`. This is a string, you'll notice that the filename also contains a folder name `my_zipped_files_folder`—you don't have to include a folder but if you do CodeIgniter will automatically create a folder in the ZIP archive.

We then create some data—in this case it is written as a string of text; however, it could easily be output from a database. For example, we could change the `$data` line to:

```
$data = '';

foreach ($database_result->result() as $row) {
    $data .= $row->item_1;
    $data .= $row->item_2;
    $data .= $row->item_3;
}
```

After we create our `$data` we then create the date, which we'll use in the filename for our ZIP. The line `$this->zip->add_data($file_name, $data);` takes as argument the filename and data we created earlier and creates a file inside the ZIP file and fills it with the string in `$data`. `$this->zip->archive('/path/to/your/zip/folder/'.$date.'.zip');` will write the ZIP to the disc using `$date` as the ZIP filename. `$this->zip->download($date.'.zip');` forces the ZIP file to open in the client browser and `$this->zip->clear_data();` will clear the ZIP file from the cache.

Uploading files with CodeIgniter

CodeIgniter comes with very good file uploading support, which can take a lot of the hassle out of writing upload functions.

Getting ready

There are some settings you should be aware of which you'll probably need to change for your environment. Firstly, ensure that you load the upload library using:

```
$this->load->library('upload');
```

The following is a table of settings that should be placed in the $config array in the controller you are using, such as the following Fileupload controller:

Setting	Default	Change to	Description
upload_path	None	None	It specifies the path to the folder where the uploaded file should go. Ensure that you have set the correct permissions to enable CodeIgniter to write to it.
allowed_types	None	None	It specifies the allowed mime types, which are allowed in the upload. This can be useful as it allows you to white list uploaded file types; that is, it allows you to define only allowed types. You should separate each type with a pipe (|). For example: `$config['allowed_types'] = "jpg|gif|bmp|png";`
file_name	None	Desired file name	If this value is set, CodeIgniter will attempt to rename the file to this value on upload.
overwrite	FALSE	TRUE/FALSE	CodeIgniter looks in the upload destination folder to see if a file with a matching file name already exists. If this is set to TRUE that file will be overwritten; if it is set to FALSE, a number will be appended to the file name.
max_size	0	None	It specifies the maximum size in kilobytes that the file is allowed to be. Setting it to zero will tell CodeIgniter that there is no limit.
max_width	0	None	It specifies the maximum width in pixels. Setting it to zero will tell CodeIgniter that there is no limit.
max_height	0	None	It specifies the maximum height in pixels. Setting it to zero will tell CodeIgniter that there is no limit.

Setting	Default	Change to	Description
max_filename	0	None	It specifies the maximum character file name length of the uploaded file. Setting it to zero will tell CodeIgniter that there is no limit.
encrypt_name	FALSE	TRUE/FALSE	It tells CodeIgniter that you wish to encrypt the file name of the image on upload.
remove_spaces	TRUE	TRUE/FALSE	It specifies if you want whitespace removed from the filename on upload.

How to do it...

We're going to create two files:

- /path/to/codeigniter/application/controllers/fileupload.php
- /path/to/codeigniter/application/views/upload/upload.php

1. Add the following code into the file /path/to/codeigniter/application/ controllers/fileupload.php:

```php
<?php if ( ! defined('BASEPATH')) exit('No direct script access allowed');
class Fileupload extends CI_Controller {
    function __construct() {
        parent::__construct();
        $this->load->helper('form');
        $this->load->helper('url');
    }

    function index() {
        $this->load->view('upload/upload_form');
    }

    function upload() {
        $config['upload_path'] = '/path/to/upload/dir/';
        $config['allowed_types'] = 'gif|jpg|png';
        $config['max_size'] = '100';

        $this->load->library('upload', $config);

        if (!$this->upload->do_upload()) { // Upload error,
display form & errors
            $data['error'] = $this->upload->display_errors();
            $this->load->view('upload/upload_form', $data);
        } else { // Success, display success message
            $data['upload_data'] = $this->upload->data();
            $data['success'] = TRUE;
```

```
                        $this->load->view('upload/upload_success', $data);
                }
        }
}
```

2. Add the following code into the file `/path/to/codeigniter/application/` `views/upload.php`:

```
<html>
<body>
    <?php if (isset($error)) : ?>
        <?php echo $error;?>
    <?php endif ; ?>
    <?php echo form_open_multipart('fileupload/upload');?>
        <input type="file" name="userfile" size="20" /><br />
        <input type="submit" value="Upload File!" />
    </form>
<?php if (isset($success)) : ?>
        <h2>Success</h2>
        <p>The file was successfully uploaded, here's some
information about the file:</p>
        <ul>
            <?php foreach ($upload_data as $key => $value):?>
                <li><?php echo $key . " : " . $value ;?></li>
            <?php endforeach; ?>
        </ul>
<?php endif ; ?>
</body>
</html>
```

How it works...

This is thankfully very simple; when `Fileupload` is run `function index()` will `redirect()` to `function upload()`, which will in turn load the HTML upload form. Once a user has submitted that form `function upload()` will run again and attempt to upload the file with the CodeIgniter function, `do_upload()`. The `do_upload()` function will perform the task of uploading the file and preparing it for writing to the filesystem such as checking that the file size, file type, and so on match your settings, ensuring that the upload destination directory exists and is writable, and finally using the PHP function `move_uploaded_file()` it'll complete the task of uploading the file.

The `if` statement catches the result of this; if `TRUE` the file is uploaded successfully and the success form is displayed, the `$data` array is populated with the output of the CodeIgniter function `$this->upload->data()`.

However, if `do_upload()` returned `FALSE`, the HTML upload form is displayed again, this time with an error message to the user.

There's more...

You'll probably get a few errors the first time you try this, usually because you have an incorrect upload path, or that destination folder could have the wrong permissions assigned to it. It'll take a little tweaking to get it right. The following are some of the more common errors you'll get:

- ▸ **The upload path does not appear to be valid**: This means you've put the wrong value in `$config['upload_path']`, check that you have the correct path to your uploads folder. Ensure that you have a trailing slash / at the end of your path.

- ▸ **The upload destination folder does not appear to be writable**: This means the directory you want to upload doesn't have write permissions; usually this can be fixed on the command line by `chmod 777 -R [dir _name]` where `[dir_name]` is the path to the directory you want to upload to. Naturally, having a folder with permissions of `777` might cause you a headache later on, so ensure that the upload folder is outside of the web root.

Creating and using validation callbacks

Callbacks are used when you want to validate data in a way that may not be supported by the CodeIgniter's validation class. The benefit of using callbacks is that posted data can be easily validated by a custom function you define, and errors, if any, are passed into the error reporting functions.

How to do it...

We're going to amend the file:

- ▸ `/path/to/codeigniter/application/controllers/form.php`

Amend that file to show the following:

```
$this->form_validation->set_rules('first_name', 'First
  Name', 'required|min_length[1]|max_length[125]');
$this->form_validation->set_rules('last_name', 'Last
  Name', 'required|min_length[1]|max_length[125]');
$this->form_validation->set_rules('email', 'Email',
  'required|min_length[1]|max_length[255]|valid_email|
  callback_email_check');
$this->form_validation->set_rules('contact', 'Contact',
  'required|min_length[1]|max_length[1]|
  integer|is_natural');
$this->form_validation->set_rules('answer', 'Question',
  'required|min_length[1]|max_length[2]|integer|
```

```
                     is_natural');

public function email_check($email) {
  if ($email_is_unique == false) {
    $this->form_validation->set_message('email_check', 'The value
entered in %s already exists in the database.');
    return false;
  } else {
    return true;
  }
}
```

How it works...

This is actually very simple, especially if you have used callbacks in other applications. When the user submits the form, CodeIgniter validates the form as it would do normally, except that when CodeIgniter comes to validate the user's e-mail, the function, `callback_email_check($email)`, is run. This function can perform any test and return TRUE or FALSE, and if FALSE a message too.

Using the language class

One of the most useful features of CodeIgniter is its language class and support. It allows you to store content and set that content to belong to various languages; it is then possible to switch between languages to display different text in the same place holders in the view files. It's really easy to set up and this is how you do it.

Getting ready

A little information about language files. You'll need to know the rules for naming them. Language files are stored at `/path/to/codeigniter/application/system/language/[language_name]/`.

Where `[language_name]` is the name of the language you wish to support. So, for example, if you want to support English, French, and German you will create three file names:

- `/path/to/codeigniter/application/language/english/en_lang.php`
- `/path/to/codeigniter/application/language/french/fr_lang.php`
- `/path/to/codeigniter/application/language/german/de_lang.php`

You can see above that the three files are named 'en', 'fr', and 'de'. Appended to the names is `_lang.php`; you must append each file with `_lang.php` so that CodeIgniter knows it is a language file.

How to do it...

So, in order to create an English language file create the following files:

- ► /path/to/codeigniter/application/system/language/english/
  en_lang.php

- ► /path/to/codeigniter/application/controllers/lang.php

- ► /path/to/codeigniter/application/views/lang/english.php

1. Add the following code into /path/to/codeigniter/application/
   controllers/lang.php

```php
<?php if (!defined('BASEPATH')) exit('No direct script access
allowed');
class Lang extends CI_Controller {
  function __construct() {
    parent::__construct();
    $this->load->helper('form');
    $this->load->helper('url');
    $this->load->helper('language');
    $this->lang->load('en', 'english');
  }

  public function index() {
    redirect('lang/submit');
  }

  public function submit() {
    $this->load->library('form_validation');
    $this->form_validation->set_error_delimiters('', '<br
      />');

    // Set validation rules
    $this->form_validation->set_rules('email', $this->lang-
      >line('form_email'), 'required|min_length[1]
        |max_length[50]|valid_email');

    // Begin validation
    if ($this->form_validation->run() == FALSE) {
      $this->load->view('lang/form');
    } else {
      echo $this->lang->line('form_confirm_email') . $this-
        >input->post('email');
    }
  }
}
```

2. Add the following code into `/path/to/codeigniter/application/views/`
   `lang/form.php`

```
<html>
<body>

<h2><?php echo $this->lang->line('form_title') ; ?></h2>
<?php echo validation_errors() ; ?>
<?php echo form_open('lang/submit') ; ?>
<?php echo $this->lang->line('form_email') ; ?>
<?php echo form_input(array('name' => 'email','id' =>
'email','value' => '','maxlength' => '100','size' => '50','style'
=> 'width:10%')) ; ?>

<?php echo form_submit('', $this->lang->line('form_submit_
button')) ; ?>
<?php echo form_close() ; ?>

</body>
</html>
```

3. Add the following code into `/path/to/codeigniter/language/english/`
   `en_lang.php`

```
<?php
$lang['form_title'] = "Form title in English";
$lang['form_email'] = "Email";
$lang['form_submit_button'] = "Submit";
$lang['form_confirm_email'] = "Your email is: ";
?>
```

How it works...

In the constructor of the controller `/path/to/codeigniter/application/`
`controllers/lang.php` we're loading helpers, such as form and URL, but we're also doing
two language-related things, loading the language helper and setting the language to be used:

```
$this->load->helper('language');
$this->lang->load('en', 'english');
```

Where `'en'` is the language and `'English'` is the folder we're storing all English-related
content in.

We're loading the language helper and declaring the language filename and the language to
be used, specifically the line:

```
$this->lang->load('filename','language');
```

Here, the first parameter is the name of the language file minus the `_lang.php` (so en_lang. php will be just `'en'`, `fr_lang.php` will just be `'fr'` and so on). The second parameter is the language (in this case, it is the folder in the `/path/to/codeigniter/application/language/` folder).

Once we have loaded the language class and defined the correct language and filename, we can then begin to pull out items in the `$lang` array. The way we pull items out of the `$lang` array is by echoing `$this->lang->line(array_element_name);` so, to pull out the form title we would write echo `$this->lang->line('form_title');`

Confirming cookie acceptance from the user

Various states and regions now require websites to ask their users if they approve of that website writing cookies to their computer. There is some debate as to how this can be provisioned by the website and what constitutes approval from the user. You may have noticed that recently websites display a notice to the user requesting approval. Something called Implied Consent is the current thinking; a notice is shown informing the user that if they continue to use the site they are happy with the cookies being written.

The following recipe does just that; and a notice is shown to the user that will disappear if they click on a link indicating they are happy with cookies being written.

Getting ready

We need to make sure some config variables are set for us to be able to read and write cookies to a user's computer.

Open the `/path/to/codeigniter/application/config/config.php` file and make the following changes:

$config array items	Description
`$config['cookie_prefix'] = "";`	It specifies if you wish for a character to be there before the cookie name; for example, `$config['cookie_prefix'] = "thisprefix_";` will produce a cookie called `thisprefix_cookie_con'` (`cookie_conf` being the example cookie, in your application you will replace it with the cookie name you are working with).
`$config['cookie_domain'] = "";`	It specifies the domain of the server; if you are developing on local host, it is best to leave this value as blank, replacing with the domain name and path once you move out of a localhost environment.

$config array items	Description
`$config['cookie_path'] = "/";`	It specifies the path to the cookie—chances are you'll want this to remain /.
`$config['cookie_secure'] = FALSE;`	It specifies if you wish to encrypt the cookie value, TRUE if you want it to be encrypted and FALSE if not.

How to do it...

We're going to create two files:

- ▸ /path/to/codeigniter/application/controllers/cookie_conf.php
- ▸ /path/to/codeigniter/application/views/cookie_conf/cookie_conf.php

1. Create the file /path/to/codeigniter/application/controllers/cookie_conf.php and copy the following code into it:

```php
<?php if (!defined('BASEPATH')) exit('No direct script access allowed');

class Cookie_conf extends CI_Controller {
  function __construct() {
    parent::__construct();
    $this->load->helper('url');
    $this->load->helper('cookie');
  }

  public function index() {
    // If the cookie doesn't exist, make it
    if ( ! $this->input->cookie('cookie_conf')) {
      $cookie = array(
        'name'   => 'cookie_conf',
        'value'  => 'cookie-conf-unconfirmed',
        'expire' => 7200,
        'domain' => '',
        'path'   => '/',
        'prefix' => '',
        'secure' => FALSE
      );

      $this->input->set_cookie($cookie);
    }

    if ( $this->input->cookie('cookie_conf')) { // If cookie
      exists
    // Is the cookie unconfirmed?
    if ($this->input->cookie('cookie_conf', FALSE) ==
```

127

```
                'cookie-conf-unconfirmed') {
            $data['display_cookie_conf'] = TRUE;
            } else {
            $data['display_cookie_conf'] = FALSE;
            }
            } else { // If cookie doesn't exist yet
    $data['display_cookie_conf'] = TRUE;
                }

            $this->load->view('cookie_conf/cookie_conf', $data);
        }

        public function agree() {
          $cookie = array(
            'name'   => 'cookie_conf',
            'value'  => 'confirmed',
            'expire' => 7200,
            'domain' => '',
            'path'   => '/',
            'prefix' => '',
            'secure' => FALSE
          );

          // Set the cookie to confirmed
          $this->input->set_cookie($cookie);
          echo 'You agree to the cookie';
        }

        public function disagree() {
          echo 'You don\'t agree to the cookie';
        }
    }
```

2. Create the file `/path/to/codeigniter/application/views/cookie_conf/cookie_conf.php` and copy the following code into it:

```html
<html>
    <head>
        <script type="text/javascript" src="http://ajax.
googleapis.com/ajax/libs/jquery/1.9.1/jquery.min.js"></script>
        <?php if (isset($display_cookie_conf) && ($display_cookie_
conf == TRUE)) : ?>
            <script type="text/javascript">
                $(document).ready(function() {
                    // User has agreed
                    $('#agree').click(function(answer){
                        $.ajax({
                            type: "POST",
                            url: "cookie_conf/agree",
                            success: function(data) {
```

```
                                    // If they have agreed then remove
the cookie-conf-container from their browser
                                $('#cookie-conf-container').
slideUp(500);
                            },
                            error: function(){alert('error in
agree response');}
                        });
                    });

                    // User has disagreed
                    $('#disagree').click(function(answer) {
                        $.ajax({
                            type: "POST",
                            url: "cookie_conf/disagree",
                            success: function(data){
                                // They've not approved - we can
display an error if we want
                                $('#response').html(data);
                            },
                            error: function(){alert('error in
disagree response');}
                        });
                    });
                });

        </script>
        <?php endif; ?>
    </head>
    <body>
        <?php if (isset($display_cookie_conf) && ($display_cookie_
conf == TRUE)) : ?>
            <span id="cookie-conf-container">
                <p>This is a message to the user regarding cookies
- obviously replace it with the text appropriate to your site. </
p>
                <span id='agree'>Agree</span>
                <span id='disagree'>Disagree</span>
                <!-- If you want to provide a response to your
user, this is where it'll be outputted -->
                <div id='response'></div>
            </span>
        <?php endif; ?>

    </body>
</html>
```

How it works...

There are a few things going on here but essentially it's quite simple. Take a look at the following flowchart, it gives a pretty good overview of what is happening:

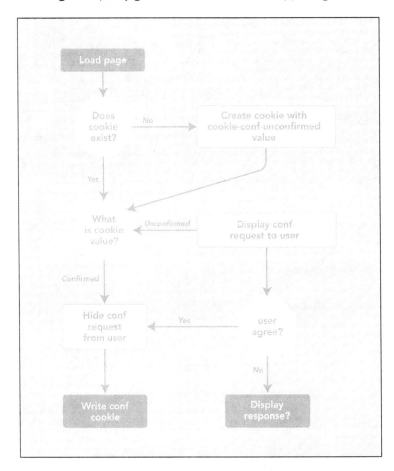

We start with the page being loaded. Does the cookie exist? The following code is from the `cookie_conf` controller. It checks to see if a cookie named `cookie_conf` already exists and if not will create that cookie with a value of `cookie-conf-unconfirmed`.

```
if ( ! $this->input->cookie('cookie_conf')) {
  $cookie = array(
    'name'   => 'cookie_conf',
    'value'  => 'cookie-conf-unconfirmed',
    'expire' => 7200,
    'domain' => '',
    'path'   => '/',
```

```
      'prefix' => '',
      'secure' => FALSE
   );

   $this->input->set_cookie($cookie);
}
```

The following code is also from `cookie_conf`. After checking for an existence of a cookie (creating one if it doesn't exist), the controller then looks at the value of that cookie. If the cookie does not exist or contains the value `cookie-conf-unconfirmed`, `$data['display_cookie_conf']` is set to `TRUE`, otherwise it is set to `FALSE`.

```
if ( $this->input->cookie('cookie_conf')) { // If cookie exists
   // Is the cookie unconfirmed?
   if ($this->input->cookie('cookie_conf', FALSE) == 'cookie-conf-
     unconfirmed') {
   $data['display_cookie_conf'] = TRUE;
   } else {
      $data['display_cookie_conf'] = FALSE;
   }
} else { // If cookie doesn't exist yet
   $data['display_cookie_conf'] = TRUE;
}
```

`cookie_conf` then loads the view. In the view is some PHP code, which checks if `$display_cookie_conf` is set and if so looks at its value. If it is `FALSE`, the code is skipped over; however, if it is `TRUE`, the HTML code is displayed. The user is given two options, one to agree with the cookie policy and the other to disagree.

If the user disagrees, you'll have to implement your own action on this event. The preceding code will respond by echoing out the text `You don't agree to the cookie`; but in real situations you'll have to decide how you want to proceed.

If the user agrees, the `cookie-conf-container` will slide up and `public function agree()` in the `Cookie_conf` controller is called by AJAX, setting the value of the cookie from `cookie-cong'unconfirmed'` to `'confirmed'`.

```
public function agree() {
   $cookie = array(
      'name'   => 'cookie_conf',
      'value'  => 'confirmed',
      'expire' => 7200,
      'domain' => '',
      'path'   => '/',
      'prefix' => '',
      'secure' => FALSE
   );

   // Set the cookie to confirmed
```

```
$this->input->set_cookie($cookie);
echo 'You agree to the cookie';
}
```

Any subsequent visit will make `cookie_conf` look for that cookie, and as long as it exists and contains the value `'confirmed'` the `'cookie-cong-container'` will not be displayed.

There's more...

I want to mention a couple of gotchas which you might experience while implementing the cookie authorization recipe.

- ▶ **Localhost and Cookies**: Firstly, the domain attribute. If you are developing on localhost, you should leave this value blank. Reason being that web browsers often have trouble with implementing cookies if domain is set to local host. Why? Because browsers are programmed to expect at least two items in the domain attribute those being the domain name and a tld, so the browser is expecting something similar to domain. com—localhost obviously doesn't look like that. So for developing in localhost, leave the domain attribute blank, replacing with the correct domain and path once you move out of the localhost environment.

- ▶ **Expire value**: Make sure that you define the expire value as an integer rather than a string; so don't put the expire value in single or double quotes, you want this: 12345, and not this: '12345'.

6
Working with Databases

In this chapter, we will cover:

- ▸ Configuring CodeIgniter for databases
- ▸ Connecting to multiple databases
- ▸ Active Record – Create (insert)
- ▸ Active Record – Read (select)
- ▸ Active Record – Update
- ▸ Active Record – Delete
- ▸ Looping through database results
- ▸ Counting the number of returned results with num_rows()
- ▸ Counting the number of returned results with count_all_results()
- ▸ Counting the number of returned results
- ▸ Query binding
- ▸ Finding the last insert ID
- ▸ Finding the number of affected rows
- ▸ Finding the last database query
- ▸ Using CodeIgniter database migrations
- ▸ Moving to the current version with current()
- ▸ Rolling back/stepping forward with version()
- ▸ Generating an XML from a database result
- ▸ Generating a CSV from a database result

Introduction

Pretty much any application you build will require database access and a functionality, from basic **Create**, **Read**, **Update**, and **Delete** (**CRUD**) operations to more sophisticated approaches. In this chapter, we'll look at some fairly simple recipes (for example, simple CRUD operations), and then some more capable recipes such as connecting to multiple databases, database caching, and generating files as output.

Some recipes are quite simple, so I won't provide all the files for you to copy (in some cases, it may be unnecessary); instead, many of the recipes are small blocks of code that you can drop into real-world scenarios as you need to.

Configuring CodeIgniter for databases

If you have already configured CodeIgniter to connect with a database, you can skip this part, as all we're going to do is make sure we can connect to a database; to do this, we're going to amend the following two files:

- `/path/to/codeigniter/application/config/database.php`
- `/path/to/codeigniter/application/config/autoload.php`

How to do it...

1. In the `database.php` config file, look for the following lines and amend them accordingly:

   ```
   $db['default']['hostname'] = 'localhost';
   $db['default']['username'] = 'Replace with database username';
   $db['default']['password'] = 'Replace with database password';
   $db['default']['database'] = 'Replace with database name';
   ```

   The chances are that you'll not need to change `$db['default']['hostname']` from the `'localhost'`, and replace other values (username, password, and database) with the specific values for your environment.

2. In the `autoload.php` config file, look for the following line (around line 55):

   ```
   $autoload['libraries'] = array();
   ```

3. Ensure that the database is being autoloaded by adding it to the `$autoload` array like this:

   ```
   $autoload['libraries'] = array('database');
   ```

Be sure to separate each library you're auto-loading with a comma, for example, `$autoload['libraries'] = array('database', 'session', 'javascript')` and so on.

How it works...

There's not a lot to this really; it's only setting the configuration settings, but one interesting point is that of autoloading the libraries. By placing a library name in this array in the autoload configuration file, you no longer need to load the library explicitly in a controller later in your application.

Connecting to multiple databases

There may be times when you require your application to connect to more than one database or database server. For example, imagine you managed an online shop, and you may wish to have one database to handle customer orders, billing, invoicing, and so on, and another database to store and maintain product and stock information. CodeIgniter can be configured to use many database instances, and the following section shows how you do it.

Getting ready

In order to let CodeIgniter interact with two or more databases, we'll need to amend a few settings in the `config` file at:

▶ `/path/to/codeigniter/application/config/database.php`

Scroll down to the bottom of the file and copy the following into it. Remember to replace `hostname`, `username`, `password`, and `database` with the correct details for your setup.

```
$db['database1']['hostname'] = '';
$db['database1']['username'] = '';
$db['database1']['password'] = '';
$db['database1']['database'] = 'database1';
$db['database1']['dbdriver'] = 'mysql';
$db['database1']['dbprefix'] = '';
$db['database1']['pconnect'] = FALSE;
$db['database1']['db_debug'] = FALSE;
$db['database1']['cache_on'] = FALSE;
$db['database1']['cachedir'] = '';
$db['database1']['char_set'] = 'utf8';
$db['database1']['dbcollat'] = 'utf8_general_ci';
$db['database1']['swap_pre'] = '';
```

```
$db['database1']['autoinit']  = TRUE;
$db['database1']['stricton']  = FALSE;

$db['database2']['hostname']  = '';
$db['database2']['username']  = '';
$db['database2']['password']  = '';
$db['database2']['database']  = 'database2';
$db['database2']['dbdriver']  = 'mysql';
$db['database2']['dbprefix']  = '';
$db['database2']['pconnect']  = FALSE;
$db['database2']['db_debug']  = FALSE;
$db['database2']['cache_on']  = FALSE;
$db['database2']['cachedir']  = '';
$db['database2']['char_set']  = 'utf8';
$db['database2']['dbcollat']  = 'utf8_general_ci';
$db['database2']['swap_pre']  = '';
$db['database2']['autoinit']  = TRUE;
$db['database2']['stricton']  = FALSE;
```

Look closely at the lines in bold. The first four lines in each database group details the standard host, username, password, and database name for each database you wish to use. But, also look at the following lines:

```
$db['database1']['pconnect']  = FALSE;
$db['database2']['pconnect']  = FALSE;
```

The database configuration setting 'pconnect' tells CodeIgniter whether you wish to have persistent connections or not. Setting this value to False in each database group allows CodeIgniter to communicate with more than one database. We're going to create two databases with one table in each. Obviously, your requirements will be different, but you can adapt to the recipe as necessary. Copy the following code into your database:

```
CREATE DATABASE `database1` ;
USE `database1`;

CREATE TABLE `table1` (
  `t1_id` int(11) NOT NULL AUTO_INCREMENT,
  `t1_first_name` varchar(255) NOT NULL,
  `t1_last_name` varchar(255) NOT NULL,
  PRIMARY KEY (`t1_id`)
) ENGINE=InnoDB  DEFAULT CHARSET=latin1 AUTO_INCREMENT=3 ;

INSERT INTO `table1` (`t1_id`, `t1_first_name`, `t1_last_name`) VALUES
(1, 'Lucy', 'Welsh'),
(2, 'Rob', 'Foster');

CREATE DATABASE  `database2` ;
```

```
USE `database2`;

CREATE TABLE `table2` (
  `t2_id` int(11) NOT NULL AUTO_INCREMENT,
  `t2_first_name` varchar(255) NOT NULL,
  `t2_last_name` varchar(255) NOT NULL,
  PRIMARY KEY (`t2_id`)
) ENGINE=InnoDB  DEFAULT CHARSET=latin1 AUTO_INCREMENT=3 ;

INSERT INTO `table2` (`t2_id`, `t2_first_name`, `t2_last_name`) VALUES
(1, 'Oliver', 'Welsh'),
(2, 'Chloe', 'Graves');
```

How to do it...

Now, we have two databases to work with and have configured the `database.php` configuration file to communicate with both of them, so now we can begin to access each database in turn.

We're going to create the controller, `'database1'`, and `'database2'` files that would be available at:

- `/path/to/codeigniter/application/controllers/multi_database.php`: This is the controller file; it will call models for both databases `'database1'` and `'database2'`
- `/path/to/codeigniter/application/models/multi_database_model_db_1.php`: This model will communicate with the first database `'database1'`.
- `/path/to/codeigniter/application/models/multi_database_model_db_2.php`: This model will communicate with the second database `'database2'`.

The following steps will help us in accessing each database:

1. Ensure that `$db['users']['pconnect']` in `/config/database.php` is set to `FALSE`, and you have entered the correct access information for each database.

2. Create the file `/path/to/codeigniter/application/controllers/multi_database.php`. This controller will call the two database models and output results from each. Add the following code to the controller file `multi_database.php`:

```php
<?php if (!defined('BASEPATH')) exit('No direct script
  access allowed');

class Multi_database extends CI_Controller {

  function __construct() {
    parent::__construct();
```

```
        $this->load->helper('url');
    }

    public function index() {
        redirect('multi_database/select');
    }

    public function select() {
        $this->load->model('Multi_database_model_db_1');
        $query1 = $this->Multi_database_model_db_1->select_1();

        $this->load->model('Multi_database_model_db_2');
        $query2 = $this->Multi_database_model_db_2->select_2();

        foreach ($query1->result() as $row1) {
            echo $row1->t1_first_name . ' ' . $row1-
                >t1_last_name;
            echo '<br />';
        }

        foreach ($query2->result() as $row2) {
            echo $row2->t2_first_name . ' ' . $row2-
                >t2_last_name;
            echo '<br />';
        }
    }
}
```

3. Create the model /path/to/codeigniter/application/models/multi_
database_model_db_1php. This model will communicate with 'database1'.
Add the following code to the model:

```
<?php if ( ! defined('BASEPATH')) exit('No direct script
    access allowed');
class Multi_database_model_db_1 extends CI_Model {
    function __construct() {
        parent::__construct();
    }

    function select_1() {
        $DBconn1 = $this->load->database('database1', TRUE);
        $query1 = $DBconn1->query("SELECT * FROM `table1`");
        return $query1;
    }
}
```

4. Create the model `/path/to/codeigniter/application/models/multi_database_model_db_2.php`. This model will communicate with `'database2'`. Add the following code to the model:

```php
<?php if ( ! defined('BASEPATH')) exit('No direct script
  access allowed');

class Multi_database_model_db_2 extends CI_Model {
  function __construct() {
    parent::__construct();
  }

  function select_2() {
    $DBconn2 = $this->load->database('database2', TRUE);
    $query2 = $DBconn2->query("SELECT * FROM `table2`");
    return $query2;
  }
}
```

How it works...

Firstly, let's pay attention to the settings we've defined for each one of our databases in the file `/path/to/codeigniter/application/config/database.php`. These database settings are specific to each database we want to connect to. We have also set the configuration variable `'pconnect'` to `FALSE` for each of our databases (see the preceding bold text). When we run the controller `Multi_database` in the browser, the controller will load our two database models named—for ease of explanation—`'Multi_database_model_db_1'` and `'Multi_database_model_db_2'`. The `Multi_database` controller will then call one function from each model, again named `select_1` and `select_2` for ease of explanation. The following code shows the same:

```php
$this->load->model('Multi_database_model_db_1');
$query1 = $this->Multi_database_model_db_1->select_1();

$this->load->model('Multi_database_model_db_2');
$query2 = $this->Multi_database_model_db_2->select_2();
```

Okay! So far so good. There's nothing new here—just calling some database models; however, it's inside those models that things get interesting. Let's take a look at the code for the model `Multi_database_model_db_1`:

```php
function select_1() {
  $DBconn1 = $this->load->database('database1', TRUE);
  $query1 = $DBconn1->query("SELECT * FROM `table1`");
  return $query1;
}
```

We're loading the database `'database1'`—meaning, we're connecting to a database called `'database1'` using the settings defined for `'database1'` in the `database.php` configuration file—and storing that in the object which we're calling, that is, `$DBconn1`:

```
$DBconn1 = $this->load->database('database1', TRUE);
```

Next, we're using the database object `$DBconn1` to run a query and store the database result object in the variable `$query1`:

```
$query1 = $DBconn1->query("SELECT * FROM `table1`");
```

We then return `$query` to the calling controller. The controller `Multi_database` then loops through the `$query1` result object, echoing as we go:

```
foreach ($query1->result() as $row1) {
  echo $row1->t1_first_name . ' ' . $row1->t1_last_name;
  echo '<br />';
}
```

Active Record – create (insert)

There are several ways to insert data into a database using CodeIgniter Active Record; for example, `$this->db->insert()` and `$this->db->insert_batch()`. The first will insert only one record at a time, and the second will insert an array of data as individual rows into the database; this can be quite useful if you know you need to insert more than one record at a time, thereby saving you the trouble of calling `insert()` more than once.

Getting ready

This is the SQL code required to support this recipe; you'll need to adapt it to your circumstances. Copy the following SQL code into your database:

```
CREATE TABLE IF NOT EXISTS `ch6_users` (
  `id` int(11) NOT NULL AUTO_INCREMENT,
  `firstname` varchar(50) NOT NULL,
  `lastname` varchar(50) NOT NULL,
  `username` varchar(20) NOT NULL,
  `password` varchar(20) NOT NULL,
  `created_date` int(11) NOT NULL,
  `is_active` varchar(3) NOT NULL,
  PRIMARY KEY (`id`)
) ENGINE=InnoDB  DEFAULT CHARSET=latin1 AUTO_INCREMENT=1 ;
```

How to do it...

We're going to create the following two files (or amend those files if you have already created them):

- ► /path/to/codeigniter/application/controllers/database.php
- ► /path/to/codeigniter/application/models/database_model.php

The following steps will demonstrate how to insert data into a database using CodeIgniter Active Record:

1. Add the following code into the controller database.php:

```php
<?php if (!defined('BASEPATH')) exit('No direct script
  access allowed');

class Database extends CI_Controller {

  function __construct() {
    parent::__construct();
  }

  public function index() {
    redirect('database/create');
  }

  public function create() {
    $data = array(
      'firstname' => 'Lucy',
      'lastname' => 'Welsh',
      'username' => 'lucywelsh',
      'password' => 'password',
      'created_date' => time(),
      'is_active' => 'yes'
    );

    $this->load->model('Database_model');
    if ($this->Database_model->insert_data($data) ) {
      echo 'Success';
    }
    else
    {
      echo 'Cannot insert to database';
    }

  }

  public function create_batch() {
```

```php
$data = array(
  array(
    'firstname' => 'Lucy',
    'lastname' => 'Welsh',
    'username' => 'lwelsh',
    'password' => 'password',
    'created_date' => time(),
    'is_active' => 'yes'),
  array(
    'firstname' => 'claire',
    'lastname' => 'Strickland',
    'username' => 'cstrickland',
    'password' => 'password',
    'created_date' => time(),
    'is_active' => 'yes'),
   array(
    'firstname' => 'Douglas',
    'lastname' => 'Morrisson',
    'username' => 'dmorrisson',
    'password' => 'password',
    'created_date' => time(),
    'is_active' => 'yes')
  );

$this->load->model('Database_model');
if ($this->Database_model->insert_batch_data($data)) {
  echo 'Success';
}
else
{
  echo 'Cannot insert to database';
}
}
}
```

2. Add the following code into the model `database_model.php`:

```php
<?php if ( ! defined('BASEPATH')) exit('No direct script access
allowed');
class Database_model extends CI_Model {

  function __construct() {
    parent::__construct();
  }

  function insert_data($data) {
    $this->db->insert('ch6_users', $data);
  }

  function insert_batch_data($data) {
```

```
        $this->db->insert_batch('ch6_users',$data);
    }
}
```

How it works...

There are two methods used here: `create()` and `create_batch()`. Let's take each function in turn and go through how they work.

The public function create()

The `create()` function should be fairly familiar; we're creating an array (named `$data`) and populating it with the data for one user or equivalent to one row's insert. The `create()` method then passes the `$data` array to the model function `insert_data()` with the following code:

```
$this->load->model('Database_model');
$this->Database_model->insert_data($data);
```

The model will then insert one row into the table `ch6_users`:

```
function insert_data($data) {
    $this->db->insert('ch6_users', $data);
}
```

The public function create_batch()

The `create_batch()` public function similar to the preceding functionality of `create()`, but rather than passing an array with one set of items, we create a multidimensional array with multiple rows of data as follows:

```
$data = array(
    array(
        'firstname' => 'Lucy',
        'lastname' => 'Welsh',
        'username' => 'lwelsh',
        'password' => 'password',
        'created_date' => time(),
        'is_active' => 'yes'),
    array(
        'firstname' => 'claire',
        'lastname' => 'Strickland',
        'username' => 'cstrickland',
        'password' => 'password',
        'created_date' => time(),
        'is_active' => 'yes'),
    array(
        'firstname' => 'Douglas',
        'lastname' => 'Morrisson',
```

```
                     'username' => 'dmorrisson',
                     'password' => 'password',
                     'created_date' => time(),
                     'is_active' => 'yes')
            );
```

We then send that array to a new model function `create_batch()`:

```
            function insert_batch_data($data) {
              $this->db->insert_batch('ch6_users',$data);
            }
```

The `function create_batch()` function uses the CodeIgniter `function insert_batch()` to INSERT each row into the database.

Active Record – read (select)

The R of CRUD represents the process to select data from a database. CodeIgniter uses the `$this->db->get()` database function to fetch rows from the database. Its usage is explained in the following sections.

Getting ready

The following is the SQL code required to support this recipe; you'll need to adapt it to your circumstances.

```
CREATE TABLE IF NOT EXISTS `ch6_users` (
  `id` int(11) NOT NULL AUTO_INCREMENT,
  `firstname` varchar(50) NOT NULL,
  `lastname` varchar(50) NOT NULL,
  `username` varchar(20) NOT NULL,
  `password` varchar(20) NOT NULL,
  `created_date` int(11) NOT NULL,
  `is_active` varchar(3) NOT NULL,
  PRIMARY KEY (`id`)
) ENGINE=InnoDB  DEFAULT CHARSET=latin1 AUTO_INCREMENT=1 ;

INSERT INTO `ch6_users` (`firstname`, `lastname`, `username`,
  `password`, `created_date`, `is_active`) VALUES
('claire', 'Strickland', 'cstrickland', 'password', 1366114115,
  'yes'),
('Douglas', 'Morrisson', 'dmorrisson', 'password', 1366114115,
  'yes'),
('Jessica', 'Welsh', 'jesswelsh', 'password', 1366114115, 'yes');
```

How to do it...

We're going to create the following two files (or amend those files if you have already created them):

- ▸ `/path/to/codeigniter/application/controllers/database.php`
- ▸ `/path/to/codeigniter/application/models/database_model.php\`

The following steps will demonstrate how to read data into a database using CodeIgniter Active Record:

1. Add the following code into the file `/path/to/codeigniter/application/controllers/database.php`:

   ```php
   public function select_row() {
       $id = 1;
       $this->load->model('Database_model');
       $result = $this->Database_model->select_row($id);
       echo '<pre>';

       var_dump($result->result());
   }
   ```

2. Add the following code into the file `/path/to/codeigniter/application/models/database_model.php`:

   ```php
   function select_row($id) {
       $this->db->where('id', $id);
       $query = $this->db->get('ch6_users');
       return $query;
   }
   ```

You know it has worked if you see the following output:

```
array(1) {
  [0]=>
  object(stdClass)#20 (7) {
    ["id"]=>
    string(1) "1"
    ["firstname"]=>
    string(4) "Lucy"
    ["lastname"]=>
    string(5) "Welsh"
    ["username"]=>
    string(6) "lwelsh"
    ["password"]=>
    string(8) "password"
    ["created_date"]=>
    string(10) "1366114115"
```

```
        ["is_active"]=>
        string(3) "yes"
    }
}
```

How it works...

In the preceding controller, `public function select_row()` assigns `$id` with the value 1—however, this can also be done from **post**, **get**, **session**, or another source—and loads the database model, passing the variable `$id` to it as follows:

```
$this->load->model('Database_model');
$this->Database_model->insert_batch_data($data);
```

The model function `select_row()` pulls the matching record from the table `'ch6_users'` and returns it to the calling controller.

Active Record – update

The U of CRUD represents the process to update data record(s) from a database in a database. CodeIgniter uses the database function `$this->db->update()` to update database records; this recipe will explain how it is done.

Getting ready

The following is the SQL code required to support this recipe; you'll need to adapt it to your circumstances.

```
CREATE TABLE IF NOT EXISTS `ch6_users` (
  `id` int(11) NOT NULL AUTO_INCREMENT,
  `firstname` varchar(50) NOT NULL,
  `lastname` varchar(50) NOT NULL,
  `username` varchar(20) NOT NULL,
  `password` varchar(20) NOT NULL,
  `created_date` int(11) NOT NULL,
  `is_active` varchar(3) NOT NULL,
  PRIMARY KEY (`id`)
) ENGINE=InnoDB  DEFAULT CHARSET=latin1 AUTO_INCREMENT=1 ;

INSERT INTO `ch6_users` (`firstname`, `lastname`, `username`,
  `password`, `created_date`, `is_active`) VALUES ('Jessica',
    'Welsh', 'jesswelsh', 'password', 1366114115, 'yes');
```

How to do it...

We're going to create the following two files (or amend those files if you have already created them):

▶ /path/to/codeigniter/application/controllers/database.php

▶ /path/to/codeigniter/application/models/database_model.php

The following step will demonstrate how to update data into a database using CodeIgniter Active Record:

1. Add the following code into the file: /path/to/codeigniter/application/controllers/database.php:

```
public function update_row() {
  $id = 1;

  $data = array(
    'firstname' => 'Jessica',
    'lastname' => 'Welsh',
    'username' => 'jesswelsh',
    'password' => 'password',
    'created_date' => time(),
    'is_active' => 'yes'
  );

  $this->load->model('Database_model');
  $result = $this->Database_model->update_row($id, $data);

  redirect('database/select_row');
}
```

Add the following code into the file: /path/to/codeigniter/application/models/database_model.php:::

```
function update_row($id, $data) {
  $this->db->where('id', $id);
  $this->db->update('ch6_users', $data);
}

array(1) {
  [0]=>
  object(stdClass)#20 (7) {
    ["id"]=>
    string(1) "1"
    ["firstname"]=>
    string(7) "Jessica"
    ["lastname"]=>
```

```
          string(5) "Welsh"
          ["username"]=>
          string(9) "jesswelsh"
          ["password"]=>
          string(8) "password"
          ["created_date"]=>
          string(10) "1366117753"
          ["is_active"]=>
          string(3) "yes"
      }
    }
```

How it works...

In the controller we just saw, `public function update_row()` assigns `$id` with the value 1—however this can be from post, get, session or another source—and loads the database model, passing the variable `$id` to it as follows:

```
$this->load->model('Database_model');
$result = $this->Database_model->update_row($id, $data);
```

The model function `update_row()` updates the matching record from the table as follows:

```
function update_row($id, $data) {
  $this->db->where('id', $id);
  $this->db->update('ch6_users', $data);
}
```

ActiveRecord – delete

The D of CRUD is used for deleting rows of data in a database table. CodeIgniter uses the `$this->db->delete()` database function to remove rows from a database; it is used in the following section.

Getting ready

The following is the SQL code required to support this recipe; you'll need to adapt it to your circumstances:

```
CREATE TABLE IF NOT EXISTS `ch6_users` (
  `id` int(11) NOT NULL AUTO_INCREMENT,
  `firstname` varchar(50) NOT NULL,
  `lastname` varchar(50) NOT NULL,
  `username` varchar(20) NOT NULL,
  `password` varchar(20) NOT NULL,
  `created_date` int(11) NOT NULL,
  `is_active` varchar(3) NOT NULL,
```

```
PRIMARY KEY (`id`)
) ENGINE=InnoDB  DEFAULT CHARSET=latin1 AUTO_INCREMENT=1 ;

INSERT INTO `ch6_users` (`firstname`, `lastname`, `username`,
   `password`, `created_date`, `is_active`) VALUES ('Jessica',
    'Welsh', 'jesswelsh', 'password', 1366114115, 'yes');
```

How to do it...

We're going to create the following two files (or amend those files if you have already created them):

- `/path/to/codeigniter/application/controllers/database.php`
- `/path/to/codeigniter/application/models/database_model.php`

The following steps will demonstrate how to delete data from a database using CodeIgniter Active Record:

1. Add the following code into the file `/path/to/codeigniter/application/controllers/database.php`:

   ```php
   public function delete_row() {
     $id = 1;

     $this->load->model('Database_model');
     $result = $this->Database_model->delete_row($id);

     redirect('database/select_row');
   }
   ```

2. Add the following code into the file `/path/to/codeigniter/application/models/database_model.php`:

   ```php
   function delete_row($id) {
     $this->db->where('id', $id);
     $this->db->delete('ch6_users');
   }
   ```

How it works...

In the preceding controller, `public function delete_row()` assigns `$id` with the value 1—however, this can be from post, get, session or another source—and loads the database model, passing the variable `$id` to it as follows:

```php
$this->load->model('Database_model');
$result = $this->Database_model->delete_row($id);
```

The model function `delete_row()` deletes the matching record from the table:

```
function delete_row($id) {
  $this->db->where('id', $id);
  $this->db->delete('ch6_users');
}
```

Looping through the database results

In any application with database connectivity, you'll probably need to display records from a database; looping through rows of data returned from a query is one of the most common tasks you'll perform in programming. CodeIgniter handles looping through database results using PHP for each statement. In this recipe, we will loop through each record at a time, echoing out the relevant information.

Getting ready

To support this recipe, we are going to create a database table and write some data to it. If you already have the data, you can skip this recipe; if not, copy the following code into your database:

```
CREATE TABLE IF NOT EXISTS `loop_table` (
  `id` int(11) NOT NULL AUTO_INCREMENT,
  `first_name` varchar(255) NOT NULL,
  `last_name` varchar(255) NOT NULL,
  PRIMARY KEY (`id`)
) ENGINE=InnoDB  DEFAULT CHARSET=latin1 AUTO_INCREMENT=3 ;

INSERT INTO `loop_table` (`id`, `first_name`, `last_name`) VALUES
(1, 'Lucy', 'Welsh'),
(2, 'Rob', 'Foster');
```

How to do it...

1. Add or adapt the following code into your controller:

   ```
   public function loop_through_data() {
     $this->load->model('Some_model');
     $data['query'] = $this->Some_model->select_data();
     $this->load->view('some_view', $data);
   }
   ```

2. Add or adapt the following code into your model:

   ```
   function select_data() {
     $query = $this->db->get('loop_table');
     return $query;
   }
   ```

3. Add or adapt the following code into your view:

```
foreach ($query->result() as $row) {
  echo $row->first_name . ' ' . $row->last_name;
  echo '<br />';
}
```

How it works...

Firstly, let's look at the SQL code; if you used the preceding SQL code, all we would have done is create a very simple table and populate it with two rows of data.

Next, we call the controller function `loop_through_data()`, which loads a model; in this case, rename `Some_model` to the model relevant to your application. We call the model function `select_data()`, storing its returned result in the `$data` array, or more specifically, in a section of the `$data` array that we're calling `'query'`:

```
$data['query'] = $this->Some_model->select_data();
```

The model function `select_data()` fetches all the rows from the database table `loop_table` and returns it to the calling controller function.

Returning to our controller, now that we have the database result in our `$data` array, we can call the `view` file `some_view.php`—you obviously need to rename it to something else in your application—and pass the `$data` array to it:

```
$this->load->view('some_view', $data);
```

The `view` file then uses a simple `foreach()` loop to cycle through each result in `$query`. Let's look at this `foreach()` loop more closely. Look at the following line of code:

```
foreach ($query->result() as $row) {
```

Remember how we stored the database result in `$data['query']`? Well, we're going to use the `'query'` part of the `$data` array, which has stored the database results, and we're going to use the CodeIgniter function `result()` on it. I hear you ask, "What does `result()` do?" The `result()` function will take an object or array and allow you to iterate through each row, allowing you to act on the individual data items within that row.

So, we're using `result()` to split apart `$query` into each row, passing that row to `$row` (because it's obvious) and allowing us to do something like:

```
echo $row->first_name . ' ' . $row->last_name;
```

This is displaying the first and last name of each person in `$row`.

Counting the number of returned results with num_rows()

It's useful to count the number of results returned—often bugs can arise if a section of the code that expects to have at least one row is passed with zero rows. Without handling the eventuality of a zero result, an application may become unpredictably unstable and may give away hints to a malicious user about the architecture of the app. Ensuring correct handling of zero results is what we're going to focus on here.

How to do it...

1. We're going to create a block of code for a model and controller. You may already have code in a controller, model, or view that does all or some of the following—obviously, you can skip any step that you do not need. Add or adapt the ensuing code into your controller:

```
$this->load->model('Some_model');
$data['query'] = $this->Some_model->some_model_function();
$this->load->view('some_view', $data);
```

2. Add or adapt the following code into your model:

```
function some_model_function() {
        $query = $this->db->get('database_table_name');
        return $query;
}
```

3. Add or adapt the following code into your view:

```
if ($query->num_rows() > 0) {
  foreach ($query->result() as $row) {
    echo $row->item1;
    echo $row->item2;
  }
} else {
  echo 'No results returned';
}
```

How it works...

This is quite common; a controller loads the required model and calls a function within that model; the result of this model is stored in an array. This is then passed to a view. It is here in the view that we'd count the number of rows. Take a look at the line in bold. We're using the CodeIgniter function `num_rows()` to look into the `$query` result and count the number of rows returned by the model. We're asking whether the number of rows is greater than zero. If it is, there must be at least one result from the model—we then look through the `$query` array as we would normally. However, if the number of results isn't greater than zero, it would mean that there were no results returned by the model. So, we use an else statement to display a brief message stating that there were `No results returned`.

Counting the number of returned results with count_all_results()

It's useful to count the number of results returned—often bugs can arise if a section of code which expects to have at least one row is passed zero rows. Without handling the eventuality of a zero result, an application may become unpredictably unstable and may give away hints to a malicious user about the architecture of the app. Ensuring correct handling of zero results is what we're going to focus on here.

How to do it...

1. Add or adapt the following code into your controller:

    ```
    $this->load->model('Some_model');
    $data['num_results'] = $this->Some_model->some_model_function();
    $this->load->view('some_view', $data);
    ```

2. Add or adapt the following code into your model:

    ```
    function some_model_function() {
      $this->db->from('table');
      return $num_rows = $this->db->count_all_results();
    }
    ```

3. Add or adapt the following code into your view:

    ```
    if (isset($num_results)) {
      echo 'There are ' . $num_results . ' returned';
    }
    ```

This is fairly similar to the recipe above `num_rows()`, but there are a few key differences. We start off by calling a controller that loads the required model and calls a function within it. Take a look at the code in bold: `$this->db->count_all_results();`. This will return the number of results returned in a given query. The result of this code is stored in an array and passed to a view where we test whether the variable `$num_results` is set; if it is, we echo a brief message indicating the number of results.

Query binding

Binding queries is another useful security process; if you use binding with your queries, values are automatically escaped by CodeIgniter, and there is no need for you to manually do so.

Getting ready

Copy the following SQL into your database:

```sql
CREATE TABLE IF NOT EXISTS `users` (
  `user_id` int(11) NOT NULL AUTO_INCREMENT,
  `user_first_name` varchar(125) NOT NULL,
  `user_last_name` varchar(125) NOT NULL,
  `user_email` varchar(255) NOT NULL,
  `user_created_date` int(11) NOT NULL COMMENT 'unix timestamp',
  `user_is_active` varchar(3) NOT NULL COMMENT 'yes or no',
  PRIMARY KEY (`user_id`)
) ENGINE=InnoDB  DEFAULT CHARSET=latin1 AUTO_INCREMENT=1 ;

INSERT INTO `users` (`user_first_name`, `user_last_name`, `user_email`, `user_created_date`, `user_is_active`) VALUES
('Chloe', 'Graves', 'cgraves@domain.com', 1366114115, 'yes'),
('Mark', 'Brookes', 'mbrookes@domain.com', 1366114115, 'yes');
```

How to do it...

In any of your models, adapt your query code to reflect the following:

```php
$query = "SELECT * FROM users WHERE users.is_active = ? AND users.created_date > ?";
$this->db->query($query, 'yes', '1366114114');
```

How it works

Using a table called `users` as an example, the query will try to fetch all records where `users.is_active` equals `Y` and `users.created_date` is greater than `1359706809` `(02/01/2013 - 03:20)`. But, you'll notice that there are two question marks in the query, and each question mark represents an item in the `$data array`. The values in the `$data` array are passed in order and into the query by the line `$this->db->query($query, $data);`. So, the first question mark in the query will be replaced with the first item in the array, the second question mark in the query will be replaced by the second item in the array, and so on.

Finding the last insert ID

Returning the Primary Key of the last inserted row can be useful in instances where you may wish to write data to more than one table and whose data may be related via the keys. CodeIgniter provides support for returning the last inserted key.

How to do it...

1. Add or adapt the following code into a model:

```
function insert($data) {
  if ($this->db->insert($data, 'table_name')) {
    return $this->db->last_id();
  } else {
return false;
  }
}
```

How it works...

Take a look at the lines in bold. We test for the returned value of `$this->db->insert($data);`, which will return true if successful and false if there was an error. If the returned value is true, we grab the Primary Key of the last inserted record for this connection; this value along with `return $this->db->insert_id();` is returned from the model to the code that called the function. If the database insert was unsuccessful, it would return false. You can adapt the above recipe easily; just drop the lines in bold into your model.

Finding the number of affected rows

Finding the number of affected rows can be useful in several ways—perhaps you want to update some records and only proceed if a certain number of records are updated, or perhaps you simply want to display the number of rows that have been deleted or updated by a query.

How to do it...

1. Add or adapt the following code into your model:

```
function update($id, $data) {
    $this->db->where('id', $id);
    if ($data->db->update($data, 'table_name')) {
        return $this->db->affected_rows();
    } else {
        return false;
    }
}
```

How it works...

The model `function update()` accepts two parameters: a `$data` array and the `$id` array of the database row we wish to update.

Next, we test for the returned value of `$this->db->update($data);`, which will return true if successful and false if there was an error. If the returned value is true, we grab the number of affected rows for the update with the following line:

```
return $this->db->affected_rows();
```

If the update doesn't happen, the returned value will be false.

Finding the last database query

Sometimes, it is useful to know about the last query that was run against the database, either for debugging purposes or for reasons where you wish to have an audit trail of every interaction with the database—you'll be surprised at the number of times you'll need to do this. CodeIgniter comes with a really handy function that you can use to write out the most recent query that CodeIgniter sent to the database.

How to do it...

1. Add or adapt the following line of code into your controller or model:

```
$this->db->last_query();
```

How it works...

Quite simply, this function will return the last query to be sent to the database; you can place it in the controller or model (even the view if you wish, but it's better to keep it at the logical side of your application rather than the view). It will return the query that you can use as an audit in the form of a string; for example, consider the following line of code:

```
log_message('level', $this->db->last_query())
```

The preceding line of code will write the last query to your log files, where `'level'` denotes the type of message. We will go through some error reporting and logging recipes in *Chapter 9, Extending the core*.

Using CodeIgniter database migrations

Imagine that you work in a team of other developers, and everyone is busy working, making changes to the code and the database structure. Keeping up with all of those changes to a database can become a challenge, particularly if many people are working on roughly the same area of the project.

CodeIgniter Migration gives you the option to install (or rollback) the changes of a database structure that might support the changes in the code. For example, if you were working on coding changes for, say, a user registration script—this change requires a column to be added to a database table; you could include a CodeIgniter database migration script with your version control commit (assuming you're using version control)—other developers will now know that for your code change to work they must run the migration which would amend their database.

Migration also allows you to roll back changes. This should not be confused with the database concept of rolling back with transactions; think of rolling back using migrations as uninstalling previously installed changes.

Getting ready

There are some configuration settings we need to change before we do this, so open `/path/to/codeigniter/application/config/migration.php` and find the following options:

Preference	Default Value	Options	Description
migration_enabled	FALSE	TRUE/ FALSE	Specifies whether or not you wish migrations to be enabled; TRUE is enabled, and FALSE is disabled.
migration_version	0	None	Specifies the current migration version your database uses or rather the most suitable migration version you wish to work with. We'll talk more about this later in the chapter. By using `current()`, we will install the up-to-date value set in 'migration_version'.
migration_path	APPPATH.'migrations/'	None	Specifies the path of the folder where you store the migration files. Migration files are PHP scripts where those queries located that define the necessary database changes. Ensure that you have set the `migrations` folder to be writable.

Be sure to load the migration library in your controller with the following line:

```
$this->load->library('migration');
```

In this recipe, we're going to create a simple users table and use a migration library to add and then remove a column from it. Enter the following SQL into your database:

```
CREATE TABLE IF NOT EXISTS `users` (
    `user_id` int(11) NOT NULL AUTO_INCREMENT,
    `user_first_name` varchar(125) NOT NULL,
    `user_last_name` varchar(125) NOT NULL,
    `user_email` varchar(255) NOT NULL,
    PRIMARY KEY (`user_id`)
) ENGINE=InnoDB DEFAULT CHARSET=latin1 AUTO_INCREMENT=1 ;
```

How to do it...

First off, all your database migration files should be placed in the `migrations` folder at `/path/to/codeigniter/application/migrations/`.

If the folder does not already exist, you'll need to create it in the `/path/to/codeigniter/application/` folder—be sure to give write permissions to it.

1. We're going to create the following two files:

   ❑ `/path/to/codeigniter/application/migrations/001_add_icon.php`

   ❑ `/path/to/codeigniter/application/controllers/migrate.php`

> Notice the filename `001_add_icon.php`. The first part (001) is the migration number; this will increment every time you add a new migration file. The second part (add_icon) is a descriptive indication of the purpose of the migration file. Add the following code into the file `001_add_icon.php`. This migration file defines the queries to be run to effect the migration change or to roll back from that change.

```php
<?php defined('BASEPATH') OR exit('No direct script access
allowed');
class Migration_Add_icon extends CI_Migration {
  public function up() {
    $this->db->query("ALTER TABLE `users` ADD COLUMN `user_icon`
      TEXT NULL AFTER `user_email`;");
  }
  public function down() {
    $this->db->query("ALTER TABLE `users` DROP COLUMN
      `user_icon`;");
  }
}
```

2. Add the following code into `/path/to/codeigniter/application/controllers/migrate.php`; the migrate controller gives us access to CodeIgniter's migration functions.

```php
<?php if (!defined('BASEPATH')) exit('No direct script access
allowed');

class Migrate extends CI_Controller {
  function __construct() {
    parent::__construct();

    if ( ! $this->input->is_cli_request() ) {
      echo 'Only access via command line.';
```

```
        exit;
    }

    $this->load->library('migration');
}

public function index() {
    echo 'Config: ' . $config['migration_version'];
}

public function current() {
    if ( ! $this->migration->current()) {
        show_error($this->migration->error_string());
    }
}

public function latest() {
    if ( ! $this->migration->latest()) {
    show_error($this->migration->error_string());
    }
}

public function version() {
    if ( $this->uri->segment(3) == '') {
        echo 'You must specify a migration version number';
    } else {
        if ( ! $this->migration->version($this->uri->segment(3)) ) {
            show_error($this->migration->error_string());
        }
    }
}
}
```

Okay, so what have we done so far? We've configured migrations to run in CodeIgniter, we've created our first migration file (taking care to name it properly), and we have two files: the controller `migrate.php` and the migration file `001_add_icon.php`.

In the migration file `001_add_icon.php`, there are 222 functions; out of these, `up()` and `down()` are functions where you would define SQL to go with your code changes. The function `down()` is where you would define SQL for removing your changes should someone (perhaps another developer) wish to revert a code change you might have made; therefore, it supports SQL.

In the controller `migrate.php`, we've created several functions for us to work with migrations, such as `current()` and `latest()`. The following two recipes will show you some basic usage of these migrations.

Moving to the current version with current()

To simply alter your database so that it corresponds with the version number in `$config['migration_version']`, you should use the `current()` function.

Getting ready

Ensure that you have followed the preceding recipe, *Using CodeIgniter database migrations*.

How to do it...

1. Using your command line (terminal application), navigate to the root of your CodeIgniter installation (where the `index.php` file is) and type the following:

   ```
   php index.php migrate current
   ```

How it works...

Consider the following command line:

```
php index.php migrate current
```

The first thing we should bear in mind is the constructor in the migrate controller. The constructor is looking at how the migrate controller is accessed; it'll deny access to the migrate controller if it is accessed via anything other than the command line—a useful security measure.

By typing the command we just saw, you'll run `public function current()`. The function accepts no parameter. CodeIgniter will look into the migrations folder for the file whose number corresponds with the value set in `$config['migration_version']` in the configuration file `/path/to/codeigniter/application/config/migration.php`.

Rolling back/stepping forward with version()

You may wish to deliberately alter the database by pointing it to a specific migration number. This can be achieved by use of the `version()` function within CodeIgniter.

Getting ready

Ensure that you have followed the preceding recipe, *Using CodeIgniter database migrations*.

How to do it...

1. Using your command line (terminal application), navigate to the root of your CodeIgniter installation (where the index.php file is) and type the following:

    ```
    php index.php migrate version 1
    ```

How it works...

Consider the following command line:

```
php index.php migrate version number
```

`number` is highlighted as it specifies the migration file number to move to, that is, `1`, `2`, `3`, and so on.

The first thing we should bear in mind is the constructor in the migrate controller. The constructor is looking at how the migrate controller is accessed; it'll deny access to the migrate controller if it is accessed via anything other than the command line—a useful security measure.

By typing the preceding command, you'll run `public function version()`, passing to it the third parameter (which has the value of `1`). CodeIgniter will look into the migrations folder for the file whose number corresponds with the third parameter (1), which by amazing coincidence is the number of the migration files we created—who would have known this?

CodeIgniter will load the migration file `001_add_icon.php` and immediately run `public function up()`, which will add the column `user_icon` to the database table `'users'`.

We can undo the creation of the `user_icon` column by entering the following in the command line:

```
php index.php migrate version 0
```

CodeIgniter will then run the public function `down()` in the migration file, which will remove the `user_icon` column.

Generating an XML from a database result

Generating an XML from a database may be useful in several ways, perhaps you wish to send data from a query across a network using a SOAP request, or perhaps you're using it to build some data for a web service. Whatever your purpose, this is how to do it—also we'll look at some real-world uses—for example, we'll generate the XML output from a database query.

Getting ready

Firstly, we need to create a table and enter some example data so that you'll see some data in the CSV format, so with that in mind, copy the following code into SQL:

```sql
CREATE TABLE IF NOT EXISTS `users` (
  `user_id` int(11) NOT NULL AUTO_INCREMENT,
  `user_first_name` varchar(125) NOT NULL,
  `user_last_name` varchar(125) NOT NULL,
  `user_email` varchar(255) NOT NULL,
  `user_created_date` int(11) NOT NULL COMMENT 'unix timestamp',
  `user_is_active` varchar(3) NOT NULL COMMENT 'yes or no',
  PRIMARY KEY (`user_id`)
) ENGINE=InnoDB  DEFAULT CHARSET=latin1 AUTO_INCREMENT=1 ;

INSERT INTO `users` (`user_first_name`, `user_last_name`, `user_
email`, `user_created_date`, `user_is_active`) VALUES
('Chloe', 'Graves', 'cgraves@domain.com', 1366114115, 'yes'),
('Mark', 'Brookes', 'mbrookes@domain.com', 1366114115, 'yes');
```

How to do it...

We're going to create the following file:

▶   `/path/to/codeigniter/application/controllers/export.php`

1.   Create the controller `export.php`. This controller will load the CodeIgniter `dbutil` (database utility) class, which will provide support for various database-specific operations and generate the XML. Add the following code into your `export.php` controller:

```php
<?php if (!defined('BASEPATH')) exit('No direct script access
allowed');

class Export extends CI_Controller {

  function __construct() {
    parent::__construct();
    $this->load->helper('url');
    $this->load->dbutil();
```

```
            }

            public function index() {
               redirect('export/xml');
            }

            public function xml() {
               $config = array ('root'     => 'root',
                                'element' => 'element',
                                'newline' => "\n",
                                'tab'     => "\t"
                               );

               $query = $this->db->query("SELECT * FROM users");

               echo $this->dbutil->xml_from_result($query, $config);
            }
        }
```

How it works...

Okay, take a look at the line in bold—we're loading the database utilities class in the controllers constructor. This utilities class contains some excellent functions for working with databases. We're using it to provide access to the function xml_from_result().

The export.php controller function index() redirects us to public function xml(), which runs a database query. You could, of course, have any source of data here, but we're calling a database and storing the result in the array $query. This is passed to the CodeIgniter function xml_from_result(). The xml_from_result() function takes the following two parameters:

- $query: This is the data for XML; in this case, the output of our database query.
- $config: This is the configuration parameter; in this case, the XML formatting options.

We then echo the result of xml_from_result() to the screen—the result of which can be seen by viewing the page source code in your browser. You don't have to echo it out; you can store it in a variable if you require the XML for other purposes.

Be sure to separate a database query into its own model—the query is shown in the preceding controller for explanatory purposes.

Generating a CSV from a database result

Perhaps one of the most common things you'll be asked to do, especially if you are building a complex application that may have users, products, orders, and various other metrics is to provide some sort of reporting of that data. Perhaps you'll be asked to generate a CSV file, and the following sections show how you do it.

Getting ready

Firstly, we need to create a table and enter some example data so that you'll see some data in the CSV format, so with that in mind, copy the following code into SQL:

```
CREATE TABLE IF NOT EXISTS `users` (
  `user_id` int(11) NOT NULL AUTO_INCREMENT,
  `user_first_name` varchar(125) NOT NULL,
  `user_last_name` varchar(125) NOT NULL,
  `user_email` varchar(255) NOT NULL,
  `user_created_date` int(11) NOT NULL COMMENT 'unix timestamp',
  `user_is_active` varchar(3) NOT NULL COMMENT 'yes or no',
  PRIMARY KEY (`user_id`)
) ENGINE=InnoDB  DEFAULT CHARSET=latin1 AUTO_INCREMENT=1 ;

INSERT INTO `users` (`user_first_name`, `user_last_name`, `user_
email`, `user_created_date`, `user_is_active`) VALUES
('Chloe', 'Graves', 'cgraves@domain.com', 1366114115, 'yes'),
('Mark', 'Brookes', 'mbrookes@domain.com', 1366114115, 'yes');
```

Now that the database is ready we'll need to ensure that you're calling the database utility class; make sure that you call it with the following line:

```
$this->load->dbutil();
```

You can either put this line in the constructor of your controller or call it in your controller function.

Also, as we're going to be creating a file, we need the support of the `'file'` helper, so make sure you're calling the helper with the following line:

```
$this->load->helper('file');
```

How to do it...

We're going to create the following file:

▶ `/path/to/codeigniter/application/controllers/export.php`

Forcing download

Add the following code into your `export.php` controller:

```php
<?php if (!defined('BASEPATH')) exit('No direct script access
allowed');

class Export extends CI_Controller {

    function __construct() {
        parent::__construct();
        $this->load->helper('download');
        $this->load->dbutil();
        $this->load->helper('url');
    }

    public function index() {
        redirect('export/csv');
    }

    public function csv() {
        $query = $this->db->query("SELECT * FROM users");
        $delimiter = ",";
        $newline = "\r\n";

        force_download('myfile.csv', $this->dbutil->csv_from_
result($query, $delimiter, $newline));
    }
```

How it works...

Okay, take a look at the lines in bold—we're loading the CodeIgniter helper `'download'` and the database utilities class in the controller constructor. This'll help us with this recipe.

The `export.php` controller function `index()` redirects us to `public function csv()`, which runs a database query. You could, of course, have any source of data here, but we're calling a database and storing the result in the array `$query`. This is passed to the CodeIgniter function `force_download()`, which accepts the following two parameters:

▸ The name and extension of the file to be created (or in this case, downloaded)

▸ The data that will go into the file; in this case, we're using the CodeIgniter function `csv_from_result()` that will take a row of data from a database query and convert it into a delimiter-separated string of text. `csv_from_result()` takes the following three parameters:

  ▫ `$query`: This is the data for the CSV; in this case, the output of our database query

❑ `$delimiter`: This is the data delimiter, that is, it specifies how we are separating each cell worth of data; this is usually a comma (,).

❑ `$newline`: This is the new line character; it is usually '\n\n'

If all goes according to plan, `force_download()` will, as the name says, force a download of the CSV file.

Saving to file

Add the following code into your `export.php` controller:

```php
<?php if (!defined('BASEPATH')) exit('No direct script access
allowed');

class Export extends CI_Controller {

  function __construct() {
    parent::__construct();
    $this->load->helper('url');
    $this->load->helper('file');
    $this->load->dbutil();
  }

  public function index() {
    redirect('export/csv');
  }

  public function csv() {
    $query = $this->db->query("SELECT * FROM users");

    $delimiter = ",";
    $newline = "\r\n";

    $data = $this->dbutil->csv_from_result($query, $delimiter,
$newline);
    $path = '/path/to/write/to/myfile.csv';

    if ( ! write_file($path, $data)) {
        echo 'Cannot write file - permissions maybe?';
    } else {
        echo 'File write OK';
    }
  }
}
```

How it works...

Okay, take a look at the lines in bold; we're loading the CodeIgniter helpers `'download'`, and `'file'` and the database utilities class in the controller constructor. This'll help us with this recipe. We're also adding CodeIgniter-specific syntax to write a file to a disk.

The `export.php` controller `function index()` redirects us to `public function csv()`, which runs a database query. You could, of course, have any source of data here, but we're calling a database query and storing the result in the `$query` array. We then call the CodeIgniter `csv_from_result()` function where `csv_from_result()` takes the following three parameters:

- `$query`: The data for the CSV; in this case, the output of our database query
- `$delimiter`: The data delimiter, that is, it specifies how we are separating each cell worth of data
- `$newline`: The new line character; it is usually set to `'\n\n'`

The `csv_from_result()` function will store its output in the variable $data. We then try to run the CodeIgniter `function write_file()`, which accepts the following two parameters:

- The path to write the file, including the filename and extension; remember that this path should be writeable
- The data to write to the file

Should all go as per the plan, the recipe will return the message `File write OK`—of course, you should replace it with your own code as you see fit. Should it fail, it'll return an error message and again replace it with your own code where necessary.

There's more...

The chances are that if the file isn't being written, you don't have the necessary permissions to write to the desired destination folder. You will need to amend the permissions for the destination folder so that they are at a level high enough to allow CodeIgniter to write to it. For example, in Linux/Mac, you would use the `chmod` command in the terminal.

7
Creating a Secure User Environment

In this chapter, we will cover:

- ▶ Escaping user input
- ▶ Preventing cross-site request forgery
- ▶ Escaping data – for a database
- ▶ Using HTTPS with CodeIgniter

Introduction

Firstly, a disclaimer: no method or system can ever be entirely foolproof and secure all the time, and you should be aware of the correct security measures that you should apply for the programming task or context in which you are coding. I will put some links to other information resources at the end of this chapter. Having said that, CodeIgniter offers some useful techniques for reducing the chance that something can go wrong, for example, in this chapter are several recipes that can help reduce the chances of something untoward–however, you should always remain vigilant and ensure that you're building securely.

Escaping user input

The CodeIgniter security class function, `xss_clean()`, attempts to clean input from the POST or COOKIE data to mitigate against techniques that can allow for the injection of code into a website. For example, it would seek to prevent JavaScript code from being executed if it is included in a blog post submitted by a user, or look at the data submitted in a text input field and escape disallowed characters.

You can apply this to any controller you're creating, or if you've extended using `MY_Controller`, you can add it to that if you wish. You can also autoload the security helper by adding it to `$autoload['helper'] = array()` in the `/path/to/codeigniter/application/config/autoload.php` file. To be explicitly clear, here we're loading the security helper in the constructor of the controller (that is, any controller you have):

```
function __construct() {
    parent::__construct();
    $this->load->helper('security');
}
```

There are two ways to do this, globally (CodeIgniter does it every time it encounters the `POST` or `COOKIE` data), and individually (CodeIgniter lets you define when to call the clean `COOKIE` or `POST` data).

Globally

1. CodeIgniter can call xss_clean() automatically each time it encounters the POST or COOKIE data without you needing to explicitly call xss_clean(). To do this, you'll need to amend the following file:

    `/path/to/codeigniter/application/config/config.php`

2. Change the value of `$config['global_xss_filtering']` to TRUE, as follows:

    `$config['global_xss_filtering'] = TRUE;`

    However, be aware that there is a computational overhead in doing so and it may not always be necessary for you to run this all the time.

Individually

Ensure that `$config['global_xss_filtering']` is set to FALSE, as follows:

`$config['global_xss_filtering'] = FALSE`

This will turn off global XSS filtering. When you wish to use `xss_cean()`, enter the following code into your controller or model:

`$cleaned_data = $this->security->xss_clean($data_to_be_cleaned);`

How it works...

In either example, you're calling the same CodeIgniter method; one is being called automatically and the other is calling it on a case-by-case basis. The code in question can be found at `/path/to/codeigniter/system/core/Security.php` (find the function, `xss_clean()`).

Preventing cross-site request forgery

A cross-site request forgery is where an attacker pretends to be a user that the website recognizes (such as a logged-in user), and the attacker is then able to access a logged-in user's profile as though they were the genuine user. There is a wealth of technical information available, such as websites, books, and so on, on how that happens, which is why we're not going to look into that here. Instead, we're going to look at how CodeIgniter mitigates against cross-site request forgeries.

How to do it...

We're going to amend one file and create two files by performing the following steps:

1. First, we need to amend some configuration items. To do that, we'll need to open the following file: `/path/to/codeigniter/application/config/config.php`

   Find the following configuration options and make the amendments as listed in the table:

Configuration Item	Default Value	Change to/Description
`$config['csrf_ protection']`	TRUE	Specifies whether to turn request forgery protection on or off
`$config['csrf_token_ name']`	`csrf_test_name`	Specifies the name of the hidden form element used in a form (see the *How it works...* section)
`$config['csrf_ cookie_name']`	`csrf_cookie_name`	Specifies the name of the cookie that is set on the user's machine
`$config['csrf_ expire']`	7200	The number of seconds that a single token is allowed to exist for; after this time, if a form is submitted, CodeIgniter will throw an error

2. Next, we create the following two files:
   - ❏ /path/to/codeigniter/application/controllers/csrf.php
   - ❏ /path/to/codeigniter/application/views/csrf/csrf.php

3. Add the following code into the, csrf.php controller. This controller will load the required helpers and display the simple form in the views/csrf/csrf.php file:

```php
<?php if (! defined('BASEPATH')) exit('No direct script
  access allowed');

class Csrf extends CI_Controller {
    function __construct() {
        parent::__construct();
        $this->load->helper('form');
        $this->load->helper('security');
    }

    public function index() {
        $this->load->view('csrf/csrf');
        if ($this->input->post()) {
            var_dump($this->input->post());
        }
    }
}
```

4. Add the following code into the, csrf.php view file. This view will create the HTML form. We're using CodeIgniter's form_open() facility to do the work for us so that we don't have to it:

```php
<?php echo form_open('csrf') ; ?>
  What's your name? <input type="text" name="firstname" />
  <input type="submit" value="Submit" />
<?php echo form_close() ; ?>
```

How it works...

If you load the controller in the web browser and view the HTML source of the page, you should see the following code snippet:

```html
<form action="http://path/to/codeigniter/csrf" method="post"
  accept-charset="utf-8"><div style="display:none">
<input type="hidden" name="csrf_test_name"
  value="577052974b00424157586e40b4c09756" />
</div>What's your name? <input type="text" name="firstname" />
  <input type="submit" value="Submit" />
</form>
```

Take a close look at the highlighted line. CodeIgniter has added a hidden form element named `csrf_test_name`. We set the name in the configuration file, `config.php` (details explained earlier) The actual value of this field will be different every time you run it.

So, what happens when you click on the **Submit** button? Well, CodeIgniter compares the value set in the cookie on the user's machine (set as `csrf_cookie_name` in `config.php`) to the value set in the hidden form element (set as `csrf_test_name` in `config.php`). If the two values do not match, CodeIgniter assumes that there is a problem and throws an error, as shown in the following screenshot:

An Error Was Encountered

The action you have requested is not allowed.

You can see this yourself by adjusting the `csrf_exipre` value from the default, `7200` seconds, to something a little easier to wait for, such as `10` seconds. Then load the controller in a browser, wait for the new set value of seconds, and click on the **Submit** button. You'll see the preceding error. Remember to put this value back to `7200` (or whatever you wish) after you have finished.

This CSRF check enables CodeIgniter to mitigate against CSRF as the cookie set on a user's machine is unlikely to be guessed and imitated by an attacker on another machine who can then set that value in `csrf_cookie_name` and `csrf_test_name`.

 CSRF protection in CodeIgniter is unsuitable for AJAX forms.

Escaping data – for a database

It's never a good idea to trust any information or data that comes the user; you should always consider any data from the user to be untrustworthy and potentially dangerous. You are strongly advised to ensure that you escape any data coming in from the user, and never trust any data from the user unless you have passed it through various processes that should make that data safe enough to work with. One of these techniques is **escaping data**. This recipe demonstrates the escaping of variables in a database query.

First, we'll need to create a database table. For this example, let's assume the database table is named `escape`. Enter the following SQL into your database:

```
CREATE TABLE `escape` (
`id` INT NOT NULL AUTO_INCREMENT PRIMARY KEY ,
`firstname` VARCHAR( 25 ) NOT NULL ,
`lastname` VARCHAR( 25 ) NOT NULL
) ENGINE = INNODB;
```

How to do it...

Now that we've created the database table, we'll begin escaping input from the user. We're going to create the following three files:

- ► `/path/to/codeigniter/application/controllers/escape.php`
- ► `/path/to/codeigniter/application/models/escape_model.php`
- ► `/path/to/codeigniter/application/views/escape/escape.php`

1. Create the, `/path/to/codeigniter/application/controllers/escape.php` file, and add the following code to it:

```php
<?php if (!defined('BASEPATH')) exit('No direct script
  access allowed');

class Escape extends CI_Controller {
    function __construct() {
        parent::__construct();
        $this->load->helper('form');
        $this->load->helper('security');
        $this->load->helper('url');
        $this->load->database();
    }

    public function index() {
        redirect('escape/display_form');
    }

    public function display_form() {
```

```
            $this->load->view('escape/escape');
        }

    public function escape_post() {
        $data = array(
            'firstname' => $this->input->post('firstname'),
            'lastname'  => $this->input->post('lastname')
        );

        $this->load->model('Escape_model');
        if ($this->Escape_model->insert_data($data)) {
            echo 'Success';
        } else {
            echo 'Did not write to database';
        }
    }
}
```

2. Create the, /path/to/codeigniter/application/views/escape/escape. php file, and add the following code to it. The escape.php controller will display a simple form to the user asking them to enter their first and last name, as follows:

```
<p>Please enter your first and last names.</p>
<?php echo form_open('escape/escape_post') ; ?>
    <p>First Name</p>
    <?php echo form_input(array('name' => 'firstname',
        'id' => 'firstname', 'value' => set_value(
            'firstname', ''))); ?>
    <p>Last Name</p>
    <?php echo form_input(array('name' => 'lastname',
        'id' => 'lastname', 'value' => set_value(
            'lastname', ''))); ?>
    <br />
    <?php echo form_submit('submit', 'Submit'); ?>
<?php echo form_close(); ?>
```

3. Create the, /path/to/codeigniter/application/models/escape_model. php file, and add the following code to it. As we're explicitly typing the query, we're going to use $this->db->escape() to do the escaping for us as follows:

```
<?php if ( ! defined('BASEPATH')) exit('No direct script
  access allowed');
class Escape_model extends CI_Model {

    function __construct() {
        parent::__construct();
    }

    function insert_data($data) {
```

```
$query = "INSERT INTO `escape` (`firstname`,
    `lastname`) VALUES (
        ".$this->db->escape($data['firstname'])." ,
            ".$this->db->escape(
                $data['lastname']).") ";
if ($this->db->query($query)) {
    return true;
} else {
    return false;
}
        }
    }
}
```

How it works...

Okay, if you load the controller in your browser, you'll see the form. This form asks the user to enter their first file name and last () name, so let's enter Rob's as the first name and Foster as the last name. You'll notice that there's an apostrophe at the end of word *Rob*, go ahead and click on the **Submit** button. The form should submit to the escape.php controller, which will package up the post input into an array and send to the model. This is where the work begins; take a look at the highlighted text in the preceding model script, check out the lines, $this->db->escape($data['firstname']) and $this->db->escape ($data['lastname']), the CodeIgniter function is escaping the input passed to it, and inserting it safely into the database. You can see this by looking in the database; to do this, run the command:

```
select * from escape
```

And you should see something similar to the following screenshot:

```
mysql> select * from escape;
+----+-----------+----------+
| id | firstname | lastname |
+----+-----------+----------+
|  1 | Rob's     | Foster   |
+----+-----------+----------+
```

You can, for the sake of demonstration, remove `$this->db->escape()` from the model query and see what happens. Amend the code in the model to reflect the following:

```
function insert_data($data) {
        $query = "INSERT INTO `escape` (`firstname`, `lastname`)
            VALUES ('".$data['firstname']."',
                '".$data['lastname']."') ";
        if ($this->db->query($query)) {
            return true;
        } else {
            return false;
        }
    }
```

You'll see a database error, as shown in the following screenshot:

A Database Error Occurred

Error Number: 1064

You have an error in your SQL syntax; check the manual that corresponds to your MySQL server version for the right syntax to use near 's', 'Foster') at line 1

INSERT INTO `escape` (`firstname`, `lastname`) VALUES ('Rob's', 'Foster')

Filename: /path/to/codeigniter/application/models/escape_model.php

Line Number: 10

You can see from the preceding error that the values for first name and last name haven't been properly escaped. In fact, the apostrophe in *Rob* (`Rob's`) is treated as SQL query syntax rather than an actual variable. You can see how `$this->db->escape()` works for you to make queries safer and easier.

There's more...

There are two more escaping functions you should be aware of, these are `escape_str()` and `escape_like_str()`. Their use is identical to `escape()`; however, you would call each function with `$this->db->escape_str()` and `$this->db->escape_like_str()` respectively.

What are they for? Well, `escape_str()` will still escape data passed to it like the `escape()` function does, but it can also escape data other than just strings (which `escape()` is limited to). `escape_like_str()` can be used when you're relying on wildcards to narrow down query results. For more information, go to `http://ellislab.com/codeigniter/user-guide/database/queries.html`.

Using HTTPS with CodeIgniter

Using SSL is a huge topic, as is online security in general; therefore, I strongly recommend you read widely about web security (because this recipe isn't really a security primer). However, if you specifically wish to protect certain pages with an SSL certificate, there is an easy way to do it. We can create a CodeIgniter helper file to toggle SSL support on or off. Let's see how to do it.

Getting ready

I'm sure you know of the benefits of requiring certain pages in a website to be protected with an SSL certificate. The sight of that green address bar and little padlock can go a long way in allaying a user's concerns with entering data in a website. CodeIgniter doesn't come with SSL support built-in; however, it is perfectly easy to implement using a simple helper. Obviously, SSL support isn't the be-all and end-all of website security, and should always be implemented alongside other security measures to mitigate against unwanted visitors.

How to do it...

We're going to create a recipe that enables a user to view a page that isn't secured behind a HTTPS connection, and have them click on a link that will redirect them to a page that is secured behind a HTTPS connection. The parts of the code that implement the HTTPS connection and check whether a page is being viewed via HTTPS are highlighted, so you can quickly get into the bones of what's happening.

We're going to create the following five files:

- `/path/to/codeigniter/application/views/https/with_https.php`
- `/path/to/codeigniter/application/views/https/without_https.php`
- `/path/to/codeigniter/application/controllers/with_https.php`
- `/path/to/codeigniter/application/controllers/without_https.php`
- `/path/to/codeigniter/application/helpers/ssl_helper.php`

1. Create the, `/path/to/codeigniter/application/views/https/with_https.php` file, and add the following code to it:

```php
<?php
echo '<p>This page is being viewed with HTTPS.</p>';

echo anchor ('without_https','Click here to view a page
  without HTTPS') ;
?>
```

2. Create the `/path/to/codeigniter/application/views/https/without_https.php` file, and add the following code to it:

```php
<?php
echo '<p>This page is being viewed without HTTPS.</p>';

echo anchor('with_https', 'Click here to view a page with
  HTTPS');
?>
```

3. Create the `/path/to/codeigniter/application/controllers/with_https.php` file. This controller will load the `ssl_helper` and set support to `on`. It will also display a link to the `without_https` controller. Add the following code to the `With_https` controller:

```php
<?php if ( ! defined('BASEPATH')) exit('No direct script
  access allowed');

class With_https extends CI_Controller {
    function __construct() {
        parent::__construct();
        $this->load->helper('url');
        $this->load->helper('ssl_helper');

        toggle_ssl("on");
    }

    public function index() {
        $this->load->view('https/with_https');
    }
}
```

4. Create the `/path/to/codeigniter/application/controllers/without_https.php` file, and add the following code to it. This controller will load the `ssl_helper` and set SSL support to `off`. It will also display a link to the `with_https` controller. Add the following code to the `Without_https` controller:

```php
<?php if ( ! defined('BASEPATH')) exit('No direct script
  access allowed');

class Without_https extends CI_Controller {
    function __construct() {
        parent::__construct();
        $this->load->helper('url');
```

```
            $this->load->helper('ssl_helper');

            toggle_ssl("off");
      }

      public function index() {
            $this->load->view('https/without_https');
      }
}
```

5. Create the /path/to/codeigniter/application/helpers/ssl_helper.php
   file. This helper will take one function argument passed to it by the calling controllers
   and alter the base_url value depending on whether we need SSL support or not.
   Add the following code to the helper, ssl_helper:

```php
<?php if (! defined('BASEPATH')) exit('No direct script
   access allowed');

function toggle_ssl($action) {
    $CI =& get_instance();

    if ($action == "on") {
        $CI->config->config['base_url'] = str_replace(
            'http://', 'https://',
                $CI->config->config['base_url']);

        if ($_SERVER['SERVER_PORT'] != 443) {
            redirect($CI->uri->uri_string());
        }
    } elseif ($action == "off") {
        $CI->config->config['base_url'] = str_replace(
            'https://', 'http://',
                $CI->config->config['base_url']);

        if ($_SERVER['SERVER_PORT'] != 80) {
            redirect($CI->uri->uri_string());
        }
    } else { // if neither turn https support off
        $CI->config->config['base_url'] = str_replace(
            'https://', 'http://',
                $CI->config->config['base_url']);

        if ($_SERVER['SERVER_PORT'] != 80) {
            redirect($CI->uri->uri_string());
        }
    }
}
```

Port 443 is the default HTTPS port; however, this might not always be the case, and the SSL port may be configured differently on your environment and it may be another number on the system you're developing on or developing for. Remember to use the correct port in your environment.

How it works...

Whichever controller we load (`with_https` or `without_https`), one of the first things done in the constructor is to load the helper, `ssl_helper`, with the following line:

```
$this->load->helper('ssl_helper')
```

You can see this line highlighted in each controller. We then need to call the helper function, `toggle_ssl(string)`, passing a string of either on or off to it. Obviously, on will enforce SSL and off will remove it. When the `ssl_helper` is called, it immediately calls (by reference: using & to copy by reference) the main CodeIgniter super object. We can see it being called by reference by inclusion of the ampersand character before the PHP function, `get_instance()`. The object is then stored for us to use in the helper as the variable, `$CI`, as follows:

```
$CI =& get_instance()
```

Depending on the value passed to it, the helper will do one of the following three things:

- If the value is on, then we wish to turn on SSL support. Using the PHP function, `str_replace`, we swap the `http://` part of the `base_url` value to `https://`, saving that on the fly as CodeIgniter's new `base_url` value as follows:

```
$CI->config->config['base_url'] = str_replace('https://',
  'http://', $CI->config->config['base_url']);
```

- If the value is off, we do exactly the same but in reverse. We swap the `https://` part of the current `base_url` value to `http://` as follows:

```
$CI->config->config['base_url'] = str_replace('https://',
  'http://', $CI->config->config['base_url']);
```

  - After both preceding `str_replace`, we test the current value of the `$_SERVER` array element, `SERVER_PORT;`, redirecting accordingly.

- If the value passed to `toggle_ssl` isn't either on or off, then the default action will set SSL support to off.

There's more...

Some of you may not be familiar with setting up SSL on your machine. Setting SSL up is out of the scope of this book; however, it's quite simple to do. There's a great link from the Apache Foundation in the following section that details how to set up an SSL certificate.

Setting up HTTPS on localhost

It is possible to set up HTTPS on localhost (assuming that's what you're developing on). I've found an URL that's particularly helpful in getting a self-certified SSL certificate on localhost.

A self-certified SSL certificate is just an SSL certificate which you've made yourself. It's going to be just as good as one you purchase; however, if you push it to a live production environment and an actual user visits. Their browser will tell them the issuing authority is unknown (because you made it yourself), the user will probably think that this means that the site is dangerous and leave. Therefore, for a live site, you'll need a certificate from a recognized issuing authority while for testing, you can make one yourself. The following links will help you make one:

```
http://httpd.apache.org/docs/2.2/ssl/ssl_faq.html
```

```
https://www.verisign.com
```

```
https://www.globalsign.co.uk/
```

Alternatively, if you have managed hosting a lot, your package or product from the host providing company will come with an SSL certificate, or it is likely that the host provider will be able to set one up for you (check the terms of the contract).

8
Calendaring, Right Place, and Right Time

In this chapter, we will cover:

- ▸ Building a CodeIgniter Calendar helper with database results
- ▸ Building an appointment manager with Calendar Library
- ▸ Creating a helper to work with a person's date of birth
- ▸ Working with fuzzy dates in CodeIgniter

Introduction

CodeIgniter comes bundled with many functions and helpers to help support your application when working with time and dates, calendars, and so on. We're going to use a few of them in this chapter, but we will also create a few helpers of our own, which can be useful in everyday tasks, such as calculating a person's age (useful for an age verification script) and working with fuzzy dates (that is, writing a description of the date or time rather than just writing out an accurate date).

Building a CodeIgniter Calendar helper with database results

CodeIgniter comes with a really useful calendar helper that allows you to display months in a grid. It is possible to develop functionality to pull events from a database (such as a table that stores diary appointments) and indicate to the user if there is an appointment on a given day.

Getting ready

As we're storing appointments in a database, we'll need a database table. Copy the following code into your database:

```sql
CREATE TABLE `appointments` (
  `app_id` int(11) NOT NULL AUTO_INCREMENT,
  `app_date` varchar(11) NOT NULL,
  `app_url` varchar(255) NOT NULL,
  `app_name` varchar(255) NOT NULL,
  PRIMARY KEY (`app_id`)
) ENGINE=InnoDB  DEFAULT CHARSET=latin1 AUTO_INCREMENT=5 ;

INSERT INTO `appointments` (`app_id`, `app_date`, `app_url`, `app_name`) VALUES
(1, '1375465528', 'http://localhost/1', 'My Appointment'),
(2, '1375638327', 'http://localhost/2', 'My Second Appointment'),
(3, '1375897527', 'http://localhost/3', 'My Third Appointment'),
(4, '1381167927', 'http://localhost/4', 'My Forth Name');
```

How to do it...

We're going to create two files:

- `/path/to/codeigniter/application/controllers/app_cal.php`
- `/path/to/codeigniter/application/models/app_cal_model.php`
- `/path/to/codeigniter/application/views/app_cal/view.php`

In order to create those two files we execute the following steps:

1. Create the file `/path/to/codeigniter/application/controllers/app_cal.php` and add the following code to it:

```php
<?php if ( ! defined('BASEPATH')) exit('No direct script access allowed');

class App_cal extends CI_Controller {
    function __construct() {
        parent::__construct();
        $this->load->helper('url');
        $this->load->helper('date');
    }

    public function index() {
        redirect('app_cal/show');
```

```
        }

    public function show() {
        $prefs = array (
            'start_day'      => 'monday',
            'month_type'     => 'long',
            'day_type'       => 'short',
            'show_next_prev' => TRUE,
            'next_prev_url'  => 'http://www.your_domain.com/app_
cal/show/'
            );

        $this->load->library('calendar', $prefs);

        if ($this->uri->segment(4)) {
            $year= $this->uri->segment(3);
            $month = $this->uri->segment(4);
        } else {
            $year = date("Y", time());
            $month = date("m", time());
        }

        $this->load->model('App_cal_model');
        $appointments = $this->App_cal_model->get_
appointments($year, $month);
        $data = array();

        foreach ($appointments->result() as $row) {
            $data[(int)date("d",$row->app_date)] = $row->app_url;
        }

        $data['cal_data'] = $this->calendar->generate($year,
$month, $data);

        $this->load->view('app_cal/view', $data);
    }
}
```

2. Create the file /path/to/codeigniter/application/models/app_cal_
   model.php and add the following code to it:

```php
<?php if ( ! defined('BASEPATH')) exit('No direct script access
allowed');

class App_cal_model extends CI_Model {
    function __construct() {
        parent::__construct();
    }

    function get_appointments($year, $month) {
```

```
$month_as_written = array(
    '01' => 'January',
    '02' => 'February',
    '03' => 'March',
    '04' => 'April',
    '05' => 'May',
    '06' => 'June',
    '07' => 'July',
    '08' => 'August',
    '09' => 'September',
    '10' => 'October',
    '11' => 'November',
    '12' => 'December'
);

$start_date = '01' . ' ' . $month_as_written[$month] . ' '
. $year;
$start_of_month = strtotime($start_date);

$end_date = days_in_month($month, $year) . ' ' . $month_
as_written[$month] . ' ' . $year;
$end_of_month = strtotime($end_date);

$this->db->where('app_date > ', $start_of_month);
$this->db->where('app_date < ', $end_of_month);
$query = $this->db->get('appointments');

return $query;
    }
}
```

3. Create the file `/path/to/codeigniter/application/views/app_cal/view.php` and add the following code to it:

```
<?php echo $cal_data ; ?>
```

How it works...

We start off by loading the controller `app_cal` (that stands for Appointment Calendar, in case you were wondering) in our web browser. Note that we load the helpers `'url'` and `'date'` in the constructor:

```
$this->load->helper('url');
$this->load->helper('date');
```

The first function loaded is `index()`, which redirects us to the `show()` function, where we immediately begin to define some preferences for the calendar functionality:

```
$prefs = array (
    'start_day'      => 'monday',
    'month_type'     => 'long',
    'day_type'       => 'short',
    'show_next_prev' => TRUE,
    'next_prev_url'  => 'http://www.your_domain.com/app_cal/
show/'
    );
```

Each item is fairly self-explanatory but I'll go into them anyway:

Preference	Description
start_day	Specifies which day of the week is leftmost in the calendar grid, so if you entered 'sunday', the day row (the row which describes the days) in the calendar grid will start at Sunday. If for some peculiar reason you wanted your calendar to start on a Wednesday, you would enter 'wednesday' and the calendar week would start with Wednesday. But don't really do that; it would look odd!
month_type	Specifies how the month is written. 'long' is the full month name, such as August, and 'short' is a shortened version, such as Aug.
day_type	Specifies how the days of the week are written in the days row of the calendar grid. 'long' is Monday, Tuesday, Wednesday, and so on, and 'short' is Mon, Tue, Wed, and so on.
show_next_prev	Could be either TRUE or FALSE. This lets CodeIgniter know if it should display the next and previous chevrons (<< and >>); clicking these will advance the calendar forward or backward one month at a time. If this is set to TRUE (which it is in this recipe) you'll need to specify next_prev_url.
next_prev_url	Specifies the URL CodeIgniter should use for the << or >> links.

Next, we load the calendar library and pass the `$prefs` array to it as a second parameter. Then, we test for the existence of a fourth `uri` segment:

```
if ($this->uri->segment(4)) {
$year= $this->uri->segment(3);
$month = $this->uri->segment(4);
} else {
$year = date("Y", time());
$month = date("m", time());
}
```

The third and fourth `uri` segments are years (YYYY) and months (MM) respectively, and if they don't exist, it is probably the first time the calendar is being loaded (or the calendar isn't being accessed via `'next_prev_url'`). Either way, because we don't have a third or fourth `uri` segment to pass to our model, we'll have to make them up. But what should we use? How about the current month and current year (see the preceding highlighted code)?

Now, we load the model `App_model` and pass to it our `$year` and `$month` variables:

```
$this->load->model('App_cal_model');
$appointments = $this->App_cal_model->get_appointments($year, $month);
```

Let's take a look at the model now and see what's happening. We store our appointments in the database using timestamps, and because the years and months are being passed to the `app_cal` controller as the strings 'YYYY' and 'MM' we'll need to convert the 'YYYY', 'MM' strings to timestamps, so we can query the database and work out whether we have an appointment for a particular day in the selected month. This means we'll need to use the PHP function `strtotime`.

Those of you who are familiar with the function (or even those who just read the function name) will understand that `strtotime` converts a string of written English to a Unix timestamp, so writing "last Wednesday", for example, will make `strtotime` return whatever the timestamp was for last Wednesday. It's a great way to get a timestamp, but it does mean that you'll need to generate some sort of string description for the date you wish to calculate.

We want to grab all the appointments for a particular month, which means generating a database query with a WHERE clause looking for "appointments greater than the timestamp representing the first day of a month and less than a timestamp representing the last day of a month". So, to get ready for that, let's take a look at the following `$month_as_written` array in the code:

```
$month_as_written = array(
'01' => 'January',
'02' => 'February',
'03' => 'March',
'04' => 'April',
'05' => 'May',
'06' => 'June',
'07' => 'July',
'08' => 'August',
'09' => 'September',
'10' => 'October',
'11' => 'November',
'12' => 'December'
);
```

You'll see that the key of each item in the array matches the format of `$month` (MM). That's important, as we'll use the value in `$month` to write out in English the required month name.

We'll prepend it with `'01 '` to indicate the first of the month and append it with `$year`, like this:

```
$start_date = '01' . ' ' . $month_as_written[$month] . ' ' . $year;
$start_of_month = strtotime($start_date);
```

The written string is stored in the variable `$start_date`, which is then passed to `strtotime()`, which in turn returns the Unix timestamp for the start of the month. Next, we calculate the end date:

```
$end_date = days_in_month($month, $year) . ' ' . $month_as_
written[$month] . ' ' . $year;
$end_of_month = strtotime($end_date);
```

Next, we use the CodeIgniter function `days_in_month()`; passing it `$month` and `$year` it will return the number of days in the month as an integer. We then concatenate this value with a space `' '` and the written month from the `$month_as_written` array before finishing with `$year`. The string is then passed to `strtotime($end_date)`, which gives us the Unix timestamp for the end of the month; this value is stored in the variable `$end_of_month`.

Well use the two variables `$start_of_month` and `$end_of_month` in our database query, asking it to return appointments after the start but before the end of the calculated month:

```
$this->db->where('app_date > ', $start_of_month);
$this->db->where('app_date < ', $end_of_month);
$query = $this->db->get('appointments');

return $query;
```

Next up, we need to build an array to store the appointments and URLs. First, let's declare the array:

```
$data = array();
```

Now, we'll loop through the `App_model` result (contained in the variable `$appointments`) building the array as we go:

```
foreach ($appointments->result() as $row) {
$data[(int)date("d",$row->app_date)] = $row->app_url;
}
```

Once finished, the array should take this structure:

```
array(3) {
  [2]=>
  string(18) "http://localhost/1"
  [4]=>
  string(18) "http://localhost/2"
  [7]=>
  string(18) "http://localhost/3"
}
```

The `$data` array is passed along with `$year` and `$month` to the calendar library function `generate()`:

```
$data['cal_data'] = $this->calendar->generate($year, $month, $data);

$this->load->view('app_cal/view', $data);
```

The product of this is stored in `$data['cal_data']` and then passed to the view `app_cal/view`, from where it is rendered to the screen.

Building an appointment manager with Calendar Library

The preceding recipe used the CodeIgniter Calendar library to help build an interactive calendar. However, you could only view items in the calendar that were already in the database. The next logical step is building a small application that allows you to create items for the calendar with a form; a simple appointment manager would do the trick. We're basing this recipe on the previous one; however, you don't need to go back and work through that recipe. Everything you need is contained in this recipe.

Getting ready

We'll need to make a database table to store our appointments. If you have used the previous recipe, you should have the database table already; if so, run the following code in your database:

```
ALTER TABLE `appointments` ADD `app_description` VARCHAR( 255 ) NOT
NULL AFTER `app_name`
```

Alternatively, if you haven't already got the table, run this code in your database:

```
CREATE TABLE `appointments` (
  `app_id` int(11) NOT NULL AUTO_INCREMENT,
  `app_date` varchar(11) NOT NULL,
  `app_url` varchar(255) NOT NULL,
  `app_name` varchar(255) NOT NULL,
  `app_description` varchar(255) NOT NULL,
  PRIMARY KEY (`app_id`)
) ENGINE=InnoDB  DEFAULT CHARSET=latin1 AUTO_INCREMENT=1 ;
```

Now that the database is sorted, let's look at the code:

How to do it...

We're going to create the following six files:

- ▶ `/path/to/codeigniter/application/controllers/app_cal.php`: This contains all the code necessary to run the show, including the HTML 6 template for the calendar

- ▶ `/path/to/codeigniter/application/models/app_cal_model.php`: This contains all necessary code for interacting with the database

- ▶ `/path/to/codeigniter/application/views/app_cal/view.php`: This will display the calendar

- ▶ `/path/to/codeigniter/application/views/app_cal/appointment.php`: This will display a form where you can add appointments

- ▶ `/path/to/codeigniter/application/views/app_cal/new.php`: This displays a form allowing the user to create a new appointment

- ▶ `/path/to/codeigniter/application/views/app_cal/delete.php`: This displays a delete confirmation message

We need to execute the following steps to create those files:

1. Create the file `/path/to/codeigniter/application/controllers/app_cal.php` and add to it the following code (this is quite a big controller, so I'm going to break down the bigger functions to explain what they do):

```php
<?php if ( ! defined('BASEPATH')) exit('No direct script access
allowed');

class App_cal extends CI_Controller {
    function __construct() {
        parent::__construct();
        $this->load->helper('url');
        $this->load->helper('date');
        $this->load->helper('form');
        $this->load->model('App_cal_model');
    }

    public function index() {
        redirect('app_cal/show');
    }
```

The public function `show()` will display the Calendar on the screen; it is responsible for deciding what month and what year to show.

```php
    public function show() {
        if ($this->uri->segment(4)) {
```

```
                $year= $this->uri->segment(3);
                $month = $this->uri->segment(4);
        } else {
            $year = date("Y", time());
            $month = date("m", time());
        }


        $tpl = '
            {table_open}<table border="1" cellpadding="15"
cellspacing="1">{/table_open}

            {heading_row_start}<tr>{/heading_row_start}

            {heading_previous_cell}<th><a href="{previous_
url}">&lt;&lt;</a></th>{/heading_previous_cell}
            {heading_title_cell}<th colspan="{colspan}">{heading}</
th>{/heading_title_cell}
            {heading_next_cell}<th><a href="{next_url}">&gt;&gt;</
a></th>{/heading_next_cell}

            {heading_row_end}</tr>{/heading_row_end}

            {week_row_start}<tr>{/week_row_start}
            {week_day_cell}<td>{week_day}</td>{/week_day_cell}
            {week_row_end}</tr>{/week_row_end}

            {cal_row_start}<tr>{/cal_row_start}
            {cal_cell_start}<td>{/cal_cell_start}

            {cal_cell_content}'.anchor('app_cal/
create/'.$year.'/'.$month.'/{day}', '+').' <a
href="{content}">{day}</a>{/cal_cell_content}
            {cal_cell_content_today}<div class="highlight">'.
anchor('app_cal/create/'.$year.'/'.$month.'/{day}', '+').'<a
href="{content}">{day}</a></div>{/cal_cell_content_today}

            {cal_cell_no_content}'.anchor('app_cal/
create/'.$year.'/'.$month.'/{day}', '+').' {day}{/cal_cell_no_
content}
            {cal_cell_no_content_today}<div class="highlight">'.
anchor('app_cal/create/'.$year.'/'.$month.'/{day}', '+').'{day}</
div>{/cal_cell_no_content_today}

            {cal_cell_blank} {/cal_cell_blank}

            {cal_cell_end}</td>{/cal_cell_end}
```

```
                    {cal_row_end}</tr>{/cal_row_end}

                    {table_close}</table>{/table_close}' ;

            $prefs = array (
                'start_day'          => 'monday',
                'month_type'         => 'long',
                'day_type'           => 'short',
                'show_next_prev'     => TRUE,
                'next_prev_url'      => 'http://www.your_domain.com/
app_cal/show/',
                'template'           => $tpl
            );


            $this->load->library('calendar', $prefs);

            $appointments = $this->App_cal_model->get_
appointments($year, $month);
            $data = array();

            foreach ($appointments->result() as $row) {
                $data[(int)date("d",$row->app_date)] = $row->app_url;
            }

            $data['cal_data'] = $this->calendar->generate($year,
$month, $data);

            $this->load->view('app_cal/view', $data);
        }
```

The public function `create()` will handle the creation of appointments, so it'll display the appointment form, validate input, and send data to the model for insertion into the database.

```
    public function create() {
        $this->load->library('form_validation');
        $this->form_validation->set_error_delimiters('', '<br
/>');

        $this->form_validation->set_rules('app_
name', 'Appointment Name', 'required|min_length[1]|max_
length[255]|trim');
        $this->form_validation->set_rules('app_description',
'Appointment Description', 'min_length[1]|max_length[255]|trim');
        $this->form_validation->set_rules('day', 'Appointment
Start Day', 'required|min_length[1]|max_length[11]|trim');
```

```
        $this->form_validation->set_rules('month',  'Appointment
Start Month', 'required|min_length[1]|max_length[11]|trim');
        $this->form_validation->set_rules('year', 'Appointment
Start Year', 'required|min_length[1]|max_length[11]|trim');

        if ($this->uri->segment(3)) {
            $year   = $this->uri->segment(3);
            $month  = $this->uri->segment(4);
            $day    = $this->uri->segment(5);
        } elseif ($this->input->post()) {
            $year   = $this->input->post('year');
            $month  = $this->input->post('month');
            $day    = $this->input->post('day');
        } else {
            $year   = date("Y", time());
            $month  = date("m", time());
            $day    = date("j", time());
        }

        if ($this->form_validation->run() == FALSE) { // First
load, or problem with form
            $data['app_name']           = array('name' => 'app_
name', 'id' => 'app_name', 'value' => set_value('app_name', ''),
'maxlength'   => '100', 'size' => '35');
            $data['app_description']       = array('name' =>
'app_description', 'id' => 'app_description', 'value' => set_
value('app_description', ''), 'maxlength' => '100', 'size' =>
'35');

            $days_in_this_month = days_in_month($month,$year);

            $days_i = array();
            for ($i=1;$i<=$days_in_this_month;$i++) {
                ($i<10 ? $days_i['0'.$i] = '0'.$i : $days_i[$i] =
$i) ;
            }

            $data['days']   = $days_i;
            $data['months'] = array('01' => 'January','02' =>
'February','03' => 'March','04' => 'April','05' => 'May','06' =>
'June','07' => 'July','08' => 'August','09' => 'September','10' =>
'October','11' => 'November','12' => 'December');
            $data['years']   = array('2013' => '2013');
            $data['day']     = $day;
            $data['month']   = $month;
            $data['year']    = $year;
```

```
        $this->load->view('app_cal/new', $data);
    } else {
        $app_date = mktime(0,0,0,$month,$day,$year);

        $data = array(
            'app_name'           => $this->input->post('app_
name'),
            'app_description'    => $this->input->post('app_
description'),
            'app_date'           => $app_date,
            'app_url'            => base_url('index.php/app_
cal/appointment/'.$year.'/'.$month.'/'.$day)
            );

        if ($this->App_cal_model->create($data)) {
            redirect('app_cal/show/'.$year.'/'.$month);
        } else {
            redirect('app_cal/index');
        }
    }
}
```

The public function delete() is responsible for removing (deleting) an appointment. It will load the delete confirmation form, validate the input, and pass data to the model for deletion from the database.

```
public function delete() {
$this->load->library('form_validation');
$this->form_validation->set_error_delimiters('', '<br
/>');

    if ($this->input->post('app_id')) {
        $id = $this->input->post('app_id');
    } else {
        $id = $this->uri->segment(3);
    }

    $this->form_validation->set_rules('app_id', 'Appointment
ID', 'min_length[1]|max_length[11]|is_natural|trim');

    if ($this->form_validation->run() == FALSE) { // First
load, or problem with form
        $appointment = $this->App_cal_model->get_single($id);
        $data['id'] = $id;

        foreach ($appointment->result() as $row) {
```

```
                $data['app_name'] = $row->app_name;
                $data['app_date'] = $row->app_date;
            }

            $this->load->view('app_cal/delete', $data);
        } else {
            if ($this->App_cal_model->delete($id)) {
                redirect('app_cal/index');
            } else {
                redirect('app_cal/index');
            }
        }
    }

    public function appointment() {
        if ($this->uri->segment(3)) {
            $year   = $this->uri->segment(3);
            $month  = $this->uri->segment(4);
            $day    = $this->uri->segment(5);

            $data['appointments'] = $this->App_cal_model->get_
appointment($year, $month, $day);
            $this->load->view('app_cal/appointment', $data);
        } else {

        }
    }
}
```

2. Create the file `/path/to/codeigniter/application/models/app_cal_
    model.php` and add the following code to it:

```php
<?php if ( ! defined('BASEPATH')) exit('No direct script access
allowed');

class App_cal_model extends CI_Model {

    function __construct() {
        parent::__construct();
    }

    function get_appointments($year, $month) {
        $month_as_written = array(
            '01' => 'January',
            '02' => 'February',
```

```
                  '03' => 'March',
                  '04' => 'April',
                  '05' => 'May',
                  '06' => 'June',
                  '07' => 'July',
                  '08' => 'August',
                  '09' => 'September',
                  '10' => 'October',
                  '11' => 'November',
                  '12' => 'December'
          );

          $sd = '01' . ' ' . $month_as_written[$month] . ' ' .
$year;
          $start_of_month = strtotime($sd);

          $ed = days_in_month($month, $year) . ' ' . $month_as_
written[$month] . ' ' . $year;
          $end_of_month = strtotime($ed);

          $this->db->where('app_date > ', $start_of_month);
          $this->db->where('app_date < ', $end_of_month);
          $query = $this->db->get('appointments');
          $this->db->last_query();

          return $query;
      }

      function get_appointment($year, $month, $day) {
          $start_of_day = mktime(0,0,0,$month,$day,$year);
          $end_of_day = $start_of_day + 86400;
          $this->db->where('app_date >= ', $start_of_day);
          $this->db->where('app_date <= ', $end_of_day);
          $query = $this->db->get('appointments');

          return $query;
      }

      function create($data) {
          if ($this->db->insert('appointments', $data)) {
              return true;
          } else {
              return false;
          }
```

```
        }

        function delete($id) {
            $this->db->where('app_id', $id);
            if ($this->db->delete('appointments')) {
                return true;
            } else {
                return false;
            }
        }

        function get_single($id) {
            $this->db->where('app_id', $id);
            $query = $this->db->get('appointments');
            return $query;
        }
    }
```

3. Create the file /path/to/codeigniter/application/views/app_cal/view.
php and add the following code to it:

```
<?php echo anchor ('app_cal/create', 'New Appointment') ; ?>
<?php echo $cal_data ; ?>
```

4. Create the file /path/to/codeigniter/application/views/app_cal/
appointment.php and add the following code to it:

```
<?php echo anchor ('app_cal/index', 'View Calendar') ; ?>
<a href=""></a><h2>Appointments</h2>

<?php foreach ($appointments->result() as $row) : ?>
        <?php echo anchor('app_cal/delete/'.$row->app_id, 'Delete')
; ?><br />
        <?php echo date("j-m-Y",$row->app_date) ; ?><br />
        <?php echo $row->app_name ; ?><br />
        <?php echo $row->app_description ; ?>
        <hr>
<?php endforeach ; ?>
```

5. Create the file /path/to/codeigniter/application/views/app_cal/
delete.php and add the following code to it:

```
<h2>Delete Appointment</h2>

<?php if (validation_errors()) : ?>
```

```
    <p><?php echo validation_errors() ;?></p>
<?php endif ; ?>

<?php echo form_open('app_cal/delete') ; ?>
<h4>Are you sure you want to delete the following appointment?</
h4>

<?php echo $app_name . ' on ' . date("d-m-Y h:i:s", $app_date); ?>

<?php echo form_hidden('app_id', $id) ; ?>

<br /><br />

<input type="submit" value="Delete" />
or <?php echo anchor ('app_cal', 'Cancel') ; ?>
<?php echo form_close() ; ?>
```

6. Create the file `/path/to/codeigniter/application/views/app_cal/new.php` and add the following code to it:

```
<h2>New Appointment</h2>
<h4>Appointment Name</h4>

<?php if (validation_errors()) : ?>
    <p><?php echo validation_errors() ;?></p>
<?php endif ; ?>

<?php echo form_open('app_cal/create') ; ?>
<?php echo form_input($app_name); ?>
<h4>Appointment Description</h4>
<?php echo form_input($app_description); ?>
<h4>Appointment Date</h4>
<?php echo form_dropdown('day', $days, $day); ?>
<?php echo form_dropdown('month', $months, $month); ?>
<?php echo form_dropdown('year', $years, $year); ?>


<br /><br />

<input type="submit" value="Save" />
or <?php echo anchor ('app_cal', 'Cancel') ; ?>
<?php echo form_close() ; ?>
```

How it works...

For the most part the functionality is broadly similar to the previous recipe, but there are some differences; we've added support to manage appointments. So, let's begin with looking at `public function view()`. You'll notice that we have moved some code around; the code which either grabs the dates from the uri or makes the date on the fly is now before the `$prefs` array — this is because of the `$tpl` variable. What's `$tpl` then?

The content of the `$tpl` variable string, more specifically it is a calendar template used by the Calendar library; the template supports a tag for days—`{day}`—but not for the month or year. This means that we have to insert these values manually into the template. But to do that, we need to know the year and month values beforehand; that's why the code to calculate the month and day is now moved up before the `$prefs` array. The template code that I use is a modified version of what is available from the CodeIgniter website user guide: `http://ellislab.com/codeigniter/user-guide/libraries/calendar.html`.

From here onwards it's the same functionality as the `view()` function in the previous recipe: we load the Calendar library, fetch all appointments for the current month, and pass it to the `app_cal/view.php` view file. Let's go through some of the newer functions in more detail:

The public function create()

When the user enters the new appointment's details and posts the create form, the public function `create()` first declares the validation rules for the new appointment. We'll then need to grab the year, month, and day for the specific appointment from either the `post` or `get` arrays. The public `create()` function checks for this and stores the date values in variables:

```
if ($this->uri->segment(3)) {
    $year   = $this->uri->segment(3);
    $month  = $this->uri->segment(4);
    $day    = $this->uri->segment(5);
} elseif ($this->input->post()) {
    $year   = $this->input->post('year');
    $month  = $this->input->post('month');
    $day    = $this->input->post('day');
} else {
    $year   = date("Y", time());
    $month  = date("m", time());
    $day    = date("j", time());
}
```

There are three tests here as the public function `create()` can be accessed in different ways. The first test looks for whether the page is accessed by someone by clicking on an add appointment link **+** in the calendar grid, the second test looks for the variables if the page has been posted, and the third (an else) is for when the **New Appointment** link is clicked.

Next, we check if the page validation is passed or not; FALSE can mean a failure of validation or that create() is being accessed for the first time.

We set some form values for CodeIgniter to render in the view and begin to build the variables necessary for the date dropdowns:

```
$days_in_this_month = days_in_month($month,$year);
$days_i = array();
for ($i=1;$i<=$days_in_this_month;$i++) {
    ($i<10 ? $days_i['0'.$i] = '0'.$i : $days_i[$i] = $i) ;
}
```

We then show the view file and wait for the user to submit. Upon successful submission (that is, when the form passes validation), we calculate the Unix timestamp for the appointment date variable (day, month, and year) and package everything into the $data array, ready for insertion into the database. A successful insertion will redirect the user to the month and year in which their appointment sits.

The public function delete()

This is quite simple; we check for the existence of an appointment ID in either the get or post arrays:

```
if ($this->input->post('app_id')) {
$id = $this->input->post('app_id');
} else {
$id = $this->uri->segment(3);
}
```

We look in both get and post because the function can be accessed for the first time by someone clicking on a URL, and the second time by someone posting (when they click on the **confirm delete** button in the view).

If the form is being submitted with errors, or run for the first time, the appointment details are fetched from the database (having been passed $id from the preceding code).

```
$appointment = $this->App_cal_model->get_single($id);

foreach ($appointment->result() as $row) {
$data['app_name'] = $row->app_name;
$data['app_date'] = $row->app_date;
}

$this->load->view('app_cal/delete', $data);
```

We then fetch `app_name` and `app_date` from the database result and store them as items in the `$data` array for passing to the `app_cal/delete.php` view file. Upon a successful submit (if nothing failed the validation) the model function `delete()` is called, and if a delete occurred the user is redirected to the same month and year where their deleted appointment previously sat.

Creating a helper to work with a person's date of birth

From time to time, you'll need an age verification script, a method to ascertain whether or not a user is of a certain age. Based on their age, they may be allowed, or disallowed, from viewing content, for example, a website that promotes adult products, such as alcohol or tobacco or a games site that promotes a game rated for certain ages. The code in this recipe helps you to ascertain a user's age, compares that against a minimum age requirement, and displays an HTML file accordingly.

How to do it...

We're going to create five files:

- `/path/to/codeigniter/application/controllers/register.php`: This is the controller for our recipe

- `/path/to/codeigniter/application/helpers/dob_val_helper.php`: This file calculates the user's age, compares it to the required age, and returns true or false depending on the result

- `/path/to/codeigniter/application/views/register/signup.php`: This file displays the age verification form

- `/path/to/codeigniter/application/views/register/enter.php`: This is displayed if the user can enter

- `/path/to/codeigniter/application/views/register/noenter.php`: This is displayed if the user cannot enter

1. Create the controller file, `register.php`, and add the following code to it:

```php
<?php if ( ! defined('BASEPATH')) exit('No direct script access allowed');

class Register extends CI_Controller {
  function __construct() {
    parent::__construct();
    $this->load->helper('form');
    $this->load->helper('dob_val');
  }
```

```php
    public function index() {
      $this->load->library('form_validation');
      $this->form_validation->set_error_delimiters('', '<br />');
      $this->form_validation->set_rules('year', 'Year',
'required|min_length[4]|max_length[4]|trim');
      $this->form_validation->set_rules('month', 'Month',
'required|min_length[2]|max_length[2]|trim');
      $this->form_validation->set_rules('day', 'Day', 'required|min_
length[2]|max_length[2]|trim');

      if ($this->form_validation->run() == FALSE) {
        $this->load->view('register/signup');
      } else {
        $dob = array(
          'year' => $this->input->post('year'),
          'month' => $this->input->post('month'),
          'day' => $this->input->post('day')
        );
        $at_least = 18;
        if (are_they_old_enough($dob, $at_least = 18)) {
          $this->load->view('register/enter');
        } else {
          $this->load->view('register/noenter');
        }
      }
    }
  }
}
```

2. Create the helper file, `dob_val_helper.php`, and add the following code to it:

```php
<?php if ( ! defined('BASEPATH')) exit('No direct script access
allowed');
function are_they_old_enough($dob, $at_least = 18) {
  $birthday = strtotime($dob['year'].'-'.$dob['month'].'-
'.$dob['day']);
  $diff = floor((time() - $birthday) / (60 * 60 * 24 * 365));

  if ($diff >= $at_least) {
    return true;
  } else {
    return false;
  }
}
```

3. Create the view file, `signup.php`, and add the following code to it:

```php
<?php echo form_open() ; ?>

    <?php echo validation_errors() ; ?>

    Day <input type="text" name="day" size="5" value="<?php echo
set_value('day') ; ?>"/>

    Month <input type="text" name="month" size="5" value="<?php echo
set_value('month') ; ?>"/>

    Year <input type="text" name="year" size="5" value="<?php echo
set_value('year') ; ?>"/>

    <input type="submit" value="go" />

<?php echo form_close() ; ?>
```

4. Create the view file `enter.php` and add the following code to it:

```php
<p>You are old enough to view page</p>
```

5. Create the view file `noenter.php` and add the following code to it:

```php
<p>You are NOT old enough to view page</p>
```

How it works...

First off, we come to the controller; the controller loads the URL helper (as we're using the `redirect()` function and a helper we will create called `dob_val`):

```php
function __construct() {
  parent::__construct();
  $this->load->helper('form');
  $this->load->helper('dob_val');
}
```

We then set up form validation and set the rules for our day, month, and year fields from the HTML. The `register/signup.php` view file is loaded, ready for the user to enter their date of birth in the three form fields.

The user will press submit, and if the submission passes for validation, the three form values are put into the `$dob` array:

```php
$dob = array(
    'year' => $this->input->post('year'),
    'month' => $this->input->post('month'),
```

```
        'day' => $this->input->post('day')
);
```

We set our minimum age (the age the user must be in order to view age restricted content) like this:

```
$at_least = 18;
```

Then, we pass the $dob array along with the $at_least variable to the dob_val helper:

```
if (are_they_old_enough($dob, $at_least = 18)) {
    $this->load->view('register/enter');
} else {
    $this->load->view('register/noenter');
}
```

The helper calculates if the user is above or below the $at_least age, returning TRUE if they are above and FALSE if they are not. If they are, they see the register/enter view file, and if they aren't they see the register/noenter view file.

Working with fuzzy dates in CodeIgniter

What is a fuzzy date? A fuzzy date is a more familiar and general way to describe a data or time rather than an exact, precise time; it describes an event in a way that is more familiar to a reader than a precise timestamp. For example, rather than saying that an email was sent at 17:41, you could say it was sent "less than a minute ago" (assuming you sent it within the last minute) or even "a few moments ago". The precise time at which something occurred is considered unimportant—or at least unnecessary—information and it is instead replaced with a more general, informal, and conversational description of the date and time.

How to do it...

We're going to create two files:

- ▶ /path/to/codeigniter/application/controllers/fuzzy_date.php: This controller will call the fuzzy_date_helper.php file and pass to it some dates (as a Unix timestamp) for the helper to convert.

- ▶ /path/to/codeigniter/application/helpers/fuzzy_date_helper.php: This helper will be called by the controller and will convert the dates passed to it, returning a written description every time.

1. Create the controller file, fuzzy_date.php, and add the following code to it:

```
<?php if ( ! defined('BASEPATH')) exit('No direct script access
allowed');

class Fuzzy_date extends CI_Controller {
```

```php
        function __construct() {
                parent::__construct();
                $this->load->helper('url');
                $this->load->helper('fuzzy_date_helper');););

        }

        public function index() {
                echo describe_the_time(time() + 30);
        }
}
?>
```

2. Create the helper file, `fuzzy_date_helper.php`, and add the following code to it:

```php
<?php if ( ! defined('BASEPATH')) exit('No direct script access
allowed');

function describe_the_time($time_in) {
  define('SECOND', 1);
  define('MINUTE', 60 * SECOND);
  define('HOUR', 60 * MINUTE);
  define('DAY', 24 * HOUR);
  define('MONTH', 30 * DAY);
  define('YEAR', 12 * MONTH);

  $past_descriptions = array(
    1 => 'about a minute ago',
    2 => 'a few minutes ago',
    3 => 'within the last hour',
    4 => 'earlier today',
    5 => 'yesterday',
    6 => 'earlier this week',
    7 => 'earlier this month',
    8 => 'last month',
    9 => 'earlier this year',
    10 => 'last year',
    11 => 'a long time ago',
    12 => 'I don\'t know that time'
    );

  $future_descriptions = array(
    1 => 'a minute from now',
    2 => 'in the next few minutes',
    3 => 'in the next hour',
```

```
      4 => 'later today',
      5 => 'tomorrow',
      6 => 'later this week',
      7 => 'later this month',
      8 => 'next month',
      9 => 'later this year',
     10 => 'next year',
     11 => 'a long way off',
     12 => 'I don\'t know that time'
     );

  $now = time();

  if ($time_in < $now) {
    if ($time_in > $now - MINUTE) { // About a minute ago
      return $past_descriptions[1];
    } elseif ( ($time_in >= $now - (MINUTE * 5) ) && ($time_in <=
$now ) ) { // A few minutes ago
      return $past_descriptions[2];
    } elseif ( ($time_in >= $now - (MINUTE * 60)) && ($time_in <=
$now ) ) { // Within the last hour
      return $past_descriptions[3];
    } elseif ( ($time_in >= $now - (HOUR * 24)) && ($time_in <=
$now - (MINUTE * 60) ) ) { // Earlier today
      return $past_descriptions[4];
    } elseif ( ($time_in >= $now - (HOUR * 48)) && ($time_in <=
$now - (HOUR * 24) ) ) { // Yesterday
      return $past_descriptions[5];
    } elseif ( ($time_in >= $now - (DAY * 7)) && ($time_in <= $now
- (HOUR * 48) ) ) { // Earlier this week
      return $past_descriptions[6];
    } elseif ( ($time_in >= $now - (DAY * 31)) && ($time_in <=
$now - (DAY * 7) ) ) { // Earlier this month
      return $past_descriptions[7];
    } elseif ( ($time_in >= $now - (DAY * 62)) && ($time_in <=
$now - (DAY * 31) ) ) { // Last Month
      return $past_descriptions[8];
    } elseif ( ($time_in >= $now - (MONTH * 12)) && ($time_in <=
$now - (MONTH * 31) ) ) { // Earlier this year
      return $past_descriptions[9];
    } elseif ( ($time_in >= $now - (MONTH * 24)) && ($time_in <=
$now - (MONTH * 12) ) ) { // Last year
      return $past_descriptions[10];
    } elseif ( ($time_in >= $now - (MONTH * 24) && ($time_in <=
$now - (MONTH * 12) ) ) ){  // Last year
```

```
        return $past_descriptions[11];
      } else {
        return $past_descriptions[12];
      }
    } else {
      if ($time_in < $now + MINUTE) { // A minute from now
        return $future_descriptions[1];
      } elseif ( ($time_in <= $now + (MINUTE * 5) ) && ($time_in >=
$now ) ) { // In the next few minutes
        return $future_descriptions[2];
      } elseif ( ($time_in <= $now + (MINUTE * 59)) && ($time_in >=
$now ) ) { // In the next hour
        return $future_descriptions[3];
      } elseif ( ($time_in <= $now + (HOUR * 24)) && ($time_in >=
$now + (MINUTE * 59) ) ) { // Later today
        return $future_descriptions[4];
      } elseif ( ($time_in <= $now + (HOUR * 48)) && ($time_in >=
$now + (HOUR * 24) ) ) { // Yesterday
        return $future_descriptions[5];
      } elseif ( ($time_in <= $now + (DAY * 7)) && ($time_in >= $now
+ (HOUR * 48) ) ) { // Earlier this week
        return $future_descriptions[6];
      } elseif ( ($time_in <= $now + (DAY * 31)) && ($time_in >=
$now + (DAY * 7) ) ) { // Earlier this month
        return $future_descriptions[7];
      } elseif ( ($time_in <= $now + (DAY * 62)) && ($time_in >=
$now + (DAY * 31) ) ) { // Last Month
        return $future_descriptions[8];
      } elseif ( ($time_in <= $now + (MONTH * 12)) && ($time_in >=
$now + (MONTH * 31) ) ) { // Earlier this year
        return $future_descriptions[9];
      } elseif ( ($time_in <= $now + (MONTH * 24)) && ($time_in >=
$now + (MONTH * 12) ) ) { // Last year
        return $future_descriptions[10];
      } elseif ( ($time_in <= $now + (MONTH * 24) ) ) { // Last year
        return $future_descriptions[11];
      } else {
        return $future_descriptions[12];
      }
    }
  }

?>
```

How it works...

Let's take a look at the `fuzzy_date` controller, the controller loads in the constructor, which in turn loads our `fuzzy_date_helper`, this is the helper which will translate Unix timestamps into descriptive text for us:

```
function __construct() {
  parent::__construct();
  $this->load->helper('url');
  $this->load->helper('fuzzydate_helper');
}
```

We then load the public function `index()`, which calls `fuzzydate_helper,` passing to it a timestamp (at the moment, the input passed is set to be `time() + 30`).

Why `time() + 30`? Well, `time()` is the php function that returns the Unix timestamp for "now" (whenever "now" is for you), and the `+ 30` is 30 seconds added to the current timestamp value returned by `time()`, meaning "now plus 30 seconds" (or "30 seconds in the future"). I've set it to that for the initial demonstration, but I will describe how this can be altered later in the description.

In the controller we pass 'now plus 30 seconds' to the helper:

```
echo describe_the_time(time() + 30);
```

The incoming function augment (that is, what we defined in the controller) is declared locally for the helper as `$time_in`:

```
function describe_the_time($time_in) {
```

The helper takes the `$time_in` variable, looks at its value, and works out if the timestamp value is greater than, or less than, `$now` as defined in the helper as $now = time():

```
if ($time_in < $now) {
... // $time_in is in the past
} else {
... // $time_in is in the future
}
```

As 'now plus 30 seconds' is greater than now (30 seconds more, to be precise) the helper goes to the `else` part of the `if` structure and then begins a series of comparisons, trying to find a place where the value defined in `$time_in` will fit. As 'now plus 30 seconds' is less than 'now plus 60 seconds' (30 seconds less, in fact), the first `if` statement is applied and the helper returns the first item in the `$future_descriptions` array:

```
if ($time_in < $now + MINUTE) { // A minute from now
  return $future_descriptions[1];
}
```

That would be a minute from now?

You can, of course, alter the timestamp passed to the helper in the controller; you could set it to `time() + 250` (which would be now plus 250 seconds). Now, plus 250 seconds is greater than a minute (60 seconds) but less than 5 minutes (300 seconds), causing the second `if` statement to apply and return the text 'in the next few minutes'.

We can also pass a lower timestamp value than "now": `time() - 4000` (that is "now minus 4000 seconds"). Passing a lower timestamp will cause the behavior of the helper to change. How? Well, remember that initial `if` statement?

```
if ($time_in < $now) {
...
} else {
...
}
```

This time, we won't go down to the else part of it; instead, the initial `if` part will be triggered and the helper will begin to process times in the past. So, by setting the helper input to `time() - 4000` (now minus 4000 seconds, which is more than a minute ago, more than 5 minutes ago, and more than an hour ago but less than a full day ago), the helper will return the text "earlier today".

You can, of course, add many, many more detailed comparisons and descriptions; in fact, I encourage you to do so—go nuts!

In a real situation, you would amend the helper function call in the controller, removing the input of `time() +` or `- number_of_seconds` to just the timestamp of the thing you want to describe – be it a blog post created date, file upload date, appointment date...whatever...you get the idea I'm sure.

9
Extending the Core

In this chapter, you will learn:

- ▸ Using CodeIgniter Sparks
- ▸ Creating PDFs with the DOMPDF Spark
- ▸ Creating Hooks in CodeIgniter
- ▸ Clearing dead sessions from the database
- ▸ Extending your controllers
- ▸ Uploading a file with FTP
- ▸ Making your own configuration files and using the settings
- ▸ Creating libraries and giving them access to CodeIgniter resources
- ▸ Using the language class – switching languages on the go

Introduction

CodeIgniter does pretty much most of what you need it to do right out of the box; but there are going to be times when you have to extend or alter the standard setup—whether it's creating Hooks so you don't have to hack the core (you really don't want to hack the core), or installing Sparks to add extra functionality and scope for new features—there are many ways to extend and build on CodeIgniter to get more out of it.

Using CodeIgniter Sparks

Not too long ago, if you wanted to install an extension or some external software for CodeIgniter, you had to hunt it down. You'd need to search for what you were looking for on the Internet and if you were lucky, you would find a blog or someone's personal site, perhaps even a GitHub account or Google code repository where you could download and install a package. Sometimes it worked, sometimes it didn't and whatever you downloaded it almost always needed some level of editing or re-writing.

Fast forward to, now! Thankfully, we have Sparks. Think of Sparks as extensions you can use with CodeIgniter. They're kept in one place (so you don't have to hunt them down across the Internet) at `http://www.getsparks.org`.

We touched on Sparks in *Chapter 1, CodeIgniter Basics*, however, let's go into more detail and get you to install and use a couple of Sparks which I have found useful over time.

So, if you haven't installed it until now, install Sparks in your CodeIgniter instance. Either go to *Chapter 1, CodeIgniter Basics*, for instructions on how to do this, or follow the instructions on the GetSparks website.

Getting ready

First, you need to navigate to the top level (or root) of your CodeIgniter directory.

How to do it...

If you are using MAC or Linux, download CodeIgniter Sparks as follows:

1. On the command line, navigate to the root of your CodeIgniter application, and type:

   ```
   php -r "$(curl -fsSL http://getsparks.org/go-sparks)"
   ```

   This will download and install CodeIgniter Sparks to your specific CodeIgniter instance.

If you are using Windows, then you will need to download Sparks and unpack manually. To do follow these instructions or check out the instructions on the GetSparks website for the latest version:

1. Create a folder named `tools` in the top level (root) of your CodeIgniter directory.
2. Go to the following URL: `http://getsparks.org/install`.
3. Go to the **Normal Installation** section and download the Sparks package.
4. Unpack the download into the `tools` folder you created in step 1.
5. Download the `Loader` class extension from: `http://getsparks.org/static/install/MY_Loader.php.txt`.

6. Rename the `MY_Loader.php.txt` file, to `MY_Loader.php`, and move it to the `application/core/MY_Loader.php` directory in your CodeIgniter application.

How it works...

Sparks is downloaded to the `/path/to/codeigniter/tools` folder of your CodeIgniter instance ready for use. You can install any Spark you wish by issuing the following command:

```
php tools/spark install [version] spark-name
```

Here, `[version]` is the specific version of the Spark. It is optional, and if you omit it, Sparks will automatically select the latest version. `spark-name` is the name of the Spark you wish to download.

Creating PDFs with the DOMPDF Spark

The DOMPDF Spark is a great bit of kit; it's simple to set up and can handle most things. It works by grabbing the output of a HTML template file (which you previously created)—you can pass variables to the HTML just as you would with a normal view file—and DOMPDF will create a PDF file from that formatted HTML code.

Getting ready

As this recipe requires the DOMPDF Spark, we'll need to install that into our CodeIgniter instance before we do anything else. To install it, perform the following steps:

1. Grab the DOMPDF Spark from `getsparks.org` and install it. Open a terminal window, navigate to your CodeIgniter application directory, and type the following code:

   ```
   php tools/spark install dompdf
   ```

   That will download the DOMPDF Spark. The DOMPDF Spark may have been downloaded, but you'll need to do some installation to get it going.

   In the `/path/to/codeigniter/sparks/dompdf/[version-number]/helpers` folder (where `[version-number]` is the version of the Spark), there is a folder and a file. These are as follows (in bold):

   - `/path/to/codeigniter/sparks/dompdf/0.5.3/helpers/dompdf/`
   - `/path/to/codeigniter/sparks/dompdf/0.5.3/helpers/dompdf_helper.php`

2. Copy this folder and file into the `helpers` folder of your CodeIgniter application (`/path/to/codeigniter/application/helpers`).

3. We're also going to need a database table in order for our model to work, so go ahead, and type the following code into your database:

```sql
CREATE TABLE `users` (
  `user_id` int(11) NOT NULL AUTO_INCREMENT,
  `user_firstname` varchar(255) NOT NULL,
  `user_lastname` varchar(255) NOT NULL,
  `user_email` varchar(255) NOT NULL,
  PRIMARY KEY (`user_id`)
) ENGINE=InnoDB  DEFAULT CHARSET=latin1 AUTO_INCREMENT=3 ;

INSERT INTO `users` (`user_id`, `user_firstname`, `user_lastname`, `user_email`) VALUES
(1, 'Rob', 'Foster', 'rf@domain.com'),
(2, 'Lucy', 'Welsh', 'lw@domain.com');
```

How to do it...

We're going to create the following three files:

- ▶ /path/to/codeigniter/application/controllers/makepdf.php: This controller will load the DOMPDF extension and output our PDF.

- ▶ /path/to/codeigniter/application/models/makepdf_model.php: We'll use this model to get information from the database that is necessary to pass to the view file view_all_users.

- ▶ /path/to/codeigniter/application/views/makepdf/view_all_users. php: This file contains the HTML and markup for how we wish the PDF to look. It also contains some PHP code, which echoes out some data gathered from the model.

1. First add the following code to the makepdf controller:

```php
<?php if (! defined('BASEPATH')) exit('No direct script
  access allowed');

class Makepdf extends CI_Controller {
    function __construct() {
        parent::__construct();
        $this->load->helper('file');
        $this->load->helper('dompdf');
        $this->load->model('Makepdf_model');
    }

    function index() {
        $data['query'] =
          $this->Makepdf_model->get_all_users();
```

```php
        $filename = 'List-of-users';
        $html = $this->load->view('makepdf/view_all_users',
          $data, true);
        pdf_create($html, $filename);
    }
}
```

2. Then add the following code to the `makepdf_model` model:

```php
<?php if (! defined('BASEPATH')) exit('No direct script
  access allowed');

class Makepdf_model extends CI_Model {

    function __construct() {
        parent::__construct();
    }

    function get_all_users() {
        $query = $this->db->get('users');
        return $query;
    }
}
```

3. Finally, add the following code to the `makepdf/view_all_users.php` view:

```php
<table>
<tr>
    <td>First Name</td>
    <td>Last Name</td>
    <td>Email</td>
</tr>
    <?php foreach($query->result() as $row) : ?>
        <tr>
            <td><?php echo $row->user_firstname ; ?></td>
            <td><?php echo $row->user_lastname ; ?></td>
            <td><?php echo $row->user_email ; ?></td>
        </tr>
    <?php endforeach ; ?>
</table>
```

How it works...

In the constructor of our `makepdf` controller, we load the `dompdf` helper. We place the `dompdf_helper.php` file and the `dompdf` folder in the `helpers` folder of our CodeIgniter application installed earlier on in the *Getting ready* section of this recipe.

`private function index()` then calls the `Makepdf_model` function, `get_all_users()`. This model function runs a simple select operation on the users table and stores it in the `$data['query']` array, we will come back to this in a moment. The `$filename` variable is assigned the string `List-of-users`, but if you wanted, you could change this to anything you wanted, you can even add today's date if required, which would look like the following code snippet:

```
$filename = 'List-of-users-for'.date("d-m-Y", time())
```

Anyway, back to the story. We then use the standard CodeIgniter method a view file and pass the `$data` array to it: $html = $this->load->view('makepdf/view_all_users', $data, true). Remember this `$data` array contains our database query of users. Instead of letting CodeIgniter render the view as it would normally, we catch the now processed HTML to a `$html` variable, which is passed to the `dompdf` function, `pdf_createalong`, with the `$filename` variable.

If you load the controller in your browser, you should automatically be prompted to download the PDF.

You can see how this can easily be adapted to output a wide and varied HTML designs, from invoices to, purchase orders to, address contacts. Just amend the model query to pull out what you need to know from the database and alter the HTML to display that information, and there you go.

Creating Hooks in CodeIgniter

There you are, quite happily using some framework or CMS to run a website, and you've just been asked to get it to do something which it was not originally designed. You begrudgingly agreed and start to work out how to implement what's been asked. You decide that you'll amend the core system files of whatever platform you've been stuck with because it's quick and easy, and because your boss used terms such as "quick wins" and "cost efficient".

Anyway, the requested functionality works and everyone's happy—except the poor person (that may still be you) who comes along a few months later to upgrade the platform to the latest version and...*BANG!* That amendment you made to the system core, forget it! It's been lost by overwriting it with the new files from the upgrade. Now, that crazy thing you were asked to implement no longer works and you're left trying to remember what you did to get it working. Then before anyone notices, it's missing, and you're left thinking. "oh God why can't I just go home!"

Well cheer up! You're using CodeIgniter and that should never happen to you (providing you use Hooks of course). You can still hack the core if you wish—go ahead, hack away, see if I care—but you'll kick yourself when you have to upgrade. I'm only thinking about your stress levels.

Hooks allow you to override the behavior of CodeIgniter at specific points at its execution without the need to make changes to the CodeIgniter core files. Fantastic! That means that with CodeIgniter, you can implement any number of ludicrous management change requests and it won't affect you on upgrade day one bit. Hooks work in a specific order. What does that mean? Well, it means that CodeIgniter works in a specific order, that is to say, when CodeIgniter runs, it loads specific parts of itself in a set order. This order is always the same, and you can set a Hook to execute at any one of the steps.

Getting ready

First, you need to tell CodeIgniter that it should allow Hooks to run. Open the `/application/config/config.php` file and ensure that the setting for `enable_hooks` is `TRUE`, as shown in the following code snippet:

```
$config['enable_hooks'] = TRUE;
```

You'll also have to decide the best time for your Hook to run. There are seven points in the execution of CodeIgniter where you can set your Hook to run, as follows:

- `pre_system`: This is the earliest place you can set a Hook to run. Only Benchmarking and Hooks are brought into play at this stage

- `pre_controller`: This is executed before any of your controllers are called

- `post_controller_constructor`: This makes your Hooks run after a controller constructor but before any controller functions are called

- `post_controller`: This makes your Hook run after the controller has finished executing

- `display_override`: This will override the CodeIgniter `display()` function–this is when CodeIgniter tried to render view files or other output to screen

- `cache_override`: This overrides the `_display_cache()` function,you can use this if you wanted to implement custom caching functionality

- `post_system`: This is to be called once the normal operation has finished (that is, after the system has finished its execution of the current request)

How to do it...

1. Define an execution point for your hook. Once you've decided the point to run your Hook, you'll need to tell CodeIgniter when to run the hook. You do this, by defining the correct information in the $hook array in the config/hooks.php file.

   The key of the $hook array specifies the execution point –that is when you want the hook to run (see the list mentioned in the Getting ready section of this recipe). In the following example, the array key is post_controller, which means that the hook is executed after the controller has finished executing. The $hook array now looks like the following.

   ```php
   $hook['post_controller'] = array(
       'class'    => 'Class_name',
       'function' => 'function_name',
       'filename' => 'file_name_of_hook.php',
       'filepath' => 'path_to_hook',
       'params'   => array(param1, param2, param3 ... etc)
   );
   ```

   So what does all the preceding code mean then? Let' have a look at the following table to understand the preceding code better:

Array element	Description
class	It is the name of the class, which is in the file defined in the filename element.
function	It is the name of the function in the class.
filename	It is the name of the file which contains the class.
filepath	This is the location of the file defined in the array element filename, normally the folder hooks, but you can add subfolders or move it to a different location if you wish.
params	They are any arguments you wish to pass to the function element of your Hook class. Separate each argument by a comma.

2. You then need to create your hook class, as shown in the following code snippet:

   ```php
   <?php if ( ! defined('BASEPATH')) exit('No direct script access allowed');

   class Class_name {
     function function_name () {
     }
   }
   ```

   You put the code for your hook in this class, obviously change Class_name to something more useful for you, and the function function_name() is obviously an example--change this name too.

Should you need to gain access to CodeIgniter resources in your hook, you can do so by accessing the main CodeIgniter object, using the CodeIgniter get_instance() function shown in the following code:

```
function function_name () {
  $CI = & get_instance();
  $CI->load->thing_to_load();
}
```

Here, `thing_to_load` is the name of your model, or library, and so on. There you have it--hooks are simple really, decide on an execution point, create a class to contain the code for your hook, and away you go!

Clearing dead sessions from the database

You may have found that CodeIgniter sometimes does not successfully remove sessions from the sessions table in the database. Unused sessions are instead cleared of their `user_data field`, but that the row remains in the sessions table.

I have often had to write specific database queries to clear sessions. I usually put these queries in the `My_Controller` class(refer to the *Extending your controllers* recipe in this chapter); however, I have recently begun to use Hooks to perform this. Then it's always working in the background and I don't need to think about it.

Getting ready

We're going to amend the following file:

`/path/to/codeigniter/application/config/config.php`

Open the `/application/config/config.php` file and ensure that the setting for `enable_hooks` is TRUE, as shown in the following code snippet:

```
$config['enable_hooks'] = TRUE;
```

How to do it...

We're going create and amend the following file:

```
/path/to/codeigniter/application/hooks/clear_sessions.php
```

1. Create the preceding file and add the following code to it:

```php
<?php  if ( ! defined('BASEPATH')) exit('No direct script
  access allowed');

class Clear_sessions {
  function clear_now() {
    $CI =& get_instance();
    $query = $CI->db->query("DELETE FROM `ci_sessions`
      WHERE `user_data` = '' ");
  }
}
```

 We're using the default CodeIgniter sessions table name, that is, `ci_sessions`. In your application, you'll need to substitute this value with the name of your sessions table (assuming you've changed it from `ci_sessions`)..

2. Open the `/path/to/codeigniter/application/config/hooks.php` file and add the following code to it:

```php
$hook['post_controller'] = array(
    'class'     => 'Clear_sessions',
    'function' => 'clear_now',
    'filename' => 'clear_sessions.php',
    'filepath' => 'hooks'
    );
```

How it works...

We have defined a class (`Clear_sessions`) in the `clear_sessions.php` file into which we'll put all the logic we need for the Hook to perform its task. Within that class, we have the `clear_now()` function. CodeIgniter knows that it is to run the `clear_now()` function, in the `Clear_sessions` class, in the `clear_sessions.php` file, because we defined this in the `hooks.php` config file, as shown in the following code snippet:

```php
$hook['post_controller'] = array(
    'class'     => 'Clear_sessions',
    'function' => 'clear_now',
    'filename' => 'clear_sessions.php',
    'filepath' => 'hooks'
    );
```

We told CodeIgniter the location of the `clear_sessions.php` file with the `filepath` element of the preceding array. CodeIgniter will run this Hook at the `post_controller` stage of execution, that is to say, after a controller has been run. So, that's how CodeIgniter knows what hook to execute and when; but what of the function of the hook? What does that do?

Let's look at the following code line:

```
$CI =& get_instance();
```

This gives us access to the main CodeIgniter object, which is defined as `$CI` (for CodeIgniter). Using this object, we have access to the database functions and settings. We'll use this `$CI` object to run a database query, as shown in the following code snippet:

```
$query = $CI->db->query("DELETE FROM `ci_sessions` WHERE
    `user_data` = '' ");
```

The preceding code line deletes any sessions from the table (named here as the default CodeIgniter sessions table ci_sessions) whose `user_data` is empty (*not* not null just empty).

All spent sessions that CodeIgniter hasn't cleaned up properly should now be gone from the sessions table, leaving active sessions alone.

Extending your controllers

Inheritance is a wonderful thing; allowing you to define conceptual layers, or levels within an application, that is, allowing child classes to share traits and attributes of parent classes allows applications to model real-world examples more accurately and intuitively than standard procedural programming.

In CodeIgniter, the default design structure for your application is that the controller you create extends the main CodeIgniter controller. For example, in the following code, we have a `Signin` controller, which extends the main CodeIgniter controller, `CI_Controller`:

```
class Signin extends CI_Controller {
}
```

Your `Signin` controller will inherit the properties of the `CI_Controller`. However, CodeIgniter also allows you to parachute in a stage between the `CI_Controller` and the controller you create, you can slot in a middle layer. This middle step is named `My_Controller`. The new MY_Controller will extend the CI_Controller (inheriting everything as it goes) and any normal application-specific controller you create (users, login, invoice, and so on) will inherit from the new MY_Controller. It is defined as shown in the following code snippet:

```
class MY_Controller extends CI_Controller {
}
```

Now, your `Signin` class must be amended to inherit from your `MY_Controller` rather than CodeIgniter's `CI_Controller` as follows:

```
class Signin extends MY_Controller {
}
```

How to do it...

We're going to create the following two files:

- ▶ `/path/to/codeigniter/application/core/MY_Controller.php`
- ▶ `/path/to/codeigniter/application/controllers/days.php`

1. Create the `/path/to/codeigniter/application/core/MY_Controller.php` file and add the following code to it:

```php
<?php if (! defined('BASEPATH')) exit('No direct script
  access allowed');
class MY_Controller extends CI_Controller {
    function __construct() {
        parent::__construct();
        $this->load->helper('array');
    }
}
```

2. Next, create the `/path/to/codeigniter/application/controllers/days.php` file and add the following code to it:

```php
<?php if (! defined('BASEPATH')) exit('No direct script
  access allowed');

class Days extends MY_Controller {
    function __construct() {
        parent::__construct();
    }

    function index() {
        $days = array("Monday","Tuesday","Wednesday",
            "Thursday","Friday","Saturday","Sunday");
        echo random_element($days);
    }
}
```

How it works...

This is mostly Inheritance. Your child classes are inheriting attributes from parent classes. However, specifically here, we are demonstrating how to load the array helper in the `MY_Controller` class and have the `Days` controller inherit the helper resource in order to execute the array helper function, `random_element()`.

There are so many uses for this, for example, you could check to see if the user was logged in your `MY_Controller` Class, this would mean that you would only have to write this once rather than in every controller. Or you could go further and have an authenticated controller and unauthenticated controller extending `MY_Controller`. The `MY_Controller` file would call any files and perform any tasks common to authenticated and unauthenticated users, While, the authenticated controller would perform login checks, and so on.

Uploading a file with FTP

Every now and again, you'll be asked to generate a file—perhaps from a database export, or maybe some system logs. Most of the time, you'll be asked to e-mail that file to some location, but sometimes, you'll be asked to upload it to an FTP folder the client has access to. We're going to take a recipe from a previous chapter (*Generating a CSV from a database result* from *Chapter 6, Working with Databases*), and adapt it so that it uploads to an FTP location rather than stream an output.

Getting ready

1. We're going to be pulling some values from a database. To do that, we'll need a table to pull data from. The following is the schema for that table. Copy the following into your database:

```
CREATE TABLE `users` (
  `user_id` int(11) NOT NULL AUTO_INCREMENT,
  `user_firstname` varchar(255) NOT NULL,
  `user_lastname` varchar(255) NOT NULL,
  `user_email` varchar(255) NOT NULL,
  PRIMARY KEY (`user_id`)
) ENGINE=InnoDB  DEFAULT CHARSET=latin1 AUTO_INCREMENT=3 ;# MySQL
returned an empty result set (i.e. zero rows).

INSERT INTO `users` (`user_id`, `user_firstname`, `user_lastname`,
`user_email`) VALUES
(1, 'Rob', 'Foster', 'rf@domain.com'),
(2, 'Lucy', 'Welsh', 'lw@domain.com');# 2 rows affected.
```

2. Go to *Chapter 6, Working with Databases*, and copy out the code from the *Generating a CSV from a database result* recipe; then return here for further instructions.

How to do it...

We're going to amend one file from the *Generating a CSV from a database result* recipe, that is, `/path/to/codeigniter/application/controllers/export.php`. This is the export controller from *Chapter 6, Working with Databases*. We're going to use it as the basis for this recipe. It will grab some data from the database that eventually generates a CSV for us.

1. Open `export.php` for editing and amend it to reflect the following code snippet (changes are highlighted):

```php
<?php if (!defined('BASEPATH')) exit('No direct script
  access allowed');

class Export extends CI_Controller {
  function __construct() {
    parent::__construct();
    $this->load->helper('url');
    $this->load->helper('file');
    $this->load->library('ftp');
    $this->load->dbutil();
  }

  public function index() {
    redirect('export/csv');
  }

  public function csv() {
    $query = $this->db->query("SELECT * FROM users");

    $delimiter = ",";
    $newline = "\r\n";

    $data = $this->dbutil->csv_from_result($query,
      $delimiter, $newline);
    $filename = 'myfile.csv';
    $path = './'.$filename;

    if (! write_file($path, $data)) {
      echo 'Cannot write file - permissions maybe?';
      exit;
    }

    $config['hostname'] = 'your-hostname';
    $config['username'] = 'your-username';
    $config['password'] = 'your-password';
    $config['debug'] = TRUE;

    $this->ftp->connect($config);
```

```
$this->ftp->upload($path, '/dir_on_ftp/'.$filename,
    'ascii', 0755);
$this->ftp->close();
    }
}
```

There are some variables here that you should change to reflect the settings of your FTP environment such as:

```
$config['hostname'] = 'ftp.example.com';
$config['username'] = 'your-username';
$config['password'] = 'your-password';
```

...and the string dir_on_ftp in:

```
$this->ftp->upload($path, '/dir_on_ftp/'.$filename,
    'ascii', 0755);
```

How it works...

As you would expect from a new recipe, there are some changes in the normal export controller that we've used in *Chapter 6, Working with Databases*. These changes are necessary to support the FTP helper in its job of uploading a file to an FTP server. Let's take a look at what's going on.

First, we load the helpers we'll need--url, file, and FTP--in the Exporter controllers constructor to ensure that this export controller has the right support necessary to make the file transfer.

```
function __construct() {
    parent::__construct();
    $this->load->helper('url');
    $this->load->helper('file');
    $this->load->library('ftp');
    $this->load->dbutil();
}
```

Everything then follows the functionality of the previous controller (from *Chapter 6, Working with Databases*) ,that is, fetching a result set from the database table and using the CodeIgniter dbutil function, csv_from_result(), to generate a file for us. It's placed on the server by write_file() using the location defined in $path.

Then the FTP functionality kicks in. We define the login settings for the FTP server we want to write the file to–you can and probably should put these in your own config file (also explained in this chapter, see the *Making your own configuration files and using the settings* recipe), but for now, we'll define them here as it's easier to explain one thing at a time. The settings are fairly obvious until you see the $config['debug'] array setting. debug allows error reports to be displayed to you, the developer. Obviously, in a live production environment, you definitely want that set to be FALSE to prevent any sensitive and important information being shown.

Anyways, using the login settings that we have defined in our `$config` array, we attempt to connect to the FTP server and try to upload a file, as shown in the following code snippet:

```
$this->ftp->connect($config);
$this->ftp->upload($path, '/dir_on_ftp/'.$filename, 'ascii',
    0755);
```

If all goes well, the file should be uploaded to your server. Log in with an FTP client and take a look to see if it's there–if it's not check that you're using the correct FTP settings and that the path you're writing to on the FTP server is writable and actually exists, that is, that the path defined here in bold exists:

```
$this->ftp->upload($path, '/dir_on_ftp/'.$filename, 'ascii', 0755);
```

An interesting point is the two function arguments at the end of the preceding `upload()` function: `ascii` and `0755`. These state that we're encoding the file transfer as `ascii` (which is plain text) and setting its file permissions to `0755`. This can also be defined in the config array if you wish.

Creating libraries and giving them access to CodeIgniter resources

CodeIgniter allows you to create your own libraries and helpers in circumstances where you don't want or need to place code in controllers or models. Why would you place code in a library and not a helper? Well, some people become quite agitated by the reasoning for this and I'm sure that if you thought hard enough about it, you could come up with some strict rules that defines when a bit of code is a helper or a library. But life is far too short. As long as the code is well documented and is maintainable, stable, and secure, you can do whatever you like. However, as a general rule of thumb:

A library is for code which requires access to other resources, such as needing access to a database, or to an external system (perhaps through cURL), whereas a helper is a smaller bit of code which performs a specific task (such as checking a string being a valid e-mail or for a valid URL, for example).

I'm sure there are better definitions, but this one works for me; and I'm sure there will be times when you may want a helper to have access to a database or other resource; and I'm sure there will be times when a library doesn't need access to these resources. My point is, just make sure the code is documented and maintainable and don't get bogged down in conceptual design augments.

Having said that, let's look at creating a library and giving it access to CodeIgniter resources (because, by default, it won't).

Getting ready

We're going to access a database through a library; however, to do that we'll need a database to access (of course), so copy the following code into your database:

```
CREATE TABLE IF NOT EXISTS `person` (
  `id` int(11) NOT NULL AUTO_INCREMENT,
  `first_name` varchar(50) NOT NULL,
  `last_name` varchar(50) NOT NULL,
  `email` varchar(255) NOT NULL,
  PRIMARY KEY (`id`)
) ENGINE=InnoDB  DEFAULT CHARSET=latin1 AUTO_INCREMENT=5 ;

INSERT INTO `person` (`id`, `first_name`, `last_name`, `email`) VALUES
(1, 'Rob', 'Foster', 'rfoster@dudlydog.com'),
(2, 'Lucy', 'Welsh', 'lwelsh@cocopopet.com'),
(3, 'Chloe', 'Graves', 'cgraves@mia-cat.com'),
(4, 'Claire', 'Strickland', 'cstrickland@an-other-domain.com');
```

How to do it...

We're going to create the following three files:

▸ /path/to/codeigniter/application/controllers/call_lib.php

▸ /path/to/codeigniter/application/libraries/lib_to_call.php

▸ /path/to/codeigniter/application/models/lib_model.php

1. Create the call_lib.php controller and add the following code to it:

```php
<?php if (! defined('BASEPATH')) exit('No direct script
  access allowed');

class Call_lib extends CI_Controller {
  function __construct() {
    parent::__construct();
    $this->load->library('lib_to_call');
    $this->load->database();
  }

  public function index() {
    $result = $this->lib_to_call->get_users();

    echo '<pre>';
      var_dump($result->result());
    echo '</pre>';
  }
}
```

2. Create the `lib_to_call.php` library and add the following code to it:

```php
<?php if (! defined('BASEPATH')) exit('No direct script
  access allowed');

class Lib_to_call {
    public function get_users() {
        $CI =& get_instance();
        $CI->load->model('Lib_model');
         return $CI->Lib_model->get();
    }
}
```

3. Then create the `lib_model.php` model and add the following code to it:

```php
<?php if ( ! defined('BASEPATH')) exit('No direct script
  access allowed');

class Lib_model extends CI_Model {
    function __construct() {
        parent::__construct();
    }

    function get() {
        $query = $this->db->get('person');
        return $query;
    }
}
```

How it works...

In looking at how to give your libraries access to CodeIgniter resources, we're going to run through the preceding recipe. It's connecting to a model; however, it can be any type of CodeIgniter resource such as a Hook or a helper, and so on.

First, the `call_lib.php` controller loads in its constructor the `lib_to_call` library, as follows:

```php
function __construct() {
    parent::__construct();
    $this->load->library('lib_to_call');
}
```

This makes the library available to the entire controller.

We then call `public function index()`, which calls the library function, `get_users()`, storing the returned results in the `$result` variable. Let's look at what the library function, `get_users()`, is doing, this is where we allow the library to get access to CodeIgniter resources.

Look at the following highlighted lines in the `lib_to_call` library:

```
class Lib_to_call {
    public function get_users() {
        $CI =& get_instance();
        $CI->load->model('Lib_model');
        return $CI->Lib_model->get();
    }
}
```

We're using the PHP function, `get_instance()`, to get our hands on a copy by reference (that means we're using the initial object rather than a copy of it) or the CodeIgniter object. This object has access to the entire CodeIgniter system and its resources. We store this object in a local variable named `$CI` (standing for CodeIgniter). We can now call any CodeIgniter resource we like, just as we would from a controller, except that instead of using `$this` (as we would in a controller), we use `$CI`. So, to call a model or helper in a controller, we will do the following:

```
$this->load->helper('helper_name');
$this->load->model('model_name');
```

But to call helpers and models in the library, we now do the following:

```
$CI->load->helper('helper_name');
$CI->load->model('model_name');
```

The model we've now loaded will query the database with Active Record, returning all rows in the table to the library, which in turn returns it to the controller for processing. In this case (to demonstrate that it worked), we `var_dump()` the result. If all goes well, this recipe should output as follows:

```
array(4) {
  [0]=>
  object(stdClass)#19 (4) {
    ["id"]=>
    string(1) "1"
    ["first_name"]=>
    string(3) "Rob"
    ["last_name"]=>
    string(6) "Foster"
```

```
    ["email"]=>
    string(20) "rfoster@dudlydog.com"
  }
  [1]=>
  object(stdClass)#20 (4) {
    ["id"]=>
    string(1) "2"
    ["first_name"]=>
    string(4) "Lucy"
    ["last_name"]=>
    string(5) "Welsh"
    ["email"]=>
    string(20) "lwelsh@cocopopet.com"
  }
  [2]=>
  object(stdClass)#21 (4) {
    ["id"]=>
    string(1) "3"
    ["first_name"]=>
    string(5) "Chloe"
    ["last_name"]=>
    string(6) "Graves"
    ["email"]=>
    string(19) "cgraves@mia-cat.com"
  }
  [3]=>
  object(stdClass)#22 (4) {
    ["id"]=>
    string(1) "4"
    ["first_name"]=>
    string(6) "Claire"
    ["last_name"]=>
    string(10) "Strickland"
    ["email"]=>
    string(31) "cstrickland@an-other-domain.com"
  }
}
```

The preceding recipe access a database as a means of demonstrating how to gain access to a CodeIgniter super object from within a library. However, helpers, Hooks, and other elements can also be accessed. By using `$CI =& get_instance()`, we can gain access to the main CodeIgniter object. By using `$CI` rather than `$this`, this will give us access to all of CodeIgniter's resources, as shown in the following code snippet:

```
$CI =& get_instance();
$CI->load->model('Lib_model');
return $CI->Lib_model->get();
```

Making your own configuration files and using the settings

It's a great idea to have configuration settings in the same file—the benefits are obvious—so rather than having settings hidden in controllers, modules, helpers, libraries, or (God forbid) in views, you can put them in one location and refer to them from there. CodeIgniter comes with its own configuration files in the `config` folder; however, you can add your own files to the `config` folder and refer to them in your code. It's pretty handy and easy to do; let's take a look.

How to do it...

We're going to create the following two files:

- `/path/to/codeigniter/application/controllers/config_settings.php`
- `/path/to/codeigniter/application/config/my_config_file.php`

1. Create the `config_settings.php` controller, open it for editing, and add the following code to it:

```php
<?php if (!defined('BASEPATH')) exit('No direct script
  access allowed');

class Config_settings extends CI_Controller {
  function __construct() {
    parent::__construct();
    $this->config->load('my_config_file');
  }

  public function index() {
    echo $this->config->item('first_config_item');

    for($i = 0; $i < $this->config->item('stop_at'); $i++) {
      echo $i . '<br />';
    }
  }
}
```

2. Create the config file, `my_config_file.php`, open it for editing, and add the following code to it:

```php
<?php if (!defined('BASEPATH')) exit('No direct script
    access allowed');

$config['first_config_item'] = "This is my config setting,
    there are many like it but this one is mine<br />";
$config['stop_at'] = 10;
```

How it works...

To be honest, there are so many situations where putting information in a config file is useful that make it pointless writing a specific recipe for you, as the chances of it being the recipe you need are slim to none. So, this is just a proof of concept; it is there for you as a guide of the basic two files: a config file and another file (a controller) to grab information from it.

Take a look at the constructor in the controller, `Config_settings`. This is where we define the name of the config file. You can call it whatever you like (as long as the name isn't already taken by another config file). Here, I've called it `my_config_file`; it's a bit **1995**, but it's good enough for the explanation and I'm sure you get the idea.

The next thing to happen is that `public function index()` is executed, which does two things: prints out a string of text (the text is set in our config file) and iterates through a `for()` loop, only stopping when it reaches the value specified in our `my_config_file`.

These two approaches show you how to work with config values: either echoing out to screen or using that value in some sort of structure.

Using the language class – switching language on the go

Once you have developed your site to accommodate multiple languages, you'll obviously want to allow people to switch between them. For example, to switch from English to French, or French to German, or whatever region or language you're developing for. This can be handled in several ways, but in this example, we're going to use the CodeIgniter `Session` class to swap from one language to another.

Getting ready

We're going to use the `Session` class to store the user's language preference, which means, we'll need to use CodeIgniter sessions. This will require some configuration.

We'll be editing the following files:

- ▸ `path/to/codeigniter/application/config/config.php`
- ▸ `path/to/codeigniter/application/config/database.php`

The following are the config settings:

1. Find the following config values in the `path/to/codeigniter/application/config/config.php` file and amend them to reflect the following values:

Config Item	Data Type	Change to Value	Description
`$config['sess_cookie_name']`	String	`ci_session`	This is the name of the cookie written to the user's computer.
`$config['sess_expiration']`	Integer	7200	This is the number of seconds a session should remain active, after no user activity, before becoming void.
`$config['sess_expire_on_close']`	Boolean (True/False)	TRUE	This specifies that if the user closes their browser the session becomes void.
`$config['sess_encrypt_cookie']`	Boolean (True/False)	TRUE	This specifies if the cookie should be encrypted on the user's computer. For security purposes this should be set to TRUE.
`$config['sess_use_database']`	Boolean (True/False)	TRUE	This specifies weather or not to store sessions in the database. For security purposes this should be set to TRUE. You will also need to create the session table, the code for which can be found in the upcoming page.
`$config['sess_table_name']`	String	`sessions`	This specifies the name of the database table used to store session data. In this recipe, I have called the sessions table simple sessions; however, you can keep the original i_sessions–just make sure you amend the SQL accordingly.

Config Item	Data Type	Change to Value	Description
`$config['sess_match_ip']`	Boolean (True/False)	TRUE	This specifies whether CodeIgniter should monitor the IP address of requests and against that of the `session_id`. If the IP of an incoming request doesn't match the previous values, the session is disallowed.
`$config['sess_match_useragent']`	Boolean (True/False)	TRUE	This specifies whether CodeIgniter should monitor the user agent address of requests and against that of the `session_id`. If the user agent of an incoming request doesn't match the previous values, the session is disallowed.

2. Find the following config values in the `path/to/codeigniter/application/config/database.php` file and amend them to reflect the correct settings to enable you to connect to your database:

Config Item	Data Type	Change to Value	Description
`$db['default']['hostname']`	String	`localhost`	The hostname of your database. This is usually either `localhost` or an IP address
`$db['default']['username']`	String		The username you wish to use to connect to your database
`$db['default']['password']`	String		The password used to connect to your database
`$db['default']['database']`	String		The name of the database which you wish to connect to

3. We will be storing the user's language preference in the session, and the sessions are stored in the database table, `sessions`. The following is the schema for the sessions table. Using a method of your choice (command line, `phpMyAdmin`, and so on), enter the following MySQL schema into your database:

```
CREATE TABLE IF NOT EXISTS `sessions` (
  `session_id` varchar(40) COLLATE utf8_bin NOT NULL DEFAULT '0',
  `ip_address` varchar(16) COLLATE utf8_bin NOT NULL DEFAULT '0',
  `user_agent` varchar(120) COLLATE utf8_bin DEFAULT NULL,
  `last_activity` int(10) unsigned NOT NULL DEFAULT '0',
  `user_data` text COLLATE utf8_bin NOT NULL,
  PRIMARY KEY (`session_id`),
  KEY `last_activity_idx` (`last_activity`)
) ENGINE=InnoDB DEFAULT CHARSET=utf8 COLLATE=utf8_bin;
```

How to do it...

We're going to create the following language file:

`/path/to/codeigniter/application/language/french/fr_lang.php`

...and amend the following two files:

▶ `/path/to/codeigniter/application/controllers/lang.php`

▶ `/path/to/codeigniter/application/views/lang/lang.php`

1. Amend `/path/to/codeigniter/application/controllers/lang.php` to reflect the following code snippet:

```php
<?php if (!defined('BASEPATH')) exit('No direct script
  access allowed');
class Lang extends CI_Controller {
    function __construct() {
        parent::__construct();
        $this->load->helper('form');
        $this->load->helper('url');
        $this->load->helper('language');
        $this->load->helper('security');

        // Check for empty language values in the session
        if ($this->session->userdata('filename') == '' ||
          $this->session->userdata('language') == '') {
            $change_lang = array(
                'language'   => 'english',
                'filename'   => 'en',
```

```
                    );

                $this->session->set_userdata($change_lang);
                $this->lang->load(
                  $this->session->userdata('filename'),
                    $this->session->userdata('language'));
            } else { // Default language
                $this->lang->load(
                  $this->session->userdata('filename'),
                    $this->session->userdata('language'));
            }
        }

        public function index() {
            redirect('lang/submit');
        }

        public function submit() {
            $this->load->library('form_validation');
            $this->form_validation->set_error_delimiters(
              '', '<br />');

            // Set validation rules
            $this->form_validation->set_rules(
              'email', $this->lang->line('form_email'),
                'required|min_length[1]|max_length[50]|
                  valid_email');

            // Begin validation
            if ($this->form_validation->run() == FALSE) {
                $this->load->view('lang/lang');
            }
        }

    public function change_language() {
            $lang = xss_clean($this->uri->segment(3));

            switch ($lang) {
                    case "en":
                            $language = 'english';
                            $filename = 'en';

                            break;
                    case "fr":
                            $language = 'french';
                            $filename = 'fr';
                            break;
                    default:
                        break;
```

```
        }

        $change_lang = array(
            'language'   => $language,
            'filename'   => $filename,
        );

        $this->session->set_userdata($change_lang);

        redirect('lang/index');
        }
    }
```

2. Amend /path/to/codeigniter/application/views/lang/lang.php to reflect the following code snippet:

```
<html>
    <body>

        <?php echo anchor('lang/change_language/fr',
          'French'); ?>
         
        <?php echo anchor('lang/change_language/en',
          'English'); ?>

        <h2><?php echo $this->lang->line('form_title');
          ?></h2>
        <?php echo form_open('lang/submit'); ?>
        <?php echo $this->lang->line('form_email'); ?>
        <?php echo form_input(array('name' => 'email',
          'id' => 'email', 'value' => '',
            'maxlength' => '100', 'size' => '50',
              'style' => 'width:10%')); ?>

        <?php echo form_submit('',
          $this->lang->line('form_submit_button')); ?>
        <?php echo form_close(); ?>

    </body>
</html>
```

3. Copy the following code into the `/path/to/codeigniter/application/system/language/french/fr_lang.php` file:

```php
<?php if (!defined('BASEPATH')) exit('No direct script
  access allowed');
$lang['form_title'] = "Titre du formulaire en anglais";
$lang['form_email'] = "Votre E-Mail: ";
$lang['form_submit_button'] = "Suggérer";
```

4. Finally, add the following code into the `/path/to/codeigniter/application/system/language/engligh/en_lang.php` file:

```php
<?php if (!defined('BASEPATH')) exit('No direct script
  access allowed');
$lang['form_title'] = "Form title in English";
$lang['form_email'] = "Email: ";
$lang['form_submit_button'] = "Submit";
```

How it works...

This is an extension of the earlier language recipe. The only thing we're doing different is adding support for switching values in `$this->lang->load('', '');`. We're using CodeIgniter's session functionality to store the switched values. Thus, as we're passing the required language as a value in the URL, we'll want to use the CodeIgniter security method, `xss_clean()`, to mitigate against cross-site scripting.

So, in the constructor, we have the following code:

```php
// Check for empty language values in the session
if ($this->session->userdata('filename') ==
  '' || $this->session->userdata('language') == '') {
    $change_lang = array(
    'language'   => 'english',
    'filename'   => 'en',
    );

    $this->session->set_userdata($change_lang);
    $this->lang->load($this->session->userdata('filename'),
      $this->session->userdata('language'));
} else { // Default language
    $this->lang->load($this->session->userdata('filename'),
      $this->session->userdata('language'));
}
```

This will look to see whether there are any language variables set in a session. If there are not, we define the language in the `$change_lang` array and pass it to the `$this->lang->load('', '');` function, as follows:

```
$this->lang->load($this->session->userdata('filename'),
  $this->session->userdata('language'));
```

From there, `public function index()` is loaded and immediately redirects to `public function submit()`, which displays the HTML form.

We've amended the HTML form, adding the following two anchor tags:

```
<?php echo anchor('lang/change_language/fr', 'French'); ?>
 
<?php echo anchor('lang/change_language/en', 'English'); ?>
```

If a user clicks on either one of these links (French or English) in their browser, `public function change_language()` is run. We then grab and sanitize the third parameter of the URL with `$lang = xss_clean($this->uri->segment(3));` and pass it through a PHP Switch/Case statement, looking for either `en` or `fr`, assigning the `$language` and `$filename` variables as we go with the correct details (the default loads English).

Next, we load the `$language` and `$filename` variables into the `$change_lang` array and write to the session with `$this->session->set_userdata($change_lang);`. We finish by redirecting back to `public function index()`, which will send us back to the beginning with a new language loaded.

10
Working with Images

In this chapter, you will learn:

- ► Installing ImageMagick on MAC with Cactuslab
- ► Uploading images with CodeIgniter
- ► Generating thumbnails – resizing
- ► Rotating images
- ► Cropping images
- ► Adding watermarks with text
- ► Adding watermarks with image overlays
- ► Submitting a form with CodeIgniter CAPTCHA

Introduction

CodeIgniter has a useful array of tools to help you manipulate and amend images in the form of the image manipulation class; it's not Photoshop, but it's good enough for most of what you'll need to do in your day-to-day web development. It has functionalities to help you upload images, resize them, create thumbnails, add watermarks, crop, and rotate—all very useful things and exactly what you'll be after in a development environment. Here's how to do it.

Installing ImageMagick on MAC with Cactuslab

Some of the features of the CodeIgniter image manipulation class require GD2, however, other features require ImageMagick. If you're using MAMP on MAC, then the chances are that you won't have it installed by default. Cactuslab have produced an installer that does the job for you.

1. Go to the URL `http://www.cactuslab.com/imagemagick`.

2. Download the installer. At the time of writing this, the latest version is ImageMagick 6.8.6-3 for Mac OS X 10.5 - 10.8.

3. Run the installer, and if all goes well, you should now have ImageMagick installed. You'll need to set the `$config['library_path']` value to `/opt/ImageMagick/bin`, as follows:

   ```
   'library_path' => '/opt/ImageMagick/bin'
   ```

How it works...

The installer takes care of everything for you: it's voodoo!

Uploading images with CodeIgniter

This is similar to the file upload recipe mentioned earlier in the book; however, it differs from it, as we're making CodeIgniter upload images (rather than upload any file type) and perform specific tasks on images, which wouldn't be relevant to the other upload example in the book. Hence, consider this as a separate upload script. This script is the base script for the other recipes (apart from the CAPTCHA recipe) in this chapter—that is to say that the rotating, watermarking, resizing recipes and so on require this base recipe to function.

How to do it...

We're going to create the following two files:

- `/path/to/codeigniter/application/controllers/upload.php`
- `/path/to/codeigniter/application/views/upload/upload.php`

1. Create the controller file, `upload.php`, and add the following code to it:

   ```php
   <?php if (! defined('BASEPATH')) exit('No direct script
     access allowed');

   class Upload extends CI_Controller {
     function __construct() {
       parent::__construct();
       $this->load->helper('form');
       $this->load->helper('url');
     }

     function index() {
   ```

```
        $this->load->view('upload/upload', array(
          'error' => ' ' ));
      }

    function do_upload() {
      $config['upload_path'] = '/path/to/upload/dir/';
      $config['allowed_types'] = 'gif|jpg|png';
      $config['max_size'] = '10000';
      $config['max_width'] = '1024';
      $config['max_height'] = '768';

      $this->load->library('upload', $config);

      if (! $this->upload->do_upload()) {
        $error = array(
          'error' => $this->upload->display_errors());
        $this->load->view('upload/upload', $error);
      } else {
  $data = array('upload_data' => $this->upload->data());
        echo '<pre>';
        var_dump($data);
        echo '</pre>';
          }
      }
    }
```

2. Create the `/path/to/codeigniter/application/views/upload/upload.`
    `php` file and add the following code to it:

    ```
    <?php if ($error) : ?>
    <?php echo $error ; ?>
    <?php endif ; ?>

    <?php echo form_open_multipart('upload/do_upload');?>

    <input type = "file" name = "userfile" size = "20" />

    <br /><br />

    <input type = "submit" value = "upload" />

    <?php echo form_close() ; ?>
    ```

How it works...

When the `upload` controller is run in the browser the user is presented with the form (which is in the view file `views/ipload/upload.php`). The user selects an image and presses the **Submit** button public function `do_upload()` is then called. We immediately define some settings which the image being uploaded is checked against, such as allowed image types, maximum size and dimensions, these are:

```
$config['upload_path'] = '/path/to/upload/dir';
$config['allowed_types'] = 'gif|jpg|png';
$config['max_size'] = '10000';
$config['max_width'] = '1024';
$config['max_height'] = '768';
```

If the image being uploaded meets these requirements, the image can be moved to the location specified in `$config['upload_path']` where it is stored, ready should you need it.

Generating thumbnails – resizing

Obviously having the functionality to generate thumbnails is a useful thing to do. Most web developers have had the requirement to create thumbnails of images they are currently uploading, or images previously uploaded, from time to time. Usually that processing would have been done directly with PHP or whichever programming language you may have been using; but CodeIgniter gives you the ability to create thumbnails easily, and this is how you do it.

Getting ready

We're going to use a library of our own for this. If you haven't already done so (in the other recipes in this chapter), create the following file:

> ▶ `/path/to/codeigniter/application/libraries/image_manip.php`

1. Ensure that the `Image_manip` library class is defined as follows:

```
<?php if (! defined('BASEPATH')) exit('No direct script
  access allowed');
class Image_manip {
}
```

2. Also ensure that you have the image library, GD2, installed and that you have this chapter's "base" recipe—that is *Uploading images with CodeIgniter*—already copied and ready to go, as this recipe uses the code from *Uploading images with CodeIgniter* as a base recipe.

How to do it...

We're going to amend the following files from the previous recipe, *Uploading images with CodeIgniter*:

- /path/to/codeigniter/application/controllers/upload.php
- /path/to/codeigniter/application/libraries/image_manip.php

1. Add the following line (in bold) to the constructor so that the entire constructor looks like this code snippet:

```
function __construct() {
        parent::__construct();
        $this->load->helper('form');
        $this->load->helper('url');
        $this->load->library('image_manip');
}
```

2. Alter the do_upload() function, changing it to reflect the following:

```
if ( ! $this->upload->do_upload()) {
        $error = array('error' => $this->upload->display_errors());
        $this->load->view('upload/upload', $error);
} else {
        $data = array('upload_data' => $this->upload->data());

        $result = $this->upload->data();
        $origional_image = $result['full_path'];

        $data = array(
                'image_library' => 'gd2',
                'source_image' => $origional_image,
                'create_thumb' => TRUE,
                'maintain_ratio' => TRUE,
                'width' => '75',
                'height' => '50'
                );

        if ($this->image_manip->resize_image($data)) {
                echo 'Image successfully resized<br /><pre>';
                var_dump($result);
                echo '</pre>';
        } else {
                echo 'There was an error with the image processing.';
        }
}
```

3. Amend the `image_manip` library to add the following function:

```
function resize_image($data) {
  $CI =& get_instance();
  $CI->load->library('image_lib', $data);
  if ($CI->image_lib->resize()) {
    return true;
  } else {
    echo $CI->image_lib->display_errors();
  }
}
```

How it works...

When the `upload` controller is run in the browser the user is presented with the form (which is in the view file `views/ipload/upload.php`). The user selects an image and presses the **Submit** button after which `public function do_upload()` is called. We immediately define some settings against which the image being uploaded is checked, such as allowed image types, maximum size and dimensions - just as we would in the *Uploading images with CodeIgniter* recipe. Assuming that the upload was successful and there were no errors we call the `resize_image()` function in the `image_manip` library:

```
$this->image_manip->resize_image($data);
```

The `resize_image()` function grabs the main CodeIgniter object in `$CI` and loads its own `image_lib` library, as shown in the following code snippet:

```
$CI = & get_instance();
$CI->load->library('image_lib', $data);
```

The `image_lib` library will be used by CodeIgniter to perform the changes on the image using the parameters we provided in the `$data` array.

We call `$CI->image_lib->resize()`, testing for a returned TRUE value. If it returns FALSE, we then return any error messages from the operation. Otherwise, a thumbnail has been created, as shown in the following code snippet:

```
if ($CI->image_lib->resize()) {
  return true;
} else {
  echo $CI->image_lib->display_errors();
}
```

Rotating images

CodeIgniter allows for the rotation of images; this is useful if you need to flip something vertically or in any other direction. Here's how it's done.

Getting ready

We're going to use a library of our own for this. If you haven't already done so (in the other recipes in this chapter), create the following file:

- `/path/to/codeigniter/application/libraries/image_manip.php`

1. Ensure that the `image_manip` library class is defined as follows:

```php
<?php if ( ! defined('BASEPATH')) exit('No direct script
  access allowed');
class Image_manip {
}
```

2. Also ensure that you have the image library, ImageMagik, installed that you have this chapter's "base" recipe—that is *Uploading images with CodeIgniter*—already copied and ready to go, as this recipe uses the code from *Uploading images with CodeIgniter* as a base recipe.

How to do it...

We're going to amend the following two files:

- `/path/to/codeigniter/application/controllers/upload.php`
- `/path/to/codeigniter/application/libraries/image_manip.php`

1. Add the following function to the `image_manip.php` library file:

```php
function rotate($data) {
  $CI = & get_instance();
  $CI->load->library('image_lib', $data);

  $CI->image_lib->initialize($data);

  if ($CI->image_lib->rotate()) {
    return true;
  } else {
    echo $CI->image_lib->display_errors();
  }
}
```

2. Add the following line (in bold) to the constructor so that the entire constructor looks like this:

```
function __construct() {
  parent::__construct();
  $this->load->helper('form');
  $this->load->helper('url');
  $this->load->library('image_manip');
}
```

3. Alter the do_upload() function, changing it to reflect the following:

```
if ( ! $this->upload->do_upload()) {
        $error = array('error' => $this->upload->display_errors());
        $this->load->view('upload/upload', $error);
} else {
        $data = array('upload_data' => $this->upload->data());

        $result = $this->upload->data();
        $original_image = $result['full_path'];

        $data = array(
                'image_library' => 'imagemagick',
                'library_path' => '/opt/ImageMagick/bin',
                'source_image' => $original_image,
                'rotation_angle' => 'vrt'
                );
        if ($this->image_manip->rotate($data)) {
        echo 'Image successfully rotated<br /><pre>';
        var_dump($result);
        echo '</pre>';
} else {
        echo 'There was an error with the image processing.';
}
}
```

How it works...

When the upload controller is run in the browser the user is presented with the form (which is in the view views/ipload/upload.php file). The user selects an image and presses the **Submit** button, public function do_uplaod() is then called. We immediately define some settings against which the image being uploaded is checked, such as allowed image types, maximum size, and dimensions—just as we would in the *Uploading images with CodeIgniter* recipe. Assuming that the upload was successful and there were no errors, we fetch full_path from the upload data:

```
$original_image = $result['full_path'];
```

Assign it as a local variable `$original_image`. We then define an array (`$data`) with all the configuration settings which CodeIgniter requires to crop the image (be sure to get the `library_path` correct). We pass this `$data` array to the library function, `rotate`:

```
$this->image_manip->rotate($data);
```

This performs the rotate operation on the image.

Cropping images

This is going to be most useful and relevant when coupled with a frontend mechanic, allowing the user to select an area of an image; however, I'm including the code here as you may need it. You never know!

Getting ready

We're going to use a library of our own for this. If you haven't already done so (in the other recipes in this chapter), create the following file:

▶ `/path/to/codeigniter/application/libraries/image_manip.php`

1. Ensure that the `image_manip` library class is defined as follows:

```
<?php if (! defined('BASEPATH')) exit('No direct script
  access allowed');
class Image_manip {
}
```

2. Also ensure that you have the image library, ImageMagik, installed.

> If you're using MAMP on a MAC, chances are that you don't have ImageMagick installed by default. There is a process to installing ImageMagick on MAMP; however, there's a quicker way. There's an installer available from Cactuslab at `http://www.cactuslab.com/imagemagick`, and it works like a charm. The *Installing ImageMagick on MAC with Cactuslab* recipe is also available in this chapter explaining the installation process.

3. Ensure that you have this chapters 'base' recipe that is *Uploading images with CodeIgniter* already copied and ready to go as this recipe uses the code from *Uploading images with CodeIgniter* as a base recipe.

How to do it...

We're going to amend the following two files:

- ▸ `/path/to/codeigniter/application/controllers/upload.php`
- ▸ `/path/to/codeigniter/application/libraries/image_manip.php`

1. Add the following line (in bold) to the constructor so that the entire constructor looks like this:

```
function __construct() {
        parent::__construct();
        $this->load->helper('form');
        $this->load->helper('url');
        $this->load->library('image_manip');
}
```

2. Alter the do_upload() function, changing it to reflect the following:

```
if ( ! $this->upload->do_upload()) {
        $error = array('error' => $this->upload->display_errors());
        $this->load->view('upload/upload', $error);
} else {
        $data = array('upload_data' => $this->upload->data());

        $result = $this->upload->data();
        $original_image = $result['full_path'];

        $data = array(
                'source_image' => $original_image,
                'image_library' => 'imagemagick',
                'library_path' => '/opt/ImageMagick/bin',
                'x_axis' => '100',
                'y_axis' => '60'
        );

        if ($this->image_manip->crop_image($data)) {
                echo 'Image successfully cropped<br /><pre>';
                var_dump($result);
                echo '</pre>';
        } else {
                echo 'There was an error with the image processing.';
        }
}
```

3. Amend the following function in the `image_manip` library:

```
function crop_image($data) {
  $CI =& get_instance();
  $CI->load->library('image_lib', $data);

  $CI->image_lib->initialize($data);

  if ($CI->image_lib->crop()) {
    return true;
  } else {
    echo $CI->image_lib->display_errors();
  }
}
```

How it works...

When the `upload` controller is run in the browser the user is presented with the form (which is in the view `views/ipload/upload.php` file). The user selects an image and presses the **Submit** button, `public function do_uplaod()` is then called. We immediately define some settings against which the image being uploaded is checked, such as allowed image types, maximum size, and dimensions—just as we would in the *Uploading images with CodeIgniter* recipe. Assuming that the upload was successful and there were no errors we fetch the `full_path` from the upload data:

```
$original_image = $result['full_path'];
```

We assign it as a local variable, `$original_image`. We then define an array (`$data`) with all the configuration settings which CodeIgniter requires to crop the image (be sure to get the `library_path` variable correct). We pass this `$data` array to the library function, `crop_image`, as shown in the following code snippet:

```
$this->image_manip->crop_image($data);
```

This performs the cropping operation on the image.

Potential errors

You may see some or all (or perhaps entirely different) error messages while coding this recipe. The following are some of those errors and possible solutions (if all else fails, Google it):

Error: Image processing failed. Please verify that your server supports the chosen protocol and that the path to your image library is correct.

Possible Solution: It may be that the path to your image library is incorrect or that the configuration settings for the image library are wrong. Verify that you have the correct library installed and that the path is correct. To do this, perform the following steps:

1. Type `cd /usr/X11R6/bin` in your terminal.

2. Then type `ls` (or `dir` on Windows).

3. Look for the ImageMagick library there. If you cannot see it, then it's probably not installed, and you'll need to install it to be able to perform the cropping operation.

How do you install ImageMagick? Well, there are many instructions and tutorials on the Internet which can help. However, if you're using MAMP, go to the *Installing ImageMagick on MAC with Cactuslab* recipe in this chapter and use the installer to help that can install ImageMagick and do the leg work of the configuration.

However be aware that the library path won't be `/use/X11R6/bin/` (with the trailing slash) like it is in the CodeIgniter documentation; it will be `/opt/ImageMagick/bin` (without the trailing slash).

Adding watermarks with text

Adding a watermark can be a useful way to tag images with your copyright (just make sure you're the copyright owner). CodeIgniter comes with an easy method to apply a watermark to an image. Watermarks can be either text or an image overlay and can be positioned on an original image at any position you wish. The following is a description of how to add text watermarks.

Getting ready

We're going to use a library of our own for this. If you haven't already done so (in the other recipes in this chapter), create the following file:

▶ `/path/to/codeigniter/application/libraries/image_manip.php`

1. Ensure that the `image_manip` library class is defined as follows:
   ```php
   <?php if (! defined('BASEPATH')) exit('No direct script
     access allowed');
   class Image_manip {
   }
   ```

2. Also ensure that you have the image library, GD2, installed.

3. Ensure that you have this chapters base recipe that is *Uploading images with CodeIgniter* already copied and ready to go as this recipe uses the code from *Uploading images with CodeIgniter* as a base recipe.

How to do it...

We're going to amend the following two files:

- ▸ /path/to/codeigniter/application/controllers/uplod.php
- ▸ /path/to/codeigniter/application/libraries/image_manip.php

1. Add the following function to the image_manip.php library file:

```
function do_watermark($data) {
  $CI =& get_instance();
  $CI->load->library('image_lib', $data);

  $CI->image_lib->initialize($data);
  if ($CI->image_lib->watermark()) {
    return true;
  } else {
    echo $CI->image_lib->display_errors();
  }
}
```

2. Add the following line (in bold) to the constructor so that the entire constructor looks like this:

```
function __construct() {
  parent::__construct();
  $this->load->helper('form');
  $this->load->helper('url');
  $this->load->library('image_manip');
}
```

3. Alter the do_upload() function, changing it to reflect the following:

```
if ( ! $this->upload->do_upload()) {
  $error = array('error' => $this->upload
    ->display_errors());
  $this->load->view('upload/upload', $error);
} else {
  $data = array('upload_data' => $this->upload->data());

  $result = $this->upload->data();
  $original_image = $result['full_path'];

  $data = array(
  'image_library' => 'GD2',
  'source_image' => $original_image,
  'wm_text' => 'Copyright (c) ' . date("Y",time()) . '
    - YOUR NAME',
    'wm_type' => 'text',
    'wm_font_path' => './system/fonts/texb.ttf',
```

```
        'wm_font_size' => '16',
        'wm_font_color' => 'ffffff',
        'wm_vrt_alignment' => 'middle',
        'wm_hor_alignment' => 'left',
        'wm_padding' => '20'
    );

    if ($this->image_manip->do_watermark($data)) {
        echo 'Image successfully watermarked<br /><pre>';
        var_dump($result);
        echo '</pre>';
    } else {
        echo 'There was an error with the image processing.';
    }
}
```

How it works...

When the `upload` controller is run in the browser the user is presented with the form (which is in the view file `views/ipload/upload.php`). The user selects an image and presses the **Submit** button, `public function do_uplaod()` is then called. We immediately define some settings against which the image being uploaded is checked, such as allowed image types, maximum size and dimensions just as we would in the *Uploading images with CodeIgniter* recipe. Assuming that the upload was successful and there were no errors we fetch the `full_path` from the upload data:

```
$original_image = $result['full_path'];
```

Assign it as a local variable, `$original_image`. Next, we'll define an array (`$data`) with all the necessary settings to allow CodeIgniter to perform a watermark overlay on our uploaded image. There are a couple of interesting settings I'll go through in the following table:

Setting	Options	How we're applying it
wm_type	text, overlay	In this recipe, it's set to text, which tells CodeIgniter that it has to write text over the image, rather than call an image as the overlay. In the next recipe, we'll look at overlay watermarking.
wn_vrt_alignment	top, middle, bottom	We're telling CodeIgniter that it should place the text towards the middle of the uploaded image.
wn_hor_alignment	left, center, right	We're telling CodeIgniter that it should place the text towards the left of the uploaded image.

Setting	Options	How we're applying it
`wm_font_color`	Any hexadecimal value (see the following tip for a useful URL)	We're writing the text as white for no other reason than the image I used to test this code on was quite dark—a romantic sunset (ahh)—but you can of course change it to any hexadecimal value you wish.
`wm_font_path`	`./system/fonts/texb.ttf`	This is the font which comes with CodeIgniter; it's a bit industrial and you may want to change it for another, either copy a different true type font into the `./system/fonts/` directory, or link to one outside that directory.

The following URL has a list of hexadecimal color values: `http://www.w3schools.com/html/html_colors.asp`.

Adding watermarks with image overlays

CodeIgniter can add watermarks with text as detailed in the preceding recipe, but CodeIgniter can also by overlaying a watermark image on top of a base image. Here's how it's done...

Getting ready

We're going to use a library of our own for this. If you haven't already done so (in the other recipes in this chapter), create the following file:

- ▶ `/path/to/codeigniter/application/libraries/image_manip.php`

1. Ensure that the `image_manip` library class is defined as follows:
   ```php
   <?php if ( ! defined('BASEPATH')) exit('No direct script
     access allowed');
   class Image_manip {
   }
   ```

2. This recipe is based on the *Adding watermarks with text* recipe. Make sure you have followed that recipe first. We're going to make a few code changes to it to help us with watermark overlays.

How to do it...

We're going to amend the following files:

- ▸ `/path/to/codeigniter/application/controllers/uplod.php`
- ▸ `/path/to/codeigniter/application/libraries/image_manip.php`

1. Add the following function to the library file `image_manip.php`:

```
function do_watermark($data) {
  $CI =& get_instance();
  $CI->load->library('image_lib', $data);

  $CI->image_lib->initialize($data);
  if ($CI->image_lib->watermark()) {
    return true;
  } else {
    echo $CI->image_lib->display_errors();
  }
}
```

2. Add the following line (in bold) to the constructor so that the entire constructor looks like this:

```
function __construct() {
  parent::__construct();
  $this->load->helper('form');
  $this->load->helper('url');
  $this->load->library('image_manip');
}
```

3. Alter the `do_upload()` function, changing it to reflect the following:

```
if (! $this->upload->do_upload()) {
  $error = array(
    'error' => $this->upload->display_errors());
  $this->load->view('upload/upload', $error);
} else {
  $data = array('upload_data' => $this->upload->data());

  $result = $this->upload->data();
  $original_image = $result['full_path'];

  // Create Watermark
  $data = array(
  'image_library' => 'gd2',
  'source_image' => $original_image,
  'wm_type' => 'overlay',
  'wm_overlay_path' =>
    $config['upload_path'] . '/overlay_image_name',
```

```
'wm_font_path' => './system/fonts/texb.ttf',
'wm_font_size' => '16',
'wm_font_color' => 'ffffff',
'wm_vrt_alignment' => 'middle',
'wm_hor_alignment' => 'left',
'wm_padding' => '20'
);

$this->image_manip->do_watermark($data);
}
```

How it works...

This is the same basic functionality as the *Adding watermarks with text* recipe. However, instead of the `wm_type` being `text`, we have set it to `overlay`. We have added the config array item, `wm_overlay_path`, and set it to where we have the overlay image stored (in this case, we have placed the overlay image in the same folder as the uploads; of course, you can move it anywhere on your system, but it's here to keep it simple). We have also removed the array item, `wm_text`, which is now not needed (however, you can keep it if you wish, it'll not interfere with the image overlay).

Submitting a form with CodeIgniter CAPTCHA

It is sometimes necessary to add a little more security to a form other than escaping and validating user input; sometimes you may wish to ensure that a human and not some script or bot is entering data and submitting your form.

A tried and tested way of doing this is **CAPTCHA**. There are alternatives to CAPTCHA; for example, a mathematic question (what's 10 + 7, for example) is fairly easy to construct in your application. A new method is getting your users to play a short game. Based on how they do, they are assessed as being either a human or a bot; `areyouahuman.com` is a good resource for this. But for now, we'll concentrate on CodeIgniter's CAPTCHA functionality to make a CAPTCHA protected form for us.

Getting ready

We're going to store the CAPTCHA information CodeIgniter generates for us in a table in the database. To do that, we first need to create that table. The following is the MySQL code to do that. Copy the following into your database:

```sql
CREATE TABLE `captcha` (
  `captcha_id` bigint(13) unsigned NOT NULL AUTO_INCREMENT,
  `captcha_time` int(10) unsigned NOT NULL,
  `ip_address` varchar(16) NOT NULL DEFAULT '0',
  `word` varchar(20) NOT NULL,
  PRIMARY KEY (`captcha_id`),
  KEY `word` (`word`)
) ENGINE=InnoDB  DEFAULT CHARSET=latin1 AUTO_INCREMENT=1 ;
```

How to do it...

We're going to make the following four files:

- `/path/to/codeigniter/application/controllers/comments.php`: This is a controller which helps in processing a name, e-mail address, and comment from the user, and it also calls a helper to process the CAPTCHA data

- `/path/to/codeigniter/application/helpers/make_captcha_helper.php`: This helper contains the code necessary for generating a CAPTCHA image

- `/path/to/codeigniter/application/models/captcha_model.php`: This model is used to check the CAPTCHA value from the user against that stored in the database

- `/path/to/codeigniter/application/views/comments/post_form.php`: This view file will display the form (name, e-mail, comments, and so on) and the CAPTCHA image

1. Create the `controllers/comments.php` controller file and add the following code to it:

```php
<?php if ( ! defined('BASEPATH')) exit('No direct script
  access allowed');

class Comments extends CI_Controller {
  function __construct() {
    parent::__construct();
      $this->load->helper('form');
      $this->load->helper('url');
      $this->load->helper('make_captcha');
      $this->load->model('Captcha_model');
```

```
        }

    public function index() {
        $this->load->library('form_validation');
        $this->form_validation->set_error_delimiters(
          '', '<br />');

        $this->form_validation->set_rules('name',
          'Name', 'required|max_length[225]');
        $this->form_validation->set_rules('email',
          'Email', 'required|max_length[225]');
        $this->form_validation->set_rules('message',
          'Message', 'required|max_length[225]');
        $this->form_validation->set_rules('captcha',
          'Captcha', 'required|max_length[225]');

        // Begin validation
        if ($this->form_validation->run() == FALSE) {
          $data['img'] = make_captcha();
          $this->load->view('comments/post_form', $data);
        } else {
          $expiration = time() - 7200;

          $this->Captcha_model->delete_expired($expiration);

          $data = array(
            'captcha' => $this->input->post('captcha'),
            'ip_address' => $this->input->ip_address(),
            'expiration' => $expiration);

          $num_rows =
            $this->Captcha_model->does_exist($data);

          if ($num_rows == 0) {
            $data['error'] = "Type the word in the image.";
            $data['img'] = make_captcha();
            $this->load->view('comments/post_form', $data);
          } else {
            echo 'CAPTCHA OKAY - HERE IS YOUR POST:
              ' . '<br />';
            echo $this->input->post('name') . '<br />';
            echo $this->input->post('email') . '<br />';
            echo $this->input->post('message') . '<br />';
          }
        }
      }
    }
}
```

2. Next create the `helpers/make_captcha_helper.php` helper file and add the following code to it:

```php
<?php if (! defined('BASEPATH')) exit('No direct script
  access allowed');

function make_captcha() {
  $CI =& get_instance();
  $CI->load->helper('captcha');

  $vals = array(
      'img_path' => '/file/path/to/image/captcha/',
      'img_url' => 'http://url/to/image/captcha/',
      'font_path' => './system/fonts/texb.ttf',
      'img_width' => '150',
      'img_height' => 30,
      'expiration' => 7200
      );

  $cap = create_captcha($vals);
  $data = array(
      'captcha_time' => $cap['time'],
      'ip_address' => $CI->input->ip_address(),
      'word' => $cap['word']
      );

  $query = $CI->db->insert_string('captcha', $data);
  $CI->db->query($query);

  return $cap['image'];
}
```

 img_path and img_url are two interesting settings here. img_path should be the path to the image folder on the file system, and img_url should be the path of your image as it would be displayed in a web browser. CodeIgniter uses img_url to build a HTML img tag, and it is this that is sent to the post_form as $data['img'].

3. Create the `models/captcha_model.php` model file and add the following code to it:

```php
<?php if (! defined('BASEPATH')) exit('No direct script
  access allowed');

class Captcha_model extends CI_Model {
    function __construct() {
        parent::__construct();
```

```
        }

        public function delete_expired($expiration) {
            $this->db->where('captcha_time < ',$expiration);
            $this->db->delete('captcha');
        }

        public function does_exist($data) {
            $this->db->where('word', $data['captcha']);
            $this->db->where(
                'ip_address', $data['ip_address']);
            $this->db->where(
                'captcha_time > ', $data['expiration']);
            $query = $this->db->get('captcha');
            return $query->num_rows();
        }
    }
}
```

4. Then create the `comments/post_form.php` view file and add the following code to it:

```
<?php echo form_open() ; ?>
  <?php echo validation_errors() ; ?>
  <?php if (isset($errors)) { echo $errors ; }  ?>
  <br />
  Name <input type = "text" name = "name" size = "5"
    value = "<?php echo set_value('name') ; ?>"/><br />
  Email <input type = "text" name = "email" size = "5"
    value = "<?php echo set_value('email') ; ?>"/><br />
  Message <br />
  <textarea name = "message" rows = "4" cols = "20" />
    <?php echo set_value('message') ; ?></textarea><br />

  Please enter the string you see below
  <input type = "text" name = "captcha" value = "" />
  <br />
  <?php echo $img ; ?>
  <br />
  <input type = "submit" value = "Submit" />
<?php echo form_close() ; ?>
```

How it works...

The comments controller loads `public function index()`, which sets the validation environment for when or if the user submits the form. As `$this->form_validation->run()` will equal `FALSE` (as the form hasn't been submitted yet), the `make_captcha_helper` function, `make_captcha()`, is called, sending it's returned values to the `comments/post_form` view, as shown in the following code snippet:

```
if ($this->form_validation->run() == FALSE) {
  $data['img'] = make_captcha();
  $this->load->view('comments/post_form', $data);
} else {
... etc
```

The `make_captcha_helper` function, `make_captcha()`, will grab the main CodeIgniter object, as shown in the following code snippet:

```
$CI = & get_instance();
$CI->load->helper('captcha');
```

It defines the values necessary to build the CAPTCHA image, as shown in the following code snippet:

```
$vals = array(
  'img_path' => '/file/path/to/image/',
  'img_url' => 'http://url/to/image/',
  'font_path' => './system/fonts/texb.ttf',
  'img_width' => '150',
  'img_height' => 30,
  'expiration' => 7200
  );
```

These values are stored in the `$data` array, which is passed to the CodeIgniter helper, `captcha`, which returns to us the `$cap` array. `$cap` is passed to the database function, `insert_string()`, so the CAPTCHA information can be saved to the database, as shown in the following code snippet:

```
$cap = create_captcha($vals);
$data = array(
  'captcha_time' => $cap['time'],
  'ip_address' => $CI->input->ip_address(),
  'word' => $cap['word']
  );

$query = $CI->db->insert_string('captcha', $data);
```

We'll use this row in the database for comparison with the data entered by the user when they submit the form.

Finally, the `make_captcha` helper returns an HTML `img` tag string to our comments controller. This is saved in the `$data` array and passed to the `post_form` view file.

The user is then shown the HTML form, with name, e-mail, comments inputs, as well as an image of the CAPTCHA and a textbox in which to type the CAPTCHA string they see. The user then completes the form, carefully entering their data along with the string from the CAPTCHA image, and clicks on the **Submit** button.

Assuming validation is passed (there were no form errors), the comments controller will then begin to compare the CAPTCHA string inputted by the user to the one in the database created by the `make_captcha` helper.

It starts this process by first cleaning the database of old CAPTCHA rows (in this example, old is anything older than two hours); it does this by defining the current time (as a unix time stamp) minus two hours (or `7200` seconds), this is set as the `$expiration` time, as shown in the following code snippet:

```
$expiration = time() - 7200;

$this->Captcha_model->delete_expired($expiration);
```

The `Captcha_model` function, `delete_expired()`, is called, passing the expiration to it. This model function will delete rows in the database whose `captcha_time` is less than the expiration time, as shown in the following code snippet:

```
public function delete_expired($expiration) {
    $this->db->where('captcha_time < ',$expiration);
    $this->db->delete('captcha');
}
```

Once old CAPTCHAS are removed from the database, a `$data` array is created and populated with the user's CAPTCHA input, their IP address, and again, the `$expiration` time (the one we made to remove old rows). This `$data` array is passed to the `Captcha_model` function, `does_exist()`. This model function will check whether the CAPTCHA string entered by the user exists in the database, and if so, is valid (that is, less than two hours old and matching the provided IP address). The model function returns the number of rows found, as shown in the following code snippet

```
public function does_exist($data) {
    $this->db->where('word', $data['captcha']);
    $this->db->where('ip_address', $data['ip_address']);
    $this->db->where('captcha_time > ', $data['expiration']);
    $query = $this->db->get('captcha');
    return $query->num_rows();
}
```

If zero rows exist, then `$data['errors']` is given an error message. `make_captcha()` is called again, a new CAPTCHA image is generated and sent to the `post_form` view, and the error message is displayed to the user above the new CAPTCHA image. The system then waits for the user to fill in the form again and have another go.

However, if the result wasn't zero, then the CAPTCHA string entered by the user was correct, so we display a quick message to them and echo out their input. In reality, you can do what you like here, such as process their message and save it to a blog feed, or redirect them to another area on the site, whatever you wish.

11

SEO, Caching,
and Logging

In this chapter, you will learn:

- ► Using SEO-friendly URLs in CodeIgniter
- ► Using CodeIgniter caching
- ► Logging errors with CodeIgniter
- ► Benchmarking your application

Introduction

In this chapter, we'll be taking a look at various caching recipes, which can be used with
CodeIgniter. We'll be using the CodeIgniter caching functionality to help us store a data feed and
database results—although the data feed and database results are really only there as a means
to show you how to get data into CodeIgniter, so it can cache it—the data input can be anything
you wish. We'll also look at ways to implement SEO-friendly URLs using CodeIgniter routing.

Using SEO-friendly URLs in CodeIgniter

At some point, you might want to alter how CodeIgniter handles the routing of URLs to
controllers. By default, CodeIgniter splits a URL into several different parts. You obviously
have the domain section of the URL (`www.domain.com`), but after that there are (usually,
but not always) up to three more items, each separated by a forward slash. The first item is
the controller, the second is the function (or method, if you want) in the controller, and the
third is a parameter that you will pass to the function in the controller.

So, a standard URL in CodeIgniter might look like www.domain.com/users/edit/1. So, user number 1 is being edited using the edit function in the users controller—that seems simple enough and I'm sure you're familiar with it.

However, there may be times when you wish this to change. It is possible to alter what is displayed in the URL in the web browser's address bar to show something different from controller/function/data. It is possible to set up a rule in the config/routes.php file, which will map a URL to a controller, but hide this from the address bar; for example, you may have a controller named bulletin, which you wish to be displayed as news in the URL.

How to do it...

We're going to create one file and amend another file, by performing the following steps:

1. Create the /path/to/codeigniter/application/controllers/shop.php file and add the following code to it:

```php
<?php if ( ! defined('BASEPATH')) exit('No direct script
  access allowed');

class Shop extends CI_Controller {
  function __construct() {
    parent::__construct();
  }

  public function index() {
    echo 'Controller: ' . __CLASS__ . ',
      Method: ' . __FUNCTION__;
  }

  public function product() {
    echo 'Controller: ' . __CLASS__ . ',
      Method: ' . __FUNCTION__;
    echo '<br />';
    echo 'Product ID: ' . $this->uri->segment(2);
  }

  public function all() {
    echo 'Controller: ' . __CLASS__ . ',
      Method: ' . __FUNCTION__;
  }
}
```

2. Open the `/path/to/codeigniter/config/routes.php` file in your editor and amend accordingly (the changes are highlighted):

```
$route['default_controller'] = "default_controller";
$route['404_override'] = '';

$route['item/(:any)'] = "shop/product";
$route['item'] = "shop/all";
```

How it works...

Take a look at the following lines in the `config/routes.php` file:

```
$route['item/(:any)'] = "shop/product";
$route['item'] = "shop/all";
```

Now, think of them as being made up of a left and a right, in that before the = sign is left and anything after the = sign is right; the left maps to the right and the value in the left will be mapped to the value in the right.

In the preceding example, any URL whose controller name begins with `item` will be mapped to the `shop` controller. Let's look at each rule in turn:

By typing the name of the route into your browser (for example, `http://www.your_web_site_name.com/item`), the `item` command will cause CodeIgniter to call the `shop` controller, and within that controller the `public function all()` method. Because we defined it in the routes file, you will see this in your browser by typing `item` into the URL. CodeIgniter maps the requested URL to the path defined in the route rule, and (in our example) calls the `shop` controller, which using `__CLASS__` and `__FUNCTION__` will write the following output to the browser:

> Controller: Shop, Method: all
> Product ID:

Now, take a look at the URL in the browser address bar, it will still display the item, but the text on the screen says it's the `shop` controller that is being called. We have now mapped the URL to a controller and the user is none the wiser.

Now, let's look at the other route rule–`:any`. By typing the name of the route into your browser (for example, `http://www.your_web_site_name.com/item/123456`), the `item/123456` command will cause CodeIgniter to call the `shop` controller and `public function product()` because we defined it in the routes file. In `public function product()`, we echo out not only the `__CLASS__` and `__FUNCTION__` names, but also the second segment of the URI:

```
$this->uri->segment(2);
```

Which, in this case, is the ID of the product (`12356`), so you will see the following screenshot in the browser:

```
Controller: Shop, Method: product
Product ID: 123456
```

The key to this route is the (`:any`) flag in the route mapping rule; (`:any`) tells CodeIgniter that the second segment in the URI, whatever it is, should map to the `product` function of the `shop` controller. As we're the ones building the code, we will know that the second URI segment in the URL is a product ID, which we can use to query the database for the details of that product.

Using CodeIgniter caching

You can use CodeIgniter caching to cache (or temporarily store) practically anything. As an example of caching with CodeIgniter, we're going to cache an RSS feed. We could, of course, cache anything we wanted; however, caching an RSS feed is a good place to start. Working with RSS is quite simple and the recipe can easily be converted to cache feeds from other sources, such as a call to Twitter, for example.

How to do it...

We're going to create the `/path/to/codeigniter/application/controllers/rss_cache.php` file.

1. Create the preceding file and add the following code to it:

```php
<?php if ( ! defined('BASEPATH')) exit('No direct script
  access allowed');

class Rss_cache extends CI_Controller {
  function __construct() {
    parent::__construct();
    $this->load->helper('url');
```

```
    $this->load->helper('xml');
    $this->load->driver('cache', array(
      'adapter' => 'apc'));
  }

  public function index() {
    $raw_feed = '<?xml version = "1.0"
      encoding = "ISO-8859-1" ?>
    <rss version="2.0">
    <channel>
      <title>RSS Feed</title>
        <link>http://www.domain.com</link>
        <description>General Description</description>
      <item>
        <title>RSS Item 1 Title</title>
        <link>http://www.domain1.com/link1</link>
        <description>Description of First Item
          </description>
      </item>
      <item>
        <title>RSS Item 2 Title</title>
        <link>http://www.domain2.com/link2</link>
        <description>Description of Second Item
          </description>
      </item>
      <item>
        <title>RSS Item 3 Title</title>
        <link>http://www.domain3.com/link3</link>
        <description>Description of Third Item
          </description>
      </item>
    </channel>
    </rss>';

    $feed = new SimpleXmlElement($raw_feed);

    if (!$cached_feed = $this->cache->get('rss')) {
      foreach ($feed->channel->item as $item) {
        $cached_feed . = $item->title . '<br />' .
          $item->description . '<br /><br />';
      }

        $this->cache->save('rss', $cached_feed, 7);
    }

    echo $this->cache->get('rss');

  }

  public function clear_cache() {
```

```
        $this->cache->clean();
        redirect('rss_cache');
    }
  }
}
?>
```

How it works...

First, let's look at the constructor. We're loading one helper and one driver, as shown in the following code snippet:

```
function __construct() {
  parent::__construct();
  $this->load->helper('url');
  $this->load->driver('cache', array('adapter' => 'apc'));
}
```

 To use APC, you'll need to ensure that APC is installed on the environment you're working on. If not, you'll need to install it. To do this, visit `http://www.php.net/manual/en/apc.setup.php` for more details.

The URL helper is there as we're using the `redirect()` function and the cache driver is there to provide support to help us cache out data, in this case it's helping us cache data from the RSS feed—however, it really can be anything.

`public function index()` first defines the `$rss_feed` variable with the hardcoded RSS feed; this is for illustration purposes really. In reality, you will fetch the feed using:

```
$raw_feed =
    file_get_contents('http://www.domain.com/rss_feed_url');
```

However, it is convenient to hardcode it for this recipe, as by hard coding you will see the structure of the feed and know what it should "look" like

The feed has a simple structure containing only three items. The `$raw_feed` variable is passed to the PHP `SimpleXMLElement` class, which returns an object (`$feed`) for us to work with.

We then use CodeIgniter to check if there exists in cache an item named `rss`; if not, we'll loop through the `$feed` object, pulling out the title and description for each item in the RSS feed, and concatenate to a string, which is named `$cached_feed`.

```
if (!$cached_feed = $this->cache->get('rss')) {
  foreach ($feed->channel->item as $item) {
    $cached_feed .= $item->title . '<br />' .
      $item->description . '<br /><br />';
  }
    $this->cache->save('rss', $cached_feed, 30);
}
```

The `$cached_feed` string is saved to the cache with the name `rss` for a period of 30 seconds (for more on caching durations, refer to the following code):

```
$this->cache->save('rss', $cached_feed, 30);
```

Once all items in the RSS feed have been processed, we'll echo out the cache item `rss`, as shown in the following code snippet:

```
echo $this->cache->get('rss');
```

You should get something similar to the following output in your browser:

```
RSS Item 1 Title
Description of First Item
RSS Item 2 Title
Description of Second Item
RSS Item 3 Title
Description of Third Item
```

Why 30 seconds? Because it'll be a good length of time for you to go to your browser, run the script, see the preceding output, and quickly dash back to the code in your text editor to change something in the feed (such as the title element of the third item to `Gigantic Elephants`). Click on **Save**, and go back to the browser to refresh, which after 30 seconds (30 seconds since you first ran `rss_cache`) should give you the following output:

```
RSS Item 1 Title
Description of First Item
RSS Item 2 Title
Description of Second Item
Gigantic Elephants
Description of Third Item
```

Should 30 seconds be too long for you to wait, you can always manually clear the cache by running `public function clear_cache()`, which will call the CodeIgniter `$this->cache->clean()` function and redirect us back to the `rss_cache` controller where the whole process will begin again.

Alternatively, you can decrease the length of time a cache stays valid from 30 seconds to, say, 10 seconds (but in reality, you'll want it to be a length of time that you feel is right for your server or data).

So now, you can see how to store data in the cache, it doesn't have to be XML or an RSS feed, it really could be data from any source: a database query (although CodeIgniter has specific database caching methods for that), a feed from a social link (such as a Twitter feed, or from Instagram), or even financial data such as the value of the FTSE fetched every 5 minutes (or however long you set it).

Problems you may encounter

If you're developing on a MAC using MAMP, the chances are the the default caching method is XCache. CodeIgniter doesn't have a driver to work with XCache and you'll either need to write your own driver (go on be brave), or (as I did) change your caching engine to APC.

 APC (Alternative PHP Caching) is a caching service, which in this case is provided by MAMP.

You'll need to tell MAMP to use APC rather than XCache. To do this, open your MAMP control panel and click on **Preferences**, then click on the **PHP** tab. You should now see a section named **PHP extensions**. In that section should be a drop-down list (this is probably set to XCache); choose APC from this list, and click on the **OK** button. MAMP will restart, and after this you should be good to go.

Logging errors with CodeIgniter

Logging errors which occur within your CodeIgniter application doesn't have to be limited to looking at the PHP or Apache logs; you can enable CodeIgniter to handle and log errors and other behaviors and events at certain points in your code using CodeIgniter's logging functionality. This facility can be particularly useful (if you set it up correctly) to track a user's journey and progress through the system and should something go wrong with whatever they're doing, you can look in the logs and trace what they did and when, and get a better idea of what (if at all) went wrong and hopefully think about how to prevent it from occurring again.

In this recipe, we're going to look at using the logging functionality within CodeIgniter and to track if something goes wrong with an operation.

Getting ready

We'll need to set the log reporting level in the config file so that CodeIgniter knows which level of logging messages to report on. The log's folder should also have write access, so perform the following steps:

1. Open the `/path/to/codeigniter/application/config/config.php` file and find the following line:

   ```
   $config['log_threshold'] = 0;
   ```

   You can change the value of the `log_threshold` config array element to one of the five states, as shown in the following table:

State	Usage	Description
0	-	CodeIgniter will not log anything.
1	`log_message('error', 'Some Text')`	CodeIgniter will log error messages.
2	`log_message('debug', 'Some Text')`	CodeIgniter will log debugging messages.
3	`log_message('info', 'Some Text');`	CodeIgniter will log information messages.
4	All of the above	CodeIgniter will log everything.

   For our recipe, I have set the value to 4 as I want to log any error messages or information messages that CodeIgniter might generate for me.

2. Look for the line:

   ```
   $config['log_path'] = '/path/to/log/folder/';.
   ```

   Ensure that `/path/to/log/folder/` is set correctly in `$config[' log_path']` and that the folder specified has write permissions (otherwise, CodeIgniter cannot write a log file to that folder).

How to do it...

We're going to use (as it was convenient) the *Using CodeIgniter caching* recipe, mentioned earlier in this chapter, and alter it in such a way as to apply CodeIgniter logging. In this recipe, we've changed its name to `cache_log.php` (to keep it separate from `rss_cache.php`). So, if you haven't already done so (don't forget to change the name, highlighted in the following code):

1. Create the `/path/to/codeigniter/application/controllers/cache_log.php` file and add the following code to it (the changes are highlighted):

```php
<?php if ( ! defined('BASEPATH')) exit('No direct script
  access allowed');

class Cache_log extends CI_Controller {
  function __construct() {
    parent::__construct();
    $this->load->helper('url');
    $this->load->helper('xml');
    $this->load->driver('cache', array(
      'adapter' => 'apc'));
  }

  public function index() {
    $raw_feed = '<?xml version="1.0" encoding="ISO-8859-1"
      ?>
    <rss version="2.0">
    <channel>
      <title>RSS Feed</title>
        <link>http://www.domain.com</link>
        <description>General Description</description>
      <item>
        <title>RSS Item 1 Title</title>
        <link>http://www.domain1.com/link1</link>
        <description>Description of First Item
          </description>
      </item>
      <item>
        <title>RSS Item 2 Title</title>
        <link>http://www.domain2.com/link2</link>
        <description>Description of Second Item
          </description>
      </item>
      <item>
        <title>RSS Item 3 Title</title>
        <link>http://www.domain3.com/link3</link>
        <description>Description of Third Item
          </description>
      </item>
```

```
      </channel>
      </rss>';

  $feed = new SimpleXmlElement($raw_feed);

  if (!$feed) {
    log_message('error',
      'Unable to instantiate SimpleXmlElement.');
  } else {
    log_message('info',
      'SimpleXmlElement was instantiated correctly.');
  }

  if (!$cached_feed = $this->cache->get('rss')) {
    foreach ($feed->channel->item as $item) {
      $cached_feed .= $item->title . '<br />' .
        $item->description . '<br /><br />';
    }

      $this->cache->save('rss', $cached_feed, 7);
      log_message('info', 'Cache item saved.');
  }

  echo $this->cache->get('rss');

}

  public function clear_cache() {
    if (!$this->cache->clean()) {
      log_message('error', 'Unable to clear Cache.');
    } else {
      log_message('info', 'Cache cleared.');
    }

    redirect('rss_cache');
  }
}
?>
```

If all goes well you shouldn't have any errors, but you should have some DEBUG data in the config file. When you open that file you should see something similar to:

```
<?php  if ( ! defined('BASEPATH')) exit('No direct script access
allowed'); ?>

DEBUG - 2013-09-24 19:46:11 --> Config Class Initialized
DEBUG - 2013-09-24 19:46:11 --> Hooks Class Initialized
DEBUG - 2013-09-24 19:46:11 --> Utf8 Class Initialized
DEBUG - 2013-09-24 19:46:11 --> UTF-8 Support Enabled
DEBUG - 2013-09-24 19:46:11 --> URI Class Initialized
```

```
DEBUG - 2013-09-24 19:46:11 --> Router Class Initialized
DEBUG - 2013-09-24 19:46:11 --> Output Class Initialized
DEBUG - 2013-09-24 19:46:11 --> Security Class Initialized
DEBUG - 2013-09-24 19:46:11 --> Input Class Initialized
DEBUG - 2013-09-24 19:46:11 --> XSS Filtering completed
DEBUG - 2013-09-24 19:46:11 --> XSS Filtering completed
DEBUG - 2013-09-24 19:46:11 --> XSS Filtering completed
DEBUG - 2013-09-24 19:46:11 --> CRSF cookie Set
DEBUG - 2013-09-24 19:46:11 --> Global POST and COOKIE data
sanitized
DEBUG - 2013-09-24 19:46:11 --> Language Class Initialized
DEBUG - 2013-09-24 19:46:11 --> Loader Class Initialized
DEBUG - 2013-09-24 19:46:11 --> Database Driver Class Initialized
DEBUG - 2013-09-24 19:46:11 --> Session Class Initialized
DEBUG - 2013-09-24 19:46:11 --> Helper loaded: string_helper
DEBUG - 2013-09-24 19:46:11 --> Encrypt Class Initialized
DEBUG - 2013-09-24 19:46:11 --> Session routines successfully run
DEBUG - 2013-09-24 19:46:11 --> XML-RPC Class Initialized
DEBUG - 2013-09-24 19:46:11 --> Controller Class Initialized
DEBUG - 2013-09-24 19:46:11 --> Helper loaded: url_helper
DEBUG - 2013-09-24 19:46:11 --> Helper loaded: xml_helper
INFO  - 2013-09-24 19:46:11 --> SimpleXmlElement was instantiated
correctly.
INFO  - 2013-09-24 19:46:11 --> Cache item saved.
DEBUG - 2013-09-24 19:46:11 --> Final output sent to browser
DEBUG - 2013-09-24 19:46:11 --> Total execution time: 0.0280
```

You can see the info items we set in the code written in the log; I've highlighted them so that they stand out.

How it works...

You can see that we have added some conditional statements on various stages of the controller's execution, checking for the return value of certain CodeIgniter functions (the changes are highlighted in the previous code). Depending on that returned value (either TRUE or FALSE), we will write to the logs using the CodeIgniter log_message() function, but let's take a closer look at those messages and when each of them is triggered.

First off, we'll try to instantiate a new SimpleXmlElement() object. If we get a returned object, an info message is written to the log (SimpleXmlElement() was instantiated correctly). If there was an error, we write an error message to the log (unable to instantiate SimpleXmlElement()); take a look at the following code snippet:

```
$feed = new SimpleXmlElement($raw_feed);

if (!$feed) {
  log_message('error', 'Unable to instantiate SimpleXmlElement.');
```

```
} else {
  log_message('info', 'SimpleXmlElement was instantiated
  correctly.');
}
```

You can see that we're using CodeIgniter's logging functionality to write messages to the log file, and define those messages as either errors or info; this can be helpful in debugging the user's journey as you'll know what is a genuine error, and what is information entered by you to help you in the logs.

Logging style

I find it useful to write my log messages like the following code snippet:

```
log_message('info', ' **** ' . __LINE__ . ' - This is a
  message.');
```

In the preceding code snippet, we're defining the message as info, but we begin the message with four asterisks (****). This'll make the message stand out in the logs as we're viewing them, next comes the __LINE__ argument (to let you know where in the script it was triggered), followed by the actual message–here it is the unimaginative–' - This is a message.'

You may wish to add __FILE__, __CLASS__, or __FUNCTION__ for greater accuracy, depending on your needs.

Benchmarking your application

Benchmarking can be useful for you as it can let you know how your application is coping with the task of computing all your code. It can let you know where in your application something is slow, either because of memory constraints or perhaps because of a particularly computational intensive block of code. Using this information, you can identify whether there are any bottlenecks and if you are able to clear them, perhaps by reprogramming or allocating extra resources. Here's how it's done.

Getting ready

Many web applications will be linked to some sort of database and as an example of benchmarking database connectivity, we're going to query a database. To do that, we will obviously need a database to connect to. Copy the following MySQL code into your database:

```
CREATE TABLE `bench_table` (
  `id` int(11) NOT NULL AUTO_INCREMENT,
  `firstname` varchar(50) NOT NULL,
  `lastname` varchar(50) NOT NULL,
  PRIMARY KEY (`id`)
```

```
) ENGINE=InnoDB  DEFAULT CHARSET=latin1 AUTO_INCREMENT=3 ;

INSERT INTO `bench_table` (`id`, `firstname`, `lastname`) VALUES
(1, 'Rob', 'Foster'),
(2, 'Lucy', 'Welsh');
```

How to do it...

We're going to create the following two files:

▸   /path/to/codeigniter/application/controllers/bench.php

▸   /path/to/codeigniter/application/models/bench_model.php

1.   Create the bench.php controller file and add the following code to it:

```php
<?php if ( ! defined('BASEPATH')) exit('No direct script
  access allowed');

class Bench extends CI_Controller {
  function __construct() {
    parent::__construct();
    $this->load->helper('url');
    $this->load->model('bench_model');
    $this->load->database();
  }

  public function index() {
    // Who's in the database?
    $this->benchmark->mark('bm1_start');
    foreach ($this->bench_model->get_people()->result() as
      $row) {
      echo $row->firstname . ' ' . $row->lastname . '<br
        />';
    }
    $this->benchmark->mark('bm1_end');

    // Write some more people to the database
    $this->benchmark->mark('bm2_start');
    $data = array(
      array('firstname' => 'George',
          'lastname' => 'Foster'),
      array('firstname' => 'Jackie',
          'lastname' => 'Foster'),
      array('firstname' => 'Antony',
          'lastname' => 'Welsh'),
      array('firstname' => 'Rowena',
          'lastname' => 'Welsh'),
      array('firstname' => 'Peter',
          'lastname' => 'Foster'),
```

```
        array('firstname' => 'Jenny',
            'lastname' => 'Foster'),
        array('firstname' => 'Oliver',
            'lastname' => 'Welsh'),
        array('firstname' => 'Harrison',
            'lastname' => 'Foster'),
        array('firstname' => 'Felicity',
            'lastname' => 'Foster')
        );

    $result = $this->bench_model->add_to_db($data);
    $this->benchmark->mark('bm2_end');

    if ($result) {
      // Who's in the database now?
      $this->benchmark->mark('bm3_start');
      foreach ($this->bench_model->get_people()->result()
        as $row) {
        echo $row->firstname . ' ' . $row->lastname . '<br
          />';
      }
      $this->benchmark->mark('bm3_end');
    } else {
      echo 'Cannot write to database.';
    }

    echo '<br /> ---- BENCHMARK POINT STATS ---- <br />';
    echo 'BM1 (S) to BM1 (E): ' . $this->benchmark-
      >elapsed_time('bm1_start','bm1_end') . '<br />';
    echo 'BM2 (S) to BM2 (E): ' . $this->benchmark-
      >elapsed_time('bm2_start','bm2_end') . '<br />';
    echo 'BM3 (S) to BM3 (E): ' . $this->benchmark-
      >elapsed_time('bm3_start','bm3_end') . '<br />';
  }
}
?>
```

2. Create the `bench_model.php` model file and add the following code to it:

```
<?php if ( ! defined('BASEPATH')) exit('No direct script
  access allowed');

class Bench_model extends CI_Model {
    function __construct() {
        parent::__construct();
    }

    function get_people() {
        $query = $this->db->get('bench_table');
```

```
        return $query;
    }

    function add_to_db($data) {
        if ($this->db->insert_batch('bench_table', $data)) {
            return TRUE;
        } else {
            return FALSE;
        }
    }
}
```

How it works...

If you run the controller bench in your browser, you should see the following output on the screen:

```
Rob Foster
Lucy Welsh
Rob Foster
Lucy Welsh
George Foster
Jackie Foster
Antony Welsh
Rowena Welsh
Peter Foster
Jenny Foster
Oliver Welsh
Harrison Foster
Felicity Foster
---- BENCHMARK POINT STATS ----
BM1 (S) to BM1 (E): 0.0004
BM2 (S) to BM2 (E): 0.0010
BM3 (S) to BM3 (E): 0.0005
```

The output is a loop of the contents of the bench_table database table followed by the benchmark statistics. I've highlighted the stats for the batch_insert() operation.

BM1 (S) is the start of the BM1 benchmark, and BM1 (E) is the end of the BM1 benchmark.

You can see that it took significantly longer to perform the batch_insert() operation than the two read operations (the actual processing times will be different in your application and probably each time you run the controller; however, the BM2 item will almost always be longer, but the times will differ depending on the system you're using).

If this were a more complex situation, we could use this information to locate bottlenecks in the code and hope to fix them to ensure a more streamlined application.

So, what's happening in the code? There's no library or other resource to load as the benchmark system is always loaded by CodeIgniter and is always available for use.

When we run the bench controller, `public function index()` is called and immediately runs the `get_people()` function of `bench_model`. This performs an Active Record `SELECT` operation on the `bench_table` database table, returning the result object to the controller. This is looped over and we echo out each row to display a list of rows in the database before the `batch_insert()` operation:

```
$this->benchmark->mark('bm1_start');
foreach ($this->bench_model->get_people()->result() as $row) {
  echo $row->firstname . ' ' . $row->lastname . '<br />';
}
$this->benchmark->mark('bm1_end');
```

The keen-eyed amongst you will also notice the highlighted lines, we've defined the start and end points for CodeIgniter to pay attention to. The first we've named `bm1_start` and the second we've named `bm1_stop`. We can call them anything we like, but that's what I've decided to call them.

We then perform the `batch_ insert` operation, as shown in the following code snippet:

```
$this->benchmark->mark('bm2_start');
$data = array(
  array('firstname' => 'George',
      'lastname' => 'Foster'),
  array('firstname' => 'Jackie',
      'lastname' => 'Foster'),
  array('firstname' => 'Antony',
      'lastname' => 'Welsh'),
  array('firstname' => 'Rowena',
      'lastname' => 'Welsh'),
  array('firstname' => 'Peter',
      'lastname' => 'Foster'),
  array('firstname' => 'Jenny',
      'lastname' => 'Foster'),
  array('firstname' => 'Oliver',
      'lastname' => 'Welsh'),
  array('firstname' => 'Harrison',
      'lastname' => 'Foster'),
  array('firstname' => 'Felicity',
      'lastname' => 'Foster')
  );

  $result = $this->bench_model->add_to_db($data);
$this->benchmark->mark('bm2_end');
```

We're defining a multidimensional array with the details of people we want to add to the database and sending it to the `insert_batch()` function of `bench_model`; now the keen eyed among you will again notice the highlighted lines. These are the bm2 start and end points. If the `batch_insert()` operation returns TRUE (it is inserted into the database correctly), we then call the `get_people()` model function again, which will return all the records from the database:

```
if ($result) {
  // Who's in the database now?
  $this->benchmark->mark('bm3_start');
  foreach ($this->bench_model->get_people()->result() as $row) {
    echo $row->firstname . ' ' . $row->lastname . '<br />';
  }
  $this->benchmark->mark('bm3_end');
} else {
  echo 'Cannot write to database.';
}
```

Again, here we define (as highlighted in the previous code) the bm3 start and end points. That completes our database operations and we move over to reporting of the benchmarks.

We ask CodeIgniter to tell us the execution time between points:

```
echo '<br /> ---- BENCHMARK POINT STATS ---- <br />';
echo 'BM1 (S) to BM1 (E): ' . $this->benchmark->elapsed_time('bm1_
start','bm1_end') . '<br />';
echo 'BM2 (S) to BM2 (E): ' . $this->benchmark->elapsed_time('bm2_
start','bm2_end') . '<br />';
echo 'BM3 (S) to BM3 (E): ' . $this->benchmark->elapsed_time('bm3_
start','bm3_end') . '<br />';
```

For each bm1, bm2, and bm3, we want to know the time between the points specified using the `$this->benchmark->elapsed_time()` function. This function takes two arguments: a start point and an end point. For this recipe, we have asked CodeIgniter to report the time elapsed between each bm# point (where # is the number 1, 2, or 3), but if we wish to we can write this:

```
echo 'BM1 (S) to BM2 (E): ' . $this->benchmark-
  >elapsed_time('bm1_start','bm2_end') . '<br />'
```

The previous code will report the elapsed time between `bm1_start` and `bm2_end` (or from the beginning of the first `get_people()` query to the end of the `batch_insert()` query).

Think of each `$this->benchmark->mark('bm2_end');` as a checkpoint, and you can use `$this->benchmark->elapsed_time('checkpoint_1','checkpoint_2')` to return the time elapsed between them.

Index

E

e-mails
  bulk e-mails, sending with
      CodeIgniter Email 76-80
  HTML e-mails, sending with
      CodeIgniter Email 72, 73
  sending, with CodeIgniter Email 70, 71
encrypt_name setting 120
errors
  displaying, next to form items 112, 113
escape_like_str() 177
escape_str() 177
escaping data 173-177
escaping user input
  about 169
  globally 170
  individually 170
exact_length rule 104

F

file_name setting 119
files
  reading, from file system 113-115
  uploading, with FTP 223-226
  uploading, with CodeIgniter 118-122
  writing, to file system 116
file system
  files, reading from 113-115
  files, writing to 116
force_download() 166
foreach() loop 151
form
  submitting, with CodeIgniter
      CAPTCHA 257-264
FTP
  file, uploading with 223-225
function create_batch() function 144
function update() 156
fuzzy_date_helper 209
fuzzy dates
  working with 205-210

G

get_all() function 94
get_main_article() function 102
greater_than rule 104

H

hash
  comparing 42
  generating 41
  generating, with $config['encryption_key']
      value 42
  generating, without $config['encryption_key']
      value 42
helper
  creating, to work with persons date
      of birth 202-205
Hooks
  cache_override 217
  creating, in CodeIgniter 216-219
  display_override 217
  post_controller 217
  post_controller_constructor 217
  post_system 217
  pre_controller 217
  pre_system 217
HTML e-mails
  sending, CodeIgniter Email used 72, 73
HTML table
  using, with database 86-90
  using, with Data table 83-90
HTTPS
  setting up, on localhost 182
  using, with CodeIgniter 178-182

I

image_lib library 246
ImageMagick
  installing on MAC, with Cactuslab 241, 242
image overlays
  watermarks, adding with 255-257
images
  cropping 249, 251
  potential errors 251

Thank you for buying
CodeIgniter 2 Cookbook

About Packt Publishing

Packt, pronounced 'packed', published its first book "*Mastering phpMyAdmin for Effective MySQL Management*" in April 2004 and subsequently continued to specialize in publishing highly focused books on specific technologies and solutions.

Our books and publications share the experiences of your fellow IT professionals in adapting and customizing today's systems, applications, and frameworks. Our solution based books give you the knowledge and power to customize the software and technologies you're using to get the job done. Packt books are more specific and less general than the IT books you have seen in the past. Our unique business model allows us to bring you more focused information, giving you more of what you need to know, and less of what you don't.

Packt is a modern, yet unique publishing company, which focuses on producing quality, cutting-edge books for communities of developers, administrators, and newbies alike. For more information, please visit our website: www.packtpub.com.

About Packt Open Source

In 2010, Packt launched two new brands, Packt Open Source and Packt Enterprise, in order to continue its focus on specialization. This book is part of the Packt Open Source brand, home to books published on software built around Open Source licenses, and offering information to anybody from advanced developers to budding web designers. The Open Source brand also runs Packt's Open Source Royalty Scheme, by which Packt gives a royalty to each Open Source project about whose software a book is sold.

Writing for Packt

We welcome all inquiries from people who are interested in authoring. Book proposals should be sent to author@packtpub.com. If your book idea is still at an early stage and you would like to discuss it first before writing a formal book proposal, contact us; one of our commissioning editors will get in touch with you.

We're not just looking for published authors; if you have strong technical skills but no writing experience, our experienced editors can help you develop a writing career, or simply get some additional reward for your expertise.

Mastering phpMyAdmin 3.4 for Effective MySQL Management

ISBN: 978-1-84951-778-2   Paperback: 394 pages

A complete guide to getting started with phpMyAdmin 3.4 and mastering its features

1. A step-by-step tutorial for manipulating data with the latest version of phpmyadmin

2. Administer your MySQL databases with phpMyAdmin

3. Manage users and privileges with MySQL Server Administration tools

Programming with CodeIgniter MVC

ISBN: 978-1-84969-470-4   Paperback: 124 pages

Build feature-rich web applications using the CodeIgniter MVC framework

1. Build feature-rich web applications using the CodeIgniter MVC framework

2. Master the concepts of maximum simplicity, separation, flexibility, reusability, and performance efficiency

3. A quick guide to programming using the CodeIgniter MVC framework

Please check **www.PacktPub.com** for information on our titles

WordPress Web Application Development

ISBN: 978-1-78328-075-9   Paperback: 362 pages

Develop powerful web applications quickly using cutting-edge WordPress web development techniques

1. Develop powerful web applications rapidly with WordPress

2. Practical scenario-based approach with ready-to-test source code

3. Learning how to plan complex web applications from scratch

Real-time Web Application Development using Vert.x 2.0

ISBN: 978-1-78216-795-2   Paperback: 122 pages

An intuitive guide to building applications for the real-time web with Vert.x platform

1. Get started with developing applications for the real-time web

2. From concept to deployment, learn the full development workflow of a real-time web application

3. Utilize the Java skills you already have while stepping up to the next level

Please check **www.PacktPub.com** for information on our titles

CPSIA information can be obtained at www.ICGtesting.com
Printed in the USA
BVOW06s0022161213

339123BV00005B/136/P

9 781782 162308